The 21st Century: Meeting the Challenges to Business Education

National Business Education Association Yearbook, No. 37

1999

Editors:
Pat A. Gallo Villee
Brookdale Community College
Lincroft, New Jersey
and
Michael G. Curran
Rider University
Lawrenceville, New Jersey

Published by:
National Business Education Association
1914 Association Drive
Reston, VA 20191-1596
Tel: 703-860-8300 • Fax: 703-620-4483
www.nbea.org

The 21st Century: Meeting the Challenges to Business Education

National Business Education Association
1914 Association Drive
Reston, VA 20191-1596

ISBN 0-933964-53-6

Any views or recommendations expressed in this book do not necessarily constitute official policy of the National Business Education Association.

PREFACE

As the 20ᵗʰ century draws to a close and we prepare to enter the new millennium, a convergence of innovations in technology, learning, and business practices point to major shifts in our society and in education. How will we make sure we are ready for these challenges? How will we share the latest advances with our students?

The next century will bring many questions for business educators to answer. How we address and act on these questions will determine our future and the future of our students.

This Yearbook examines many of the educational practices, delivery systems, teaching tools, and curriculum contents that will impact tomorrow's students. When we thought of teaching strategies in the past, the traditional lecture format, not student-centered group activities, were what came to mind. Similarly, the delivery of subject matter was once confined to the four walls of a classroom; today, the Internet and interactive audio and video allow teachers and students to be located in different parts of the country, indeed the world. Because of advances in technology, reorganization in the business world, and the changing demographics of our classrooms, the learning environment will increasingly be customized to fit the diverse needs and learning styles of our students.

Think back to the time when you were trained to be a business educator. Was it just a few years ago or many years ago? It really doesn't matter; we all must continually learn, understand, and teach new ideas and concepts. Many of the "old skills" that we learned and were trained to teach are still important for today's students, but some of those skills are no longer relevant. We must accept the challenges placed before us and change in order to ensure that our students are prepared for the workplace of the 21ˢᵗ century.

The one constant amid all this change, however, is the importance of teachers to the learning process. As our role shifts from providers of information to facilitators of learning, we remain crucial in motivating and enabling our students to succeed.

This Yearbook includes a wide variety of topics to help us think about what the future holds—what the new millennium means to us. The dictionary defines millennium as a period of great happiness and freedom from imperfections in *human existence. If this is indeed what the Year 2000 will bring, we are all very lucky. As educators it is up to us to help create a safe haven of learning for our students and a vehicle for them to work on building the foundation for their careers and their relationships with one another.*

Business education's future will be shaped by what we do today. We do not really know what tomorrow will bring, but as business educators we will keep adding new ideas to our body of knowledge. We still have much to learn, but we all know that each day is a new opportunity to help mold our students' futures. With our positive attitude and our drive for success, business education will have a secure and vital role in the 21ˢᵗ century.

Many thanks go to the authors and all those who contributed to this Yearbook. We hope that the ideas and information shared in this publication will help business educators meet the challenges of the new millennium.

Please note that the listed Web site addresses were accurate when the chapters were written, but may have changed since publication.

Pat A. Gallo Villee
Brookdale Community College
Lincroft, New Jersey

and

Michael G. Curran
Rider University
Lawrenceville, New Jersey

TABLE OF CONTENTS

PART 2: WORKPLACE IMPLICATIONS FOR THE NEW MILLENNIUM

Overview — The Future We Create

Arthur McEntee
University of Maine at Machias
Machias, Maine

One of our roles as educators is to reflect on our past and use what we learn as a foundation for future planning and change. But words like "future" and "change" challenge our comfort level, especially in today's climate where, it seems, nothing is certain and every educational practice is up for discussion: class size, scheduling, teaching and learning strategies, student assessment, and, of course, how to get the most from technology.

Are we resistant to change in business education? If so, how do we move forward into the new millennium and master its challenges? Here is the key: we accept that the future is the one we create.

Inventing our future: this is our clarion call. The authors of this yearbook have thoughtfully examined six themes representative of the challenges to business educators of the 21st century: creating a thinking curriculum, providing opportunities for real-world learning, matching teaching styles to learning styles, adopting roles as knowledge facilitators and mentors, using technology as a tool, and fostering global thinking for our global society. They offer a road map for the rest of us, so that we can equip our students with skills that enable them to become full participants in the new millennium.

A Thinking Curriculum

All students need a thinking curriculum—one that provides a deep understanding of content and the ability to apply that understanding to the complex, real-world problems that they will face as adults.

Privacy in the workplace is one such problem, says Ann M. Remp. The workplace, relative to trust issues, will be much more complex than the one in which we grew up. In the chapter "Workplace Privacy, Confidentiality, and Surveillance," Remp shows how business education teachers can make significant contributions to society by fostering attitudes of hope and optimism as students think hard about how these issues affect them and their places of business.

Issues like privacy and confidentiality—and other issues yet to emerge—demand the ability to think flexibly and consider an issue from various viewpoints. Such thinking skills are critical to success in an increasingly complex world, and the more we can do to develop higher-order thinking skills in our students, the better. Kenneth L. Gorman, in his chapter "Organizational Leadership in the 21st Century," suggests activities teachers can use to develop such skills and, more importantly, to foster leadership ability. Old ways of doing business have become ineffective, he says. Major shifts in the world economic order and phenomenal advances in information and communication technologies have transformed business management practices. In the new paradigm, managers are leaders rather than autocrats. Leadership must become a key component of business students' education, Gorman says, and students should work on projects that have a real-life context so that they can apply what they learn and see what works.

Opportunities for Real-World Learning

Business-education partnerships are effective at bridging the classroom and the "real world." Terry D. Roach, in "Corporate Relationships With Business Education Programs," discusses the variety of formats these partnerships can take, from simple exchanges of goods and services to more complex arrangements such as job shadowing and preceptorships. Roach discusses characteristics of model programs and lists several considerations for teachers who wish to create and strengthen effective partnerships with business to the mutual benefit of both partners.

The case study by Cynthia Redmond and Byrdeen Warwood—"Partnership Building and Ideas for Applied Learning Projects"—offers additional examples of successful partnerships in their school district of Bozeman, Montana. The projects they describe have benefited not only businesses, but also their own community and helped develop students' skills in communication, problem solving, and interpersonal relationships. Look here for ideas on how to integrate learning objectives with the world outside the classroom.

The concept of "applied learning" presented by Redmond and Warwood may help those of us who struggle with the issue of student assessment, which continues to challenge educators. All too often, we do not include all learning experiences in determining a final assessment. One way to do this is with student exhibits such as portfolios. Applied learning projects, like those typical of business-education partnerships, lend themselves well to this kind of assessment and let students document that this portfolio truly represents, in part, what they know and can do. Self-reflection and self-evaluation are key factors in this type of assessment and can give students another avenue for increasing and demonstrating their potential for success.

Experience with the world of work also offers students an early opportunity to observe, interpret, and apply the work ethic, as Carol A. Johnson and Claudia L. Orr note in "Promoting the Work Ethic Among Generation X and N-Gen Students." Aside from the basic skills needed to do the job, Johnson and Orr state, work ethic is the most important quality sought by employers. Johnson and Orr find that today's students need instruction on initiative and dependability. They outline specific strategies for reaching the X- and N-Gen learners and understanding the culture in which they live.

Matching Teaching and Learning Styles

As Johnson and Orr already know, to reach any learner one must understand how he or she learns and modify one's teaching style accordingly. Educators in general need to become more aware of matching teaching style with student learning style. When this occurs, a more student-centered classroom is created. Student-centered classrooms maximize learning by engaging students in the learning process. In the chapter "Teaching and Learning Styles: Implications for Business Teacher Education," Wanda L. Stitt-Gohdes encourages teachers to understand and respect that different people learn differently. Lest we become overwhelmed by the research on the variety of learning styles that exist, Stitt-Gohdes suggests basic and concrete ways for "getting a handle" on creating an optimum learning environment in the business education classroom.

Pre-service teacher education is an excellent setting in which to emphasize and reinforce the importance of creating an optimum learning situation, and Patricia Arneson shares guidelines for shaping student experiences that lead to competent, effective, future business teachers. Her chapter "Strategies for Success: A Guide for Preparing Future Teachers" states that public concerns about education notwithstanding, the responsibility for preparing qualified teachers cannot rest entirely on the state or national standards, nor solely with teacher accreditation institutions, program, and faculty. Instead, those schools, administrators, and teachers that accept student teachers share such responsibility—along with student teachers themselves, who must take a proactive role in their own professional development.

Teachers as Knowledge Facilitators

Making a conscious attempt to match teaching and learning styles means the role of teacher changes from dispenser of knowledge to knowledge facilitator, mentor, and coach. This is a theme explored throughout this yearbook, and especially in the chapter by Jim Mansfield and Lonnie Echternacht entitled "Curriculum Integration: Optimized Learning for High School Students." Mansfield and Echternacht say teachers who encourage students to explore and apply subject matter content through integrating academic and business education curricula can strengthen academic and workplace competencies. They can also more effectively prepare students for the transition from high school to college or career.

Simulations, which business teachers have been using as a teaching strategy for years, and independent study are additional ways in which business education teachers can facilitate this transition. Independent study allows learners to research and create information in a way that is important for them. For 70 years, the University of Nebraska-Lincoln Independent Study High School has served 6,000 students annually in this manner. Interactions, once supported through fax, e-mail, and telephone, are now supplemented with communication via the Internet (the school reaches students throughout Nebraska and the 50 states as well as 135 countries throughout the world).

Technology as a Learning Tool

As the University of Nebraska-Lincoln Independent Study High School experience demonstrates, technology has redefined the "four walls" of the classroom. Jack E. Johnson, in "Distance Education: Learning for the 21st Century," defines terms common to this rapidly growing technology, examines model programs, and explores strategies for its use.

One of distance education's greatest applications, of course, is in rural or remote areas. Enrollments may be minimal, budgets stretched to the breaking point, curricula expertise far away. The question then becomes how can we provide a comprehensive education for our students when these challenges are present. Interactive television systems, Web-based courses, compressed video, or asynchronous delivery systems provide the means. A school with an exceptionally strong business program, for example, could broadcast courses to other schools that lack the high enrollment needed to sustain a specialized business curriculum.

Unfortunately, the use of technology—distance education or otherwise—is an area in which many educators are falling behind. It is expensive, both in time and money, to stay on the cutting edge. Yet Rodney G. Jurist's article, "The Promise of Technology," offers hope for teachers who want to lead rather than lag behind this important educational innovation. Perhaps due to its importance in education reform, funding for technology is more available and student access to computers and the Internet, as measured in surveys conducted by the Department of Education, is increasing. The outcome, Jurist says, is that technology is changing teacher beliefs and practices in ways that reinforce the relationship between learning and real life.

Thus, teachers must focus on the learning process itself and emphasize knowledge acquisition and management, analysis, and application. This places a burden on teachers to become even more technologically literate themselves. But if we remember and teach that technology is simply a tool to solve a problem and not simply an end in itself, we will achieve the goal of developing transferable

4

skills that will serve us and our students well as technology continues to advance and evolve. If the focus of the lesson is only to learn hardware or software, none of us will be able to apply this tool to situations that differ from what we currently know. Many times we are guilty of thinking that teaching and learning would improve if only we had more technology available to us. It might be better to identify the most difficult skills we are teaching and determine how a tool such as a pencil, calculator, or computer could better support student learning.

Carole A. Holden considers one aspect of this question in her chapter, "The Building Blocks of Multimedia Authoring." Holden shows how business educators can use authoring programs to create multimedia courseware that enhances the teaching and learning environment in their classrooms. The day is coming, she says, when teachers will be expected to create the instructional materials used by their students. Because students experience the instructional material produced in multimedia format in a variety of ways, Holden says, instruction becomes more efficient. Look here for ideas on how to jump-start the process.

Another way to offer multimedia learning experiences appears in the chapter "Business Education Integration: Interactive Broadcast Media Technology" by William R. Johnson and Linda I. Howard. Johnson and Howard report on a project at Mechanicsburg Area Senior High School, Mechanicsburg, Pennsylvania, in which business education and English courses merged so that students could update their computer applications skills and practice the higher-order thinking skills (visualization, creativity, organization, synthesis, and evaluation) useful for careers in television, video broadcasting, and community media organizations that rely on these technologies to get out their message.

Global Thinking for a Global Society

As we know from our own exposure to broadcast media, our world is interconnected to an unprecedented degree. Even today, companies are taking advantage of the economic opportunities that exist beyond their traditional markets. Carol Larson Jones examines how we can educate our students for an increasingly diverse and global society in her prescription for "Fostering a Diverse Workplace for Today's Global Marketplace."

Likewise, James Calvert Scott points out that globalization is the watch-word of business, and therefore business communication instruction must be internationalized. "Internationalizing Business Communication Instruction" looks at the "messaging" function of business and notes that the business communication tasks of the 21ˢᵗ century will be complex, as they transcend not only countries but also cultural conventions. The globalization of American business will demand a competitive advantage in global interaction, and American business leaders will look for students prepared to handle these increasingly complex requirements.

Fostering Full Participation in the Millennium

Precisely because the world is becoming so complex, we must help students see education not as something to be completed in 13 or 17 years, but as a continuing process, available throughout their lives, as a tool for coping with a changing world. As one community college president put it, education is a train and students must be able to get on and off as their needs change.

The challenges to business education in the 21ˢᵗ century apply to all teachers, all disciplines, and all levels. We are in the business of creating clear and effective communicators, self-directed and lifelong learners, creative and practical problem solvers, responsible and involved citizens, collaborative and quality workers, and integrative and informed thinkers: in short, citizens able to assume full participation in the new millennium. We cannot continue to meet future challenges without involving everyone: students, administrators, other faculty, parents, communities, and businesses. We must all work together to become successful.

The future demands that we "think globally, act locally." We will create the future that lies before us. It is a future of alternatives, and only global thinkers will be able to make the kinds of decisions necessary to lead their schools into the 21ˢᵗ century.

Chapter 1 — Teaching and Learning Styles: Implications for Business Teacher Education

Wanda L. Stitt-Gohdes
The University of Georgia
Athens, Georgia

All too often when teachers are asked why they teach as they do, they answer, "It's the way I was taught," or "It fits with the way I learn." Both responses reflect a teacher-centered learning situation. Neither focuses on the student as the center of the teaching-learning process, a subtle but critically important distinction. A multitude of changes in classrooms and students strongly suggest that the successful classrooms of today and tomorrow be student-centered. This chapter discusses the changes teachers face, describes teaching and learning styles, and offers some recommendations for current and future business educators.

The Forces of Change

A trip into a business education classroom today—even for a beginning teacher—would reveal a variety of changes that have become increasingly apparent over the past five or 10 years. Not only is technology everywhere, but the faces of our students reflect the changing demographics of our nation. Most students are ethnically and racially different from their teachers. These differences are accompanied by an increase in the identification of students with a myriad of learning disabilities.

If our student population has changed this dramatically, can we say the same for our teaching styles and strategies? Goodlad (as cited in Griggs, 1989) suggested that, based on his observations of many classrooms, most teachers prefer whole-group instruction. He concluded that "the climate within classrooms is flat as a result of teacher domination of instruction with many students minimally involved in the learning process" (p. 135). Much research supports the notion that when one is engaged in the learning process, learning is more likely to take place. In order to engage students, however, their needs and interests must be taken into consideration. Each learner must be viewed and valued individually.

Griggs (1989) reported that at-risk students have an assortment of learning preferences which may range from learning alone to learning in pairs to learning in a variety of ways. An especially important finding is that "the higher the grade level, the less teacher-motivated students become" (p. 136). This has special importance for business teachers as the majority of our classes are taught at the secondary school level.

Changing classroom demographics. Demographic trends indicate that African-Americans, women, Asians, Hispanics, and other races will make up the majority of new entrants into the workforce by 2000 (Apolloni, Feichtner, and West, 1991). Many of these individuals are currently and will continue to be students in our classrooms every day. While the racial and ethnic diversity of our students may be obvious, their diverse learning styles will not be. And it is the identification of these learning styles and the degree to which our teaching styles "fit" them that will determine the extent of student learning.

Changing classroom demographics are but one reason to consider the learning styles of students and the teaching-learning styles of educators. Academically at-risk students represent a growing population of students whose academic and vocational success is critically important not only for the students themselves but also for the continued economic well-being of our nation.

Meeting the needs of academically at-risk students. Gadwa and Griggs (1985) posed four categories of reasons students leave school: "familial factors, personal characteristics, socioeconomic factors, and educational achievement and school behavior" (p. 9). These authors administered the Learning Style Inventory to three groups of students, including a group of high school dropouts. The inventory helps to identify "learning preferences with regard to immediate environmental conditions and the students' emotional, sociological, and physical needs" (p. 12).

Gadwa and Griggs found that the dropouts who participated: "were motivated to learn; were easily bored by daily routines and highly structured learning requirements; and viewed tactile, kinesthetic, and auditory perceptions as strong modalities in the learning process" (p. 14). Clearly, these students would not be successful in the teacher-dominated, flat classroom environment described earlier by Goodlad. And yet how much of our daily instruction is highly structured, routinized, and teacher-dominated rather than student-centered?

Because of the large role that technology-based educational experiences play in the business education curriculum, much of our instruction provides a tactile modality. The reality, however, is that this modality is driven by the technology and probably by the teacher's preferred teaching and learning styles rather than a determination of preferred student learning styles.

Thus, it becomes important to investigate the relationship between the teacher's instructional and learning styles in an effort to best determine how they affect student learning.

Review of Related Literature

If we teach as we learn—or even as we were taught—what difference does that make in the classroom? Kaplan and Kies (1995) suggest that understanding the relationship between teaching style and learning requires these assumptions:

1. Teaching style and student learning styles can be identified.

2. Classroom teachers are most helpful when they assist students in learning through their own style preferences.

3. Students should have the opportunity to learn through their preferred styles.

4. Classroom teachers can develop a teaching style responsive to the wide variety of students in their classes (p. 30).

Some insight into the teaching and learning styles of educators and students are provided below.

Teaching styles. Hyman and Rosoff (1985) posit that "teaching is an act which has three elements—the *teacher*, the *student*, and the *subject matter*—interrelating in an *environment* and in a particular *time* period" (p. 14). Effective teaching occurs when all five of these elements work together. Key to this collaboration is the suggestion of Dunn and Dunn that people have individualized means of learning and that some students can only learn using methods that do not necessarily work for others.

The ways these students learn may also differ dramatically from the ways their teachers teach and learn themselves, causing a tension that usually results in student failure. A reflection of this mentality is, "If the majority of students have learned as I have taught, those who haven't learned aren't as capable."

In many cases nothing could be farther from the truth. This way of thinking can be compared to that of a physician who prescribes only one type of medication for all patients with the common cold. One might conclude that if they all did not get better, they probably did not follow the instructions. It is more likely, however, that their individual needs were different; consequently, the prescribed medication was ineffective. Thus, as Dunn and Dunn suggest, when teaching methods complement students' learning styles, student motivation and achievement increase.

Learning styles. Dunn and Dunn described 18 elements of learning style and grouped them into four categories:

1. Environmental elements: sound, light, temperature, and design.

2. Emotional elements: motivation, persistence, responsibility, and a need for structure.

3. Sociological elements: working alone, with peers, with an adult, or some combination.

4. Physical elements: perceptual strengths, intake, time of day, and need for mobility.

A brief examination of this list might elicit a response such as, "There's no way I have time to deal with all these!" A closer examination of these categories reveals some factors that are addressed relatively easily, such as environmental elements. All of us prefer working in a comfortable environment—why should we expect anything different for our students?

In order to facilitate learning, we must adjust the classroom conditions. We must also provide for the specific emotional, sociological, and physical needs that each student presents. Once this is done, the teaching process should be smoother and more effective.

The critical point to remember, as stated by Dr. Burton Kaliski of New Hampshire College, is that we are teachers of students first and then teachers of subjects. The extent to which we accept that premise critically affects how we approach the business of teaching. It also impacts our acceptance of the notion that learning differently is not wrong, it is simply different.

Marshall (1991) provided further evidence of the impact of the teacher's learning style on student learning. Research she reviewed supported the fact that the learning preferences of those students perceived to be slow or lower achievers "were not supported within the structure of traditional schooling" (p. 225). Her own research yielded some findings supporting this earlier inquiry. In assessing teachers' learning style preferences, she found that teachers generally taught the way they preferred to learn.

One finding bears particular mention. More than 90 percent of teachers indicated that they preferred to learn alone. "Despite overwhelming evidence regarding the effectiveness of peer tutoring and cooperative learning techniques, the majority of teachers expressed a reluctance to risk such approaches, preferring the 'control' possible within the quiet, paper and pencil, teacher-dominant classroom" (p. 226). Based on their own learning preferences, they inferred that student interaction was a deterrent or distraction to learning.

Implications of the relationship between the instructor's preferred teaching and learning styles were highlighted in Matthews' (1996) research, where she investigated the relationship between learning styles and perceived academic achievement of a selected group of high school students. Learning style was significantly related to the self-ratings of students regarding perceived academic achievement. Students' learning preferences were grouped into one of four categories: converger, diverger, assimilator, or accommodator.

Those selecting the converger learning style also perceived themselves to be higher achievers than students selecting one of the other three styles. The convergers are very task- and problem-oriented. They do well in testing situations where there is a single, correct answer or solution. Not surprisingly, these are the strengths that most schools and teachers value.

If there is a link, then, between the teaching and learning styles of the instructor, and thus for the student, what is the teacher to do who is genuinely interested in improving classroom learning and the academic achievement of students? The following recommendations provide some basic strategies to help better meet the needs of all learners.

Recommendations for Practice

The relationship between teaching and learning is important both to those currently teaching business education and to those who are preparing future business teachers. What may these two groups do to positively impact this relationship?

Current business teachers. As a starting point, business teachers may engage in some introspection and self-analysis of their own teaching styles and strategies. This may be done in a formal way via one of the instructional style inventories. A teacher may also choose to be videotaped over a period of time and with a cross-section of classes and students. These two strategies should help the teacher more clearly define how he or she teaches. It is also critical to identify the student learning preferences that must then be matched in some way with teaching style.

Dunn and Dunn (1979) suggest that once student learning preferences are identified, teachers should gradually begin to augment their current practice with alternative strategies more appropriate to learners' needs. For example, if a teacher prefers large-group, whole-class instruction but the majority of students are not successful with that style, smaller groups may be developed. The teacher may still provide group instruction, just with a smaller group. This practice also increases the likelihood that those students who prefer cooperative learning or have a shorter attention span may also have their needs met. This alternative teaching style would also permit the teacher to better respond to sociological and emotional elements of learning.

Griggs (1989) suggested the use of an individualized educational plan called Contract Activity Packages. This package may include some of the following: specific, detailed objectives; the use of "multisensory" resources in instruction; opportunities to use what has been learned; and a pretest, self-test, and posttest to determine degree of mastery. Using such an activity package would permit individual student learning preferences to be acknowledged and valued.

As a result of her research on learning style and perceived academic achievement, Matthews (1996) suggested that alternative assessment options would provide a genuine opportunity for students who learn in different ways to be able to demonstrate what they know. Such a change in assessment should also result in related changes in instruction, not the least of which is an acknowledgement that students learn in different ways.

In order for the increased likelihood that all—or at least more—students can achieve at higher levels academically, Hyman and Rosoff (1985) recommend a "reorientation of thinking about matching learning styles and teaching styles" (p. 41). They suggest that teachers need to understand that learning is much more inclusive than simply the points earned on a classroom test. Students learn as much from the aura of the teachers, the human qualities they demonstrate either overtly or covertly.

Teachers also need to realize that they can ultimately control only themselves; this realization, however, is the key to effective instruction and learning. The control of their actions means they may choose from a variety of teaching styles, depending on the students they are working with. And it is this overt act of choice of teaching style that directly impacts the level of learning and achievement for any student.

Determining the preferred learning styles of students is especially important for at-risk learners. Caldwell and Ginther (1996) reported on research suggesting that "the achievement of all students could be improved by providing initial instruction in a manner consistent with each student's learning style" (p. 142). For many high school dropouts, a clear disparity exists between learning and teaching style. The authors found that internal or motivational factors predicted achievement for low socioeconomic status students.

What meaning do these findings have for the business teacher? If the preferred teaching style is at odds with the student's preferred learning style, the student may perceive that he or she is not valued and, thus, become less and less motivated to achieve. In addition, the student's achievements will go unnoticed if there is only one acceptable type/style of response mode. Caldwell and Ginther suggested that if one accepts the premise that "individual control is a critical component of internal motivation, classrooms which allow for and encourage personal control will be effective" (p. 145). This does not mean students will take over the class but simply that they will participate in setting goals and establishing appropriate learning environments. For a business teacher, student performance may thus take on a variety of appearances. Alternative assessment strategies are key to success with these students.

Rural students often fall into the category of at-risk learners. Fitzgerald and Bloodsworth (1996) suggest a framework through which the needs of the rural learner, probably any learner, may be better met. The framework includes but is not restricted to the following.

1. Global learning: a syllabus, which not only provides objectives, but also shows their relationship to course content and activities.

2. Perception of learning as a social experience: recognition of students as individuals and the inclusion of personal experiences as learning points.

3. Modifying arbitrarily set time frames: once students know what is required, they can plan their own schedules. This permits flexibility in test taking, which may be affected by tests and assignments in other classes.

4. Overcoming a sense of powerlessness: flexibility in some course requirements gives the student the sense of control and choice. Contracts may be
developed between the student and teacher, which address the issue of
student control while at the same time clearly delineating what the student
has agreed to do.

While Fitzgerald and Bloodsworth (1996) have suggested this framework
for rural students, it would be equally appropriate for any student. In every
course we teach, there exists some flexibility and opportunity for choice, either
in content, style of instruction, or method of assessment. Student participation in
the development of course objectives and assignments makes them partners in
instruction rather than recipients of instruction.

An equally important aspect of attempting to provide the best learning
climate for all students is that of the teacher preparation programs. The effectiveness of classroom instruction has its foundation in these programs.

Business teacher education programs. Historically, teacher education
programs have been a reflection of the majority population. Anderson (1988)
proposed a reason for the lack of success in retaining minority teacher education
candidates:

*These programs have never attempted to identify the cognitive assets
and learning preferences of the non-white students [based on] the
ethnocentric assumption on the part of whites that minorities do not
have a valid and substantive cognitive framework which may be
somewhat different but equally effective for them. (p. 3)*

The far-reaching effect of this situation is that few minority students have
teachers who are a reflection of themselves. Thus, if the majority of teachers
represent the majority of the population, the likelihood of valuing diverse
learning styles diminishes.

The need, then, for teacher preparation programs to provide opportunities
for prospective teachers to identify and understand learning styles which may be
different from their own is critically important. Once one is aware of, exposed
to, and begins to value differences in learning styles, the idea of adapting one's
teaching style becomes less threatening and more reasonable.

To begin this process, business teacher education programs should help
students to:

1. Take a critical approach in the examination of education issues;

2. See beyond conventional thought about classroom practice;

3. Examine the rationales underlying classroom and school regularities;

4. Evaluate their own assumptions and biases and how these affect their
classroom practice; and

5. Examine critically the processes of their own socialization as teachers
(Hyman and Rosoff, 1985, p. 43).

Discussion and instruction focusing on these five themes will, at a minimum, develop an awareness and understanding of significant differences that exist between teachers and learners. It should also highlight the impact of these differences on the instructor's preferred teaching style. The bottom line, as suggested by Kaplan and Kies (1995), is that "teachers must see their roles in context of how students learn" (p. 30). This context will determine the level of student achievement and teaching effectiveness.

The authors suggest three additional areas that must be addressed in teacher preparation to enhance the expansion of teaching styles. They are "the role of the classroom teacher, instructional skills and strategies, and learning styles" (p. 30). The classroom teacher must be knowledgeable in the subject matter, be able to establish and modify objectives, and be able to assess student learning. Instructional skills and strategies include, at a minimum, effective communication skills, a variety of presentation skills, and the ability to engage students in the learning process. Finally, learning styles include the teacher's understanding and awareness of all those factors influencing the learning process.

The acquisition of these skills and abilities is the result of a focused, intentional process. It requires much introspection and reflection on long-held attitudes and practices in light of learning how best to meet student needs.

Summary

It would be tidy if a list could provide the prescription for success in matching teaching and learning styles so high achievement could occur. It also would be terribly arrogant and counterproductive to attempt such a list. What must happen, though, in order for *all* students to learn more is for teachers and those who prepare future teachers to develop a basic understanding of and respect for the simple fact that different people learn differently. That premise is basic to developing a classroom climate where learning occurs and students are active partners in this process. Ultimately, we are first teachers of *students* and then teachers of *subjects*.

References

Anderson, J. A. (1988). Cognitive Styles and Multicultural Populations. *Journal of Teacher Education, 39*, 2-9.

Apolloni, T., Feichtner, S. H., and West, L. L. (1991, Fall). Learners and Workers in the Year 2001. *The Journal for Vocational Special Needs Education, 14*, 5-10.

Caldwell, G. P., and Ginther, D. W. (1996). Differences in Learning Styles of Low Socioeconomic Status for Low and High Achievers. *Education, 117* (1), 141-147.

Dunn, R. S., and Dunn, K. J. (1979). Learning Styles/Teaching Styles: Should They . . . Can They . . . Be Matched? *Educational Leadership, 36* (4), 238-244.

Fitzgerald, D. F., and Bloodsworth, G. (1996). Addressing the Neglected Needs of Rural Learners: A Learning Style Approach. *The Clearing House, 69* (3), 169-170.

Gadwa, K., and Griggs, S. A. (1985, September). The School Dropout: Implications for Counselors. *The School Counselor*, 9-17.

Griggs, S. A. (1989). Students' Sociological Grouping Preferences of Learning Styles. *The Clearing House,* 63, 135-139.

Hyman, R., and Rosoff, B. (1985). Matching Learning Styles and Teaching Styles. *The Education Digest,* 50, 41-43.

Kaplan, E. J., and Kies, D. A. (1995). Teaching Styles and Learning Styles: Which Came First? *Journal of Instructional Psychology,* 22 (1), 29-33.

Marshall, C. (1991). Teachers' Learning Styles: How They Affect Student Learning. *Clearing House,* 64 (4), 225-227.

Matthews, D. B. (1996). An Investigation of Learning Styles and Perceived Academic Achievement for High School Students. *The Clearing House*, 69 (4), 249-254.

Chapter 2 — Promoting the Work Ethic Among Generation X and N-Gen Students

Carol A. Johnson and Claudia L. Orr
Northern Michigan University
Marquette, Michigan

The significance of work ethic in employment was revealed through a survey of 150 human resource managers from this country's 1,000 largest companies. Aside from the basic skills needed to do the job, work ethic was considered the most important quality sought when hiring administrative employees (Work Ethic Top Job Skill, 1994).

While employers often cite work ethic as a desirable employee characteristic, its definition is elusive. Work ethic has been defined as a system of beliefs, values, and principles that guide the way individuals interpret and act upon their rights and responsibilities within the work context at any given time; an "enabling" work ethic is defined as one that empowers an individual to adapt to and initiate change in order to sustain long-term harmony with his or her work environment (Miller and Coady in Ford and Herren, 1993). Today, work ethic is often broadly described as those attributes necessary for organizational growth and profitability and individual satisfaction and success.

Researchers have used survey instruments to identify characteristics and profiles of successful employees. In fact, using more than 50 work ethic descriptors, Hill and Petty (1995) identified three key themes of work ethic: interpersonal skills, initiative, and dependability (see Table 1). Employers want employees who have a "good work ethic" and appropriate social behavior, and for the future, workers "who have exhibited a capacity to learn, think, work effectively alone and in groups, and solve problems (National Center for Research in Vocational Education, 1998).

Status of Work Ethic

Some reports indicate that there may be a decline in the American work ethic, posing challenges for both employers and educators who help prepare the

Table 1. Work Ethic Themes		
Interpersonal Skills	**Initiative**	**Dependability**
Courteous	Perceptive	Follows Directions
Friendly	Productive	Follows Regulations
Cheerful	Resourceful	Dependable
Considerate	Initiating	Reliable
Pleasant	Ambitious	Careful
Cooperative	Efficient	Honest
Helpful	Effective	Punctual
Devoted	Enthusiastic	
Loyal	Perseverant	
Hard Working	Dedicated	
Source: Hill, R. B. and Petty, G. C. (1995). A New Look at Selected Employability Skills: A Factor Analysis of the Occupational Work Ethic. *Journal of Vocational Education Research*, 20 (4), 59–73.		

workforce. Whether a decline in work ethic really has occurred is uncertain; reports conflict. In fact, a shift in values rather than a decline in values may account for concerns voiced by both employers and educators. This values shift may have begun as early as the 1920s, when the assembly line, labor unions, and Social Security contributed to weakening the work ethic and ushering in an "ethics of leisure" (Eisenberger in Douthitt, 1990). Many workers do not respond to traditional incentives—money, fear, a sense of duty—and instead seek self-development (Douthitt, 1990).

Responsible educators should become aware of changes in the American value system, as these changes impact classroom instruction, perhaps by scanning nonfiction booksellers' lists. Recent titles such as *We Are All Self-Employed* (Hakim, 1994), *Success Redefined* (Giovannoni, 1997), and *True Work* (Toms and Toms, 1998) can intimate such value shifts.

An examination of data from nationwide public opinion surveys from 1972 through 1993 revealed few changes in work ethic behaviors in the United States (Weaver, 1997). However, there is an accompanying sense of less satisfaction with work. While employees want to work harder and more effectively, they enjoy it less; this is true across all sectors of the workforce.

Workforce Generations

Today's workforce includes three generations of employees (Filipczak, 1994): the Silent Generation, the Baby Boomers, and Generation Xers. The Silent Generation grew up during the Depression and later benefited from the economic prosperity of the '50s and '60s. Baby Boomers, born between 1946 and 1964 (Tapscott, 1998) and comprising the largest segment of the labor force, grew up during the economic boom and experienced times of great political and social change. They evolved from hippies to yuppies and now lead the majority of American businesses. Generation Xers were born between 1965 and 1976 (Tapscott, 1998) and are currently the smallest of the demographic generations in the labor force. The X in Generation X refers to a group that feels it has no identity or an identity not recognized by others. They have been labeled Twentysomethings, the Lost Generation, Baby Busters, the 13th Generation (the 13th generation since ratification of the Constitution), Slackers, and the Lurking Generation, lurking in the shadow of the Baby Boomers. As Generation Xers gradually exit today's collegiate business classrooms, the majority of which are directed by Baby Boomer instructors, they enter a labor market dominated by Baby Boomer managers and work team members. The generational differences, particularly between Baby Boomers and Generation Xers, create challenges for each other—in employment and in education.

Generation X Characteristics

Generation X college students and employees are products of broadly divergent circumstances. Filipczak (1994), Keaveney (1997), Sellers (1994), and others offer some characterizations. In contrast to Baby Boomers, Xers were not raised by stay-at-home moms. In fact, their parents may have been divorced, and they may have been part of the growing number of alternative families. They grew up in day care centers and were the first generation of latchkey kids, returning after school to empty homes. Consequently, Generation Xers became independent, self-motivated problem-solvers who dislike close supervision and prefer a coaching approach when given direction. Yet they look for authority figures with high accountability to offer feedback and reassurance—needs not met during their developmental years.

While Xers demonstrate a high level of independence, they often lack the social interaction skills necessary to function well in the work-team environment of business. For Xers, work team experiences need to support and validate individual efforts. Xers thrive in group environments where ideas are openly exchanged, goals are established by the group, and opportunities for individual accomplishments are provided.

During their formative years, Generation Xers watched their parents and other adults in their lives place employers ahead of families, only to witness these role models suffer from stress, burnout, failed marriages due to overwork, and finally, from being downsized and reengineered out of their careers. As a result, Generation X employees are often wary of workaholism and strive to maintain a "balanced" life. Having watched their parents trade personal lives for the "good of the company," Generation Xers are likely to put family before work, comfortably choosing to miss work to tend to family matters that conflict with work obligations.

Generation X employees build their portfolios by changing jobs frequently, especially when job satisfaction or income is likely to improve. To Baby Boomers, this may seem like disloyalty and lack of commitment to the company, but Xers believe professional growth comes from their own personal initiative. Xers seek a variety of challenging, immediately relevant projects through which to acquire new skills. They are intolerant of "busy work," politics, and purposeless meetings with endless discussions. They are interested in getting the job done and moving on.

Their interest in maintaining a balance among work, life, and family has often earned them the label "slacker." But from another perspective, this generation can be viewed as a group of balanced individuals who can set schedules, prioritize, and meet deadlines. Not surprisingly, Generation Xers have difficulty forgoing the needs of today for a future, uncertain payoff. They live for today and are motivated by money and other concrete, expeditious rewards.

Additionally, Xers grew up with rapidly changing technology. The information revolution was in full force by the time this generation of children learned to read and write. They learned how to read watching television and using interactive computer games and learned to write using word processors that corrected their grammar and spelling errors. As a result, Xers have a tremendous capacity to process information and are capable of handling multiple tasks and multiple sources of information. But they tend to have short attention spans, frequently seeking challenges and fearing boredom, though they are easily bored. They like to have fun and prefer a fast-paced, entertaining environment.

Generation X in the Workplace

To better understand Generation X in the workforce, James W. Sheehy (1990), a human resources professional with 14 years' experience, eight of them in management, accepted employment as a management trainee in a fast-food restaurant, working as a maintenance person, cook, custodian, and cashier. His fellow employees were high school and college students from upper- and middle-income families. More than half his coworkers were women, a third of them were minorities, and a majority of them worked only for discretionary cash.

Among this workforce, Sheehy witnessed "contempt for customers, poor work habits, lack of ethical standards, unrealistic expectations, and an overreliance on technology." He observed that long hours and hard work were counterproductive to meeting the needs of Generation X. Sheehy concluded that the values and ethics held by the workforce youth could be even more damaging to a business than its traditional competition.

A study comparing the work ethic attributes of vocational students in eight curriculum areas to those of full-time workers from business and industry (Hill, 1996) found no statistical differences between the two groups on the work ethic theme of interpersonal skills. (This did not mean that improvement was not needed, but that student and worker characteristics did not greatly differ.) On the two work ethic themes of initiative and dependability, however, employed workers scored significantly higher than did vocational school students, providing educators with evidence of the need to teach students these work ethic behaviors.

Educators may believe they are teaching work ethic to their students, but a study on determining the extent to which the concept of work ethic was being taught by work program coordinators in Georgia revealed that the teaching of work ethic in their classrooms was informal or unintentional (Ford and Herren, 1993). Coordinators most often taught work ethics through discussion of workplace problems, and findings suggested that educators should receive extensive in-service training in teaching this concept developmentally and intentionally. Teachers must then formally recognize work ethic behaviors as part of the curriculum and develop strategies for teaching them.

Ford and Herren's study asserts that the development of a work ethic is analogous to the stages of moral development identified by Kohlberg, Piaget, and others. To teach work ethic intentionally and developmentally, educators must understand the stages of moral development and use the same teaching methods as moral educators, creating a "cognitive apprenticeship" in which teachers move students along the developmental values continuum through practical-reasoning, decision-making strategies (Ford and Herren, 1993; Douthitt, 1990).

There are many avenues available for including work ethic instruction in the curriculum at all levels of instruction, elementary through postsecondary. In business education courses, work ethic should be included as a specific topic, unit, or seminar. Programs on this topic could be included as formal courses or as seminars sponsored by student organizations and workshops sponsored by civic or professional organizations. Much of this instruction will be accomplished through the "hidden curriculum" (Miller and Coady in Ford and Herren, 1993), in which instructors model work ethic behaviors and teach by example. Vocational education, by virtue of its hands-on curriculum and work/co-op experiences, is a natural setting for teaching the work ethic. Vocational educators can capitalize on opportunities to endorse the creative urge, offer real-world experience, reward high effort, and enforce high standards (Douthitt, 1990).

The Next Generation: N-Gen

As educators align their teaching strategies to student profiles, they need to be mindful of generational transitions. Following Generation X is the Net Generation, sometimes referred to as the Baby Boom Echo or the N-Gen. The Net Generation, born between 1977 and 1997 and numbering 80,000,000 (Tapscott, 1998), are similar to their Generation X counterparts. Collectively, they lack social interaction skills though they willingly share knowledge and information; they are intolerant of social and political practices and rhetoric, optimistic about personal futures, and committed to doing well.

While both generations may at times be found in the same classrooms and will have been raised with technology, it is the Net Generation's use of the Internet, referred to as the electronic miracle, that sets them apart from other learners. Like Generation Xers, the N-Gen prefers a fast-paced, fun environment. Cyberspace is their playground. Their culture is one of choice, customization, interaction, and authentication (Tapscott, in Nucifora, 1997).

They have grown accustomed to the free and open Information Superhighway. They choose where to go and how to get there. They customize their identity (using screen names) and their menu options, interacting with companies or individuals through online shopping, e-mail, message boards, newsgroups, and chat rooms. They share knowledge and infuse that knowledge into products and services. They are constantly authenticating the nature of the online information they find.

Because this culture is interactive and collaborative, N-Geners as a group value intellectual capital. The new learning model is that "everyone relies on their own resources, and on everyone else, sharing their expertise" (Tapscott, 1999). More than just a source of information, the Internet becomes a method of constructing intelligence and collaborating with others who are cities, states, or half-a-world away.

This generation, more than any other, is likely to shape what they learn in the same way that they gathered the information: by using multimedia tools. Even without instructor prompting, students sophisticated in the use of the Internet and other computer technology are likely to use presentation software and hardware when called upon to develop and present a class project (Ferguson, 1999).

Educators working with the Information Superhighway are faced with weighing the return on technology investments in terms of student achievement. While little conclusive evidence exists about the relationship between technology and achievement gains, educators must accept the pervasive use of technology among this generation of learners and appropriately direct student learning. Through classroom interaction and assignments, Net Generation learners should be expected to apply the often disorganized data acquired from the Web into meaningful information; to rely on the most significant media, whether digital or print; and to frame questions for sound inquiry and new insight (McKenzie, 1998). Using technology responsibly is the educator's challenge when working with Net Generation learners.

Strategies for Teaching Generation X and N-Gen Learners

Baby Boomer managers and instructors, raised in different times and circumstances, may experience frustration in working with Xers, initially viewing them as unmanageable, rude, demanding, uncommitted, disloyal, and impatient. But who better to fill and lead the fast-paced, ever-changing workforce of the 21ˢᵗ century than the empowered, self-directed, technoliterate, and flexible Xers? Regardless of Baby Boomer perceptions, the Generation X culture is and will be the predominant presence on college campuses for a considerable time (Jones, 1995) and faculty cannot overlook their learning styles and expectations. Neither can they overlook members of the Net Generation, who are just now making their presence felt in high school and on college campuses.

A typical college class conducted by a Baby Boomer professor is likely to include lectures, paper-and-pencil tests, and limited interaction with learners.

This traditional environment sharply contrasts with the fast-paced, engaging environment in which Xers and Net Generation learners thrive. While the traditional approach to teaching and learning may have worked for Baby Boomers, Xers respond more favorably to self-directed opportunities, interaction, multiple forms of feedback, choices, varied resources, and personally meaningful experiences. Digitally literate N-Gen learners will expect and prefer to use the Internet and related multimedia not only to learn but also to share knowledge with their peers.

Focusing on the work ethic themes of interpersonal skills, initiative, and dependability defined by Hill and Petty (1995) and responding to generational learner profiles will result in win-win situations for students, faculty, and the workforce. For students, instruction will be engaging and meaningful; for faculty, instruction will be student-centered; and for employers, instruction will be relevant to workforce needs.

Faculty can use a number of instructional strategies to promote work ethic while taking into account the profiles of Generation X and N-Gen learners. Both generations will respond to instructors who focus on outcomes rather than techniques, make learning experiential, give students control over their own learning, respect learners' ability to engage in parallel thinking, and highlight key points in a way that gives attention to the format of the learning materials (having grown up with computers and video games, these students are surfers and scanners) (Brown, 1997). Work ethic can effectively be promoted in the classroom through combinations of modeling, research, self-assessment, field experiences, journaling, guests, mentoring, collaborative learning, and limited lecturing.

Modeling. Modeling, for instance, acknowledges the importance the new generations place on authority figures with high accountability. By devoting important time to developing and maintaining appropriate personal and academic relationships with learners, by consistently and frequently interacting with students positively and in a friendly manner, and by working cooperatively with students, faculty model the interpersonal skills theme of work ethic. By seeking and using student input to develop and implement creative learner activities, faculty model the theme of initiative. By arriving for class early, beginning and ending class on time, using class time for well-planned and relevant activities, setting and meeting deadlines outlined in a syllabus, and returning graded papers promptly, faculty model the dependability theme of work ethic they want to teach. By consistently modeling the work ethic, faculty establish conduct standards and are able to expect those behaviors of students in return. Note that modeling occurs even before formal instruction begins, even before mentioning "work ethic." For modeling to be effective, these behaviors should be consistently maintained through all interactions with students, inside and outside the classroom.

Research. Rather than deliver lectures on the definition and importance of work ethic in the workforce, teachers can ask students to conduct electronic searches to define work ethic and its role in hiring and employment. Rather than asking that the research simply be written and handed in, teachers can have students share their findings with one another in small collaborative learning groups. Asking randomly selected individuals to report to the class on behalf of their groups allows them to develop and enhance their group skills and their listening and speaking skills. This strategy acknowledges students' need to self-select topics, their facility with technology, and their social interaction needs.

Self-assessment. After establishing a framework for the importance and scope of work ethic, students should have an opportunity to determine their own work ethic profile through the use of inventories such as the Occupational Work Ethic Inventory (OWEI) refined by Hill and Petty (1995). By promoting give-and-take exchanges of ideas rather than blind acceptance of characteristics revealed through administration and scoring of the OWEI, Xers and N-Gen learners have an opportunity to recognize their individuality and reflect on their possible fit in the workforce. They should be asked through writing and/or discussion (small group or class) to identify problems encountered in environments where work ethic profiles vary and to outline solutions to those problems from various points of view. Regardless of their generational profile, students are called on to acknowledge another definition of diversity.

Field experiences and journaling. Having acquired an understanding of the dimensions of work ethic through instructor modeling, research, and self-assessment, students can be required to make specific observations of their own and others' work ethic behaviors through short-term and long-term field experiences in introductory and advanced classes. Field experiences lend themselves to students' interest in getting the job done and learning in the most direct fashion. To focus on the many aspects of successful employment, students may be required to journal regularly. Initial journal entries about work ethic should include enough structure to meet an appropriate objective. If the purpose of a journal assignment is for students to demonstrate an understanding of the impact of work ethic, students could be called on to respond to a minimum number of ideas outlined for them:

- What behaviors were observed?
- What is likely to be the immediate impact of these behaviors on the organization, on others in the work environment, and on the individual whose behavior is being observed?
- What is likely to be the long-term impact of these behaviors on the organization, on others in the work environment, and on the individual whose behavior is being observed?

When the purpose of journal assignments moves to demonstrating an understanding and acceptance of different work ethic behaviors, students should be called on to describe behavior choices that conflict with their own, consider why an individual has made the choices she or he has, and cite consequences and rewards for different choices. In all instances, students should be asked to withhold personal judgment of individuals. They should consistently be asked to identify the behaviors they think they would have demonstrated in similar circumstances, and support those choices with reasons. As students devote more time to field experiences, their journal entries should reflect an understanding of the consequences and rewards of their own work behaviors. As is the case with all journal assignments, students should be given feedback. Journal entries should be evaluated on variety of ideas, development of ideas, and conclusions. Feedback should not be limited to instructor-written comments. In-class discussion should be used so that classmates' feedback on observations and reactions can reveal a variety of perspectives based on different work ethic profiles.

Invited guests. Inviting employers to share in work ethic instruction should appeal to Xers' and N-Geners' confidence in authority figures, use of varied resources, and need for self-direction and social interaction. Students could identify guests of their choice, extend invitations, outline and communicate expectations, and follow up with letters of appreciation. Rather than limiting guests to traditional lectures, teachers can ask them to present scenarios and case studies, participate in role-playing, and conduct discussions with students. Devoting a class period to guest involvement on a regular basis, perhaps monthly, enables instructors and businesspeople to communicate with solidarity the significance of work ethic in employment.

Mentoring. Mentoring programs, in lieu of or in addition to field experiences, pair students and businesspeople, again appealing to students' confidence in authority figures and preference for acquiring practical experience. At the onset, students and mentors meet one another at orientation sessions and mutually determine expectations, responsibilities, and time commitments. When field experience hosts and classroom guests serve as mentors, relationships with students mature through dedicated time commitments. Mentoring relationships help foster realistic workplace perspectives for students, provide frank feedback on their work ethic values and behaviors, and instill confidence that their interpersonal skills, initiative, and dependability are appropriate for the workplace.

Collaborative learning. Appealing to Xers' and N-Gen learners' desires for involvement without close supervision, collaborative learning is conducted in a learner-centered environment with proactive learners and coaching faculty. Effective collaborative learning experiences begin with an orientation to group skills and opportunities for all students to develop and demonstrate these skills in roles such as facilitator, recorder, reporter, and timekeeper. As each group convenes, it should be asked to develop its own list of self-governing rules. Inevitably, rules will include elements of work ethic. With round-robin sharing of ideas among groups and with faculty prompting, most groups' governing rules will include references to the value placed on interpersonal skills, initiative, and dependability. Periodic reviews of these lists and use of them to solve group process problems will remind students of the significance of work ethic in productivity and satisfaction.

Additionally, collaborative learning makes good use of limited classroom time by forcing students to remain on task. By randomly identifying students to orally report group learning, individual accountability is promoted. While group interdependence is a tenet of collaborative learning, with students learning from each other, individual performance on tests, projects, and other learning activities is used to determine grades.

Lectures. Keeping lectures to a minimum and basing them on sound research that has examined the characteristics of successful employees acknowledges students' preference for straightforward, no-nonsense information. To meet their need for stimulation, lectures should be enhanced by the use of presentation software and other multimedia support. The passive approach of lectures may contribute relatively little to an understanding and development of work ethic values. Needed work ethic behaviors are more appropriately developed through active teaching and learning strategies. Therefore, lectures followed by focused, well-planned discussions and exercises lend variety and personal relevance to classroom interaction.

Summary

Employers, regardless of industry, include work ethic as a criterion when screening applicants for employment, forming work teams, and conducting periodic employee reviews. They take into consideration employee interpersonal skills, initiative, and dependability; these are the qualities business educators need to instill and develop in students through daily lessons, unit plans, and seminars and workshops. When full-time worker and student work ethics were compared, the need for instruction in initiative and dependability was clearly revealed; educators have had some success in addressing interpersonal skills in instruction, but there is still room for improvement. Work ethic can be taught successfully if teachers formally recognize it as part of the curriculum and develop strategies for teaching it.

While a decline in the American work ethic has been speculated, the status of work ethic among people born between 1965 and 1976 may be explained as a shift of values from generation to generation, specifically from the Baby Boomer generation to Generation X. While encountering frustrations with Generation Xers in education and in the workforce, Baby Boomer instructors and managers must work to understand and accept the values and behaviors of an emerging force. Raised in times of changing family structures, downsized organizations, and rapidly changing technology, Generation Xers emerge as empowered, self-directed, technoliterate, and flexible—the very profile needed to lead the workforce of the 21st century. College faculty whose classrooms are inhabited by Generation Xers need to acknowledge their learning styles and expectations and incorporate appropriate strategies to provide effective work ethic instruction. Teaching strategies that acknowledge and appeal to the Generation X profile include modeling, research, self-assessment, field experiences and journaling, guests, mentoring, collaborative learning, and limited lecturing.

While instructional strategies for the next generation, the Net Generation, need not vary considerably from those used with Generation Xers, educators must acknowledge the widespread use of the Internet among Net Generation learners and the culture of choice, customization, interaction, and authentication it has created. Educators should focus on helping students organize data into meaningful information, use the most appropriate media to fulfill their purposes, and pose questions for sound inquiry and new insight—updated views of student learning.

References

Brown, B. L. (1997). New Learning Strategies for Generation X. ERIC Digest #184, Document ED4111414 97. [Online]. Available: http://www.ed.gov/databases/ERICDigests/ed411414.html.

Douthitt, F. (1990). Developing the Work Ethic Through Vocational/Technical Education. ERIC Document #ED 346 331. Westerville, OH: Ohio State Council on Vocational Education.

Ferguson, S. (1999, February 5). [Telephone interview]. Ms. Ferguson is a professor of teacher education at the University of Dayton, Dayton, OH.

Filipczak, B. (1994). It's Just a Job: Generation X at Work. *Training*, 3 (4), 21–27.

Ford, F. A., and Herren, R. V. (1993). The Teaching of Work Ethics: Current Practices of Work Program Coordinators in Georgia. ERIC Document ED 366809. Nashville, TN: Paper presented at the American Vocational Association Convention.

Hill, R. B. (1996). Work Ethic Differences in Vocational Education Students and Full-Time Employed Workers. *Journal of Vocational Education Research*, 21 (3), 13–29.

Hill, R. B., and Petty, G. C. (1995). A New Look at Selected Employability Skills: A Factor Analysis of the Occupational Work Ethic. *Journal of Vocational Education Research*, 20 (4), 59–73.

Jones, L. T. (1995). Generation X Goes to College. *The Michigan Community College Journal*, 1 (2), 67–75.

Keaveney, S. M. (1997). When MTV Goes CEO: What Happens When the "Unmanageables" Become Managers? *Marketing Management*, 6 (3), 21–24.

McKenzie, J. (1998). Grazing the Net: Raising a Generation of Free-Range Students. *Phi Delta Kappan*, 80 (1), 26–31.

National Center for Research in Vocational Education (NCRVE). (1998). The Ambiguity of the Problem: The Nature of Basic Skills. Document MDS 302. [Online]. Available: http://vocserve.berkeley.edu/MDS-309/MDS-309-.html.

Nucifora, A. (1997, December 15). Net Generation Needs New Market Style. *Tampa Business Journal*. [Online]. Available: http://www.amcity.com/tampabay/stories/1997/12/15/smallb1.html.

Sellers, P. (1994). Don't Call Me Slacker. *Fortune*, 130 (12), 180–182, 186, 190, 194, 196.

Tapscott, D. (1998). *Growing Up Digital: The Rise of the Net Generation*. New York, NY: McGraw-Hill.

Tapscott, D. (1999). N-Gen Learning. [Online]. Available: http://www.growingupdigtal.com/nglearn.html.

Weaver, C.N. (1997). Has the Work Ethic in the USA Declined? Evidence From Nationwide Surveys. *Psychological Reports*, 81, 491–495.

Work Ethic Top Job Skill (1994, September). *The CPA Journal*, 64 (9), 9–10.

Chapter 3 — Internationalizing Business Communication Instruction

James Calvert Scott
Utah State University
Logan, Utah

Rapid globalization of the business world necessitates the internationalization of business communication instruction in order to prepare students for the complex communication tasks they will encounter in their professional lives. The business communication discipline is the branch of learning and instruction that focuses on the exchange of message meanings in business-related settings. Among its more important components are those that draw attention to (a) basic communication processes and theories; (b) human relationships and related applied psychology; (c) written communication (writing and reading); (d) verbal communication (speaking and listening); (e) nonverbal communication (nonlinguistic signs); and (f) fundamental English language knowledge and competencies.

Historical Overview

Business communication likely has a long, but not well-documented, history that goes back thousands of years when early humans began to interact with others to acquire the necessities—and later the niceties—of life. Archeologists in such early cradles of civilization as present-day Egypt, Iraq, Iran, Turkey, Greece, and Italy have unearthed artifacts that document the increasingly sophisticated accomplishment of business-related transactions by early peoples—evidence that the practice of business communication has gone on for a very long time.

In the United States, various components of what is now the business communication discipline gradually evolved. The earliest forms of business education emphasized such subjects as bookkeeping, penmanship, and business arithmetic, all of which could be applied to facilitate and document the transaction of business. Over time these and related subjects developed as business educa-tion shifted from academies, private teachers, and apprenticeship programs to publicly supported high schools and private business schools.

The development of the typewriter and the emergence of shorthand shifted the business education instructional focus from the record-keeping functions to the secretarial—the communicative—functions of business (Nolan, Hayden, and Malsbary, 1967). Courses in business English emerged to meet the needs of secretaries, later to be replaced by business writing and business communication courses designed to meet the needs of a broader audience of business workers. Such communication challenges as increasing workplace diversity, globalization, and communication technologies are influencing the nature of business commu-nication courses now and into the next century (Johnson, 1997).

Business communication courses have often not been well received, in part because many students and business educators have not accepted the important role that communication plays in office work (Popham, Schrag, and Blockhus, 1975). In fact, the business communication discipline has developed the reputation as one of the most neglected components of the entire business education curriculum (Popham, Schrag, and Blockhus, 1975). Ironically, this enduring image thrives during a time when the business community increasingly values the possession of effective business communication knowledge, skills, and attitudes by its employees.

During the past decade and a half, international business communication courses have evolved within the business communication discipline. Their meteoric rise has been propelled by two major factors: continuing pleas by the business community for workers with better-developed international perspectives (Duetschman, 1991) and increasing pressures from accreditation groups—especially the influential American Assembly of Collegiate Schools of Busi-ness—to more fully internationalize business curricula (Martin and Chaney, 1992).

Reasons for Internationalizing Business Communication Instruction

Since business communication is the backbone that supports and facilitates the accomplishment of business transactions (Scott, 1996), business communica-tion instruction must prepare people to engage in contemporary business activities. These activities increasingly occur in international contexts, involving either foreign companies and their representatives from home or abroad or domestic companies with multiethnic or multinational representatives.

Globalization of business is the watchword of the day, and business communication instruction must reflect this new focus. Active participation in the global marketplace, with its many interdependent players, is increasingly the way for a business community to not only survive but thrive.

Skills in international business communication can help achieve the following:

- Facilitate the accomplishment of mutually beneficial international business transactions;
- Smooth the introduction and the implementation of better technologies around the world;
- Encourage the development of joint endeavors that tap undeveloped or underdeveloped markets; and
- Cultivate a climate that supports the development of immature economies through international trade.

Simply said, international business communication instruction is a tool that empowers businesspersons as they engage in business activities around the world (Scott, 1996).

Purpose and Goals of International Business Communication Instruction

The purpose of international business communication instruction is to prepare people for the complex international business communication tasks they will encounter in their professional and personal lives (Scott, 1996). Those who can benefit from such instruction are prospective and practicing businesspersons. For this group of people, the instruction is primarily vocational in nature since it has a strong workplace use orientation.

Others who can benefit from international business communication instruction are the public at large, who increasingly in their day-to-day interactions encounter people and businesses from other cultures and countries. For this group of people, the instruction is primarily general in nature since it has a strong personal use orientation. In actuality, the two complementary orientations share many basic elements and differ primarily in the contexts in which they are applied. As a result, it is often difficult, if not impossible, to tell where one orientation ends and the other begins.

The goals or objectives of international business communication instruction will vary depending on a variety of factors. Among these are who constitutes the targeted audience, what their backgrounds and needs are, the grade-level placement of the instruction, the degree of sophistication of the offered instruction, how the offered instruction fits into the curriculum, the preferences of the business community, the preferences of the local community, the standards of relevant professional bodies and accreditation groups, and the like.

Scott (1996) identified six fundamental goals or objectives for international business communication instruction that can be adapted as necessary by teachers and trainers to accommodate local circumstances. They include the following:

1. To develop an understanding of the dynamics of business communication in a culturally diverse world.

2. To develop an understanding of the major processes, theories, and concepts of international business communication.

3. To recognize the profound influence of culturally based factors on international business communication.

4. To minimize ethnocentrism (the belief that one's native culture is superior to other cultures) and to maximize respect for other cultures as credible and legitimate ways of life.

5. To develop a mind-set that is conducive to communicating effectively in the culturally diverse world of international business.

6. To develop strategies and techniques that facilitate effective communication in the global world of business. (p. 7)

For the 21ˢᵗ century, a seventh goal or objective ought be added: to develop cultural fluency ("the ability to cross cultural boundaries and to function much like a native by regularly matching the receiver's decoded and the sender's encoded message meanings" (Scott, 1999, p. 140)).

Strategies for Internationalizing Business Communication Instruction

The *National Standards for Business Education: What America's Students Should Know and Be Able to Do in Business* (1995) identify general performance expectations for business communication that include the following:

- Select and use modes of communications appropriate to specific situations;

- Identify and overcome barriers to different methods of communications;

- Recognize and use nonverbal cues in all forms of communications;

- Analyze audience to determine appropriate language, tone, style, and format for specific situations;

- Demonstrate knowledge of ethical considerations, integrity of information, and legal implications in communications;

- Use critical-thinking, decision-making, and problem-solving techniques to promote sound, effective business communications;

- Incorporate multicultural considerations in all communications to ensure appropriate sensitivity;

- Study international communications to promote positive relationships in the global marketplace; and

- Discuss the communication systems—cultural, organizational, technological, and interpersonal—and the use of systems concepts to analyze and direct the choice of communications strategies and forms. (p. 45)

The introduction to the communications section points out that while the fundamentals of communication are relatively consistent, some aspects change continuously, especially those involving technology and international communication. "As the world continues to change politically, economically, and geographically, communications strategies will evolve in a parallel manner and must be studied and incorporated into the curriculum if students are to function effectively in a global society" (*National Standards*, 1995, p. 45). This can be accomplished through the internationalization of business communication instruction using one of two major approaches: infusing international business communication content into existing courses or creating specialized international business communication courses (Scott, 1996).

Meeting Challenges by Infusing International Business Communication Content Into Existing Courses

Infusing international business communication content into existing courses has a number of advantages and disadvantages. An important advantage of the infusion approach is that it is relatively simple to implement. Teachers decide when, where, and to what extent they want to add international business communication content to the courses they regularly teach.

As their comfort level with adding such content to their course curricula grows, the teachers infuse more and more international business communication material into their courses, allowing for a gradual modification of course content in a nonthreatening, nondisrupting way. In circumstances where the process of formally gaining permission to change course curricula is cumbersome, controversial, or risky, implementing the infusion approach may be the best approach.

The updating changes are added gradually by the teachers over a period of time—perhaps over several years—and the changes are in such small increments that the course content evolution is unnoticed by other teachers and administrators. Since the infusion approach does not create a new course, it does not require another teacher, another classroom, or a revised teaching schedule, which simplifies the life of the department head.

Another feature of the infusion approach is that it allows all interested teachers to participate in the internationalization process, avoiding further perceived inequities among teachers' classroom assignments. Also, the infusion approach is quite simple and inexpensive to implement from an administrative perspective, requiring few, if any, new resources for implementation purposes (Scott, 1996).

Critics of the infusion approach often question whether teachers are infusing the correct amount of the right content in their classes since no effective mechanism exists to regulate and monitor the process. To reduce—ideally to eliminate—this concern, teachers must have a detailed coordination plan that divides the content to be infused among the departmental course offerings. There must also be a reliable mechanism to verify that the plan is implemented without significant variation by all involved teachers.

Ensuring that each business teacher infuses his or her assigned topics in a suitable manner without infringing on the topics of other teachers can be problematic. Students are sometimes overexposed to some infused topics and underexposed to others, in part because some topics are perceived as more desirable by teachers, easier to add to the courses they teach, and more appealing to students.

Another potential problem is that because most students sample from the offered business education courses rather than taking them all, they may be exposed to a hodgepodge of international business communication content even if the department has a coordinated infusion plan. Perhaps one strategy to alleviate this concern is to infuse the international business communication content into a few courses that most students complete. This ensures that more students are exposed to most of the infused international business communication content.

Still another concern associated with the infusion approach is being able to prove beyond a reasonable doubt that the international business communication infusion activities have in fact taken place. Having a detailed, coordinated departmentwide plan for infusing international business communication content into other business education courses does not prove that the plan is appropriate or actually being implemented by each and every teacher.

Skeptical members of the public, the business community, and the accreditation groups, having often observed significant gulfs between what educational institutions say they do and what they in fact do, may not find whatever confirmatory evidence the department musters that its infusion strategy is working effectively to be sufficient. Some of these individuals may question accepting infusion as a valid and viable approach for internationalizing business communication instruction, especially when the separate course approach provides more explicit evidence of significant internationalization efforts (Scott, 1996).

The best way to implement the infusion approach is for the department to develop a detailed implementation strategy that is carefully planned, carried out, and monitored by the involved teachers and administrators. Every teacher must be fully committed to using this approach and willing to infuse the specified international business communication content on an ongoing basis. The plan must thoughtfully distribute relevant international business communication content among a variety of courses that are taken by significant numbers of students.

A thorough search of the international business communication literature will suggest a number of possible topics that must then be logically integrated with existing curricular content, especially for mainstream course offerings. The literature search will also reveal ideas about how many of these aspects of international business communication might be developed. As this information is uncovered, it can be used to flesh out the details of the implementation plan that the teachers then carry out in their respective assigned courses.

The development of a detailed infusion plan will be a long-term task that can easily require several years to complete. The goals of the plan will parallel the goals that would have been appropriate had the separate course approach been selected. The infusion goals, however, may out of necessity be less specific and achieved over a longer period of time because they are spread out over and developed through one or more course offerings (Scott, 1996).

Educators will need time to develop sufficient international business communication background before they feel comfortable adding the identified content from the infusion plan into the courses they teach. Teachers can acquire through a variety of means the necessary international business communication knowledge prior to, during, and/or after the development of the related departmentwide infusion plan. Typical means include enrollment in international business, communication, and international business communication courses, as well as self-directed study. Independent international travel, international travel and study tours, international teacher exchanges, and international sabbatical leaves are other, less typical options.

Teachers need time to sort out how to make the most effective classroom use of their recently acquired international business communication competencies, as well as time to experiment with and refine related delivery methods, polishing their infusion delivery strategies in the process (Scott, 1996).

Many potential opportunities exist for infusing international business communication content into established business education courses at the secondary, undergraduate, and graduate levels. To illustrate a few of the many possibilities, examples from each level are provided below. While the examples are not comprehensive, they are designed to stimulate the thinking of creative business educators, who can then adapt the information to fit their specific teaching situations.

Secondary level. The business communication course offered at the secondary level typically emphasizes the generally accepted business communication standards used within the United States, including those for formatting and punctuating business letters.

These standards are often taught as if they were universal, which they are not. The formatting and punctuating standards that are taught in this country represent the cultural perspective of one important English-speaking country, the United States. Many other English-speaking countries, especially current and former Commonwealth countries, choose to use the formatting and punctuating conventions, or variations thereof, of the other worldwide-dominant English-speaking country, the United Kingdom of Great Britain and Northern Ireland.

After teaching, practicing, and reviewing the formatting and punctuating of business letters, teachers might ask students to critique a sample business letter—perhaps one of the illustrations from "Preparing Business Correspondence the British Way" (Scott, 1993) or another source—and discuss whether or not the letter is acceptable. Students will likely find the formatting and punctuating patterns unacceptable for a variety of reasons that they can discuss.

Teachers can then ask if this letter might be considered acceptable in another country. Most students will dismiss this idea because the formatting and punctuating details differ from what they know to be correct. Next, teachers can point out that depending on where the letter was written and received, it may be acceptable because it reflects one of several generally accepted British communication standards. The formatting and punctuating details would be acceptable in the United Kingdom and in many current and former Commonwealth countries.

Teachers can then point out that as more businesses enter the global marketplace, more employees will see greater variety in English language letter formatting and punctuating patterns. In spite of the fact that businesspersons increasingly acknowledge the desirability of being sensitive to the letter-writing conventions of the recipient, including formatting and punctuating standards, doing so is very difficult given the worldwide variations in practices, the limited international knowledge of most businesspersons, and the high costs of communicating about every matter in a culturally sensitive manner.

If time permits, teachers can discuss other generally acceptable British formatting and punctuating patterns so that in the future when students see different English language letter patterns, they will not reject them outright as substandard and unacceptable.

Keyboarding-related courses are major offerings in most secondary schools, and they also offer potential opportunities for infusing international business communication content. For example, when students learn how to format tables by manipulating various data sets, they can become acquainted with worldwide variation in a number of aspects of business communication as they manipulate these data sets.

Teachers might have students learn and practice formatting tables where the copy is composed of useful information about basic civilities in a number of languages. Students can begin the process by creating a simple table entitled Common Civilities in English and Spanish. This table can have two columns, one for the common civilities, such as Mr., Mrs., Miss, yes, no, please, thank you, you're welcome, excuse me, hello, goodbye, and the like, in English, and one for their Spanish equivalents, such as Señor, Señora, Señorita, sí, no, por favor, gracias, de nada, perdóneme, hola, adiós, and the like. Since the Spanish language has a number of diacritical marks not found in the English language, this offers an opportunity for teachers to introduce how to keyboard special characters from foreign language character sets, which will also be needed to keyboard some other languages.

Next, teachers can have students keyboard the information with the addition of two headings, English and Spanish, above their respective columns. Students can then change the title of the table to Civilities Around the World; add a subtitle, such as Courteous Expressions Used in International Business; add columnar headings for as many additional languages, such as French, German, Chinese, Arabic, Portuguese, and the like, as desired; and add the equivalent expressions in the selected languages. Teachers can provide the information for the selected languages or have their students research it on an individual or group basis.

If enough columns are added to the table, students will need to learn how to prepare tables in the landscape position since to fit all of the columns onto one page, the page must be turned horizontally. Teachers who can speak any of the keyboarded languages besides English can pronounce the equivalent expressions and ask the students to model their pronunciations of these civilities after theirs. This will help students begin the process of adding the civilities to their listening and speaking vocabularies.

Undergraduate level. Other opportunities for infusing international business communication content into existing courses occur at the undergraduate level. For example, virtually all core business communication courses address how to vary the organization of different types of business-related messages depending on the recipient's likely initial reader reaction. Most business communication authorities encourage writers delivering bad news to residents of the United States to organize their messages inductively or indirectly, sandwiching the implied bad news between at least a neutral and ideally a positive beginning and ending. Usually the recommended procedure for maintaining as much recipient goodwill as possible is to begin the letter with a buffer statement that does not suggest that bad news is coming.

Next, the writer leads up to the bad news in such a way that the recipient anticipates this news without the writer explicitly conveying it. The writer then diverts attention away from the implied bad news by presenting a more pleasant alternative, in effect burying the bad news in the middle of the letter. By ending on a more positive alternative, the writer is thought to minimize the negative consequences of the bad news for most recipients.

While teaching the organization of bad news letters, teachers should make their students aware that not all English-speaking business subcultures follow the inductive or indirect organizational approach widely recommended in United States-based business communication textbooks. Teachers should explain that the British business subculture, which is typically perceived to be quite polite and diplomatic, chooses to convey bad news directly and bluntly to the degree that it can offend American readers, who are used to having bad news buffered and implied rather than explicitly stated.

Because Britons are concerned about the possibility of being considered deceptive or misleading by implying bad news, they go to the other end of the spectrum and quickly and frankly convey such news. Thus, a letter beginning or quickly stating "I reject your application for employment at Britannia Ltd." is the norm, not the exception, in the United Kingdom. Teachers should note that after Britons have delivered the bad news, they typically do try to retain whatever goodwill remains through either an apology or a statement of regret regarding the bad news.

Teachers should point out that because cultures and subcultures differ from country to country, each may choose a different approach in response to a common problem. Even having a number of cultural elements in common does not guarantee that two business communities will organize all of their business communications in the same manner as the example of the mainstream American and British approaches to delivering bad news suggests.

The international business communication concept of beliefs, values, and assumptions differing from culture to culture can be infused into the principles of accounting course. Since no two cultures have identical values, no two cultures behave exactly alike. Accounting systems are in fact highly specialized culture-specific communication systems that reflect what is important to the most influential members of the financial community. Thus, what is taught in the principles of accounting course reflects the beliefs, values, and assumptions of the financial community of the United States.

One of the beliefs promulgated by this community and taught by account-ing teachers in the United States is that the income statement data are generally considered to be more important than the balance sheet data. This is based on the assumptions that in the United States businesspersons have a short-term orientation and most business owners are stockholders whose share prices are strongly influenced by current earnings–income-statement data.

This perspective, teachers should point out, is not universal. The predomi-nant worldwide cultural perspective is to favor balance sheet data over income sheet data because such diverse cultures as most Asian, European, and Latin American ones are focused primarily on the ownership of wealth, the assets and the related claims against those assets. Teachers can focus attention on these differing cultural priorities by presenting the financial statements of a business and then asking students to evaluate the financial position and desirability of the business in a financial sense.

If the business is asset rich but has only modest income-generating potential, then many potential United States-based investors will not find it financially attractive as a long-term investment; but potential investors from many other parts of the world may be eager to acquire it as a long-term invest-ment. Contrasting the positions of potential United States and Japanese investors relative to the financial statements of a particular business, for example, as well as the related culturally based reasons underlying their thinking, will be insight-ful to most students. They will learn that fundamental differences in financial perceptions are necessary if global market forces are to work effectively.

Graduate level. Still other potential opportunities for infusing interna-tional business communication content into existing courses occur at the gradu-ate level. For example, the topic of nonverbal communication is included in most managerial communication courses. Information about the component parts of nonverbal communication, including oculesics or eye-related behaviors, is frequently presented in these courses.

Teachers should ensure that their students understand the important influences of such behaviors in both domestic and international managerial settings. Interpretation of oculesic behaviors is culturally dependent. Where the oculesic behaviors occur and who initiates them are important factors in attaching the correct meanings to them.

In the United States, for example, frequent direct eye contact between communicators is typically expected. Although too much direct oculesic behavior constitutes staring, which is considered impolite, too little direct eye contact might suggest that the person is ill at ease, not attentive or respectful, and/or perhaps deceptive or not truthful. Nevertheless, members of some minority groups in the United States, such as Native Americans, typically engage in minimal eye contact to show respect for authority, deviating from the dominant nationwide oculesic pattern.

Teachers should also remind managers working in the United States that employees with strong ethnic affiliations may engage in eye movement behaviors that are more similar to those employed where the ethnic group originated than those socially sanctioned by the mainstream United States culture.

Teachers can then discuss oculesic behaviors in international settings, where proper interpretation can sometimes be even more challenging since the normative eye behaviors of other cultures and countries are often much different from those of the United States in similar situations. Most Arabic cultures, for example, tend to engage in direct, intense oculesic behaviors that many United States residents perceive as piercing. On the other hand, Far Eastern cultures tend to engage in indirect, diffuse oculesic behaviors that many United States residents perceive as inattentive and disrespectful–possibly even insulting–when in fact they signal attentiveness and respectfulness to their initiators.

It is important that teachers also caution United States-educated managers who interact with natives of other countries that sometimes these individuals know and follow the local rules for eye contact as well as or better than natives of the United States. Teachers must, therefore, encourage managers to use caution when attaching meaning to oculesic behaviors because of the many variables in both the domestic and international business environments that influence perceptions about their meanings.

In a course about designing business education programs for adult learners, diversity-related international business communication content can be infused. Understanding the characteristics of adult learners is essential whether education or training is provided. How the participating individuals are alike and different must be factored into the design and delivery of relevant education or training.

Teachers might begin by having students gather a variety of types of demographic information about adult learners, such as their genders, ages, ethnic groups, nationalities, educational levels, spoken languages, job titles, and the like. After the data are tabulated, teachers can then lead a discussion where students point out the ways in which the learners are alike and different. In many situations, students will be surprised to learn how diverse the adult learners are in terms of their demographic variables. In fact, during the 1990s approximately one fourth of all new entrants into the United States workforce have been immigrants, most of whom come from countries where English is not the dominant language (Andrews, 1990). This has changed the typical demographic profile of adult learners considerably.

The languages spoken by the adult learners will influence the choice of the language selected to deliver education or training to adult learners. Teachers should also point out to students that adult learners from various cultures and countries bring differing backgrounds, experiences, and expectations to the business education classroom that will need to be considered in the design of the offered instructional program. These adults from various parts of the world will have different beliefs, values, and assumptions; cultural identities; views of the world; ways of knowing; ways of learning; and ways of communicating to name but a few.

The challenge for designers of adult programs is trying to come to grips with all of these differences and finding as many mutually acceptable ways as possible of bridging the differences among the learners. Teachers must caution students not to stereotype adult learners, recognizing that while certain patterns are generally true, they are dealing with individuals who may or may not deviate from typical expectations.

Meeting Challenges by Creating Specialized International Business Communication Courses

Another approach to meeting the challenges of internationalizing business communication instruction is to create one or more specialized international business communication courses. The separate course approach has a number of advantages and disadvantages that are discussed below.

One important advantage is that the international business communication content is central rather than peripheral to the provided instruction. In other words, international business communication is the undisputed focus of instruction that can be developed for both professional and personal purposes through one or more courses designed to meet the varied backgrounds and needs of students.

By significantly developing international business communication knowledge, skills, and attitudes, these specialized courses increase the lifetime options of students. Further, the development and regular offering of one or more separate courses in international business communication provides indisputable evidence of a serious commitment toward internationalization, which is viewed favorably by community members, the business community, and accreditation groups (Scott, 1996).

The primary disadvantage of offering one or more separate courses in international business communication is the associated costs. Making international business communication instruction available requires the regular classroom and instructional materials resources typical of other courses plus a teacher who is interested in and knowledgeable about international business communication.

Securing a well-qualified teacher, ideally with firsthand international business communication experiences abroad, is difficult in many localities. If a current teacher is willing to teach the international business communication course, what can be done to help him or her get ready to teach the course? Since the international business communication field is evolving, limited instructional resources are available from publishers, especially at the secondary level, placing more than normal curricular decision-making and instructional resource creation responsibilities on the teacher.

Another concern is determining what course-specific instructional materials will need to be purchased and from what sources. Ascertaining how one or more possible international business communication courses would fit into the existing curriculum and assessing how many students are likely to enroll in such courses are other concerns. Deciding what is gained and what is lost by investing scarce resources in one or more separate international business communication courses and whether overall the students, department, educational institution, local community, and business community benefit by doing so can also be challenging (Scott, 1996).

In order to implement the separate course approach, it is necessary to follow the local curriculum approval process. The person in charge of guiding the international business communication course through that process, be it the designated teacher or the department head, must be aware and observant of the details of the approval process. When approaching the task, it is useful to create a detailed time line that allows for both planned and unplanned delays.

Since the proposal for any new course is likely to be examined in detail, the proposal must be carefully thought out and reviewed by multiple people. Most course proposals include such information as the course title, description, and outline; instructional resource requirements; staffing requirements; and implementation budget.

The person in charge must decide the best possible timing for presenting the international business communication course proposal to the involved decision makers since the timing often influences the outcome. Before presenting the proposal, he or she must prepare sound persuasive arguments that document that the proposed course is relevant, needed, and cost-effective.

Among the major arguments that might be used to build the case for offering a separate international business-communication course are:

- The world is increasingly internationalized;
- The business community must internationalize to remain competitive;
- Effective international business communication facilitates the conduct of business in the global marketplace;

- Serious existing deficiencies in the communication skills of graduates and employees handicap them in transacting business effectively in the increasingly diverse world of global business; and

- Offering a separate course in international business communication demonstrates to the public, the business community, and the accreditation groups serious commitment to the internationalization process (Scott, 1996).

A variety of potential opportunities exist for implementing the separate course approach to internationalizing business communication instruction. These opportunities exist within educational institutions at the secondary, undergraduate, and graduate levels and within business and industry. To illustrate a few of the many possibilities, several examples are provided below. Each example identifies how an international business communication course might be structured.

Educational institution level. Specialized international business communication courses can be offered within educational institutions at the secondary, undergraduate, and graduate levels. For example, the secondary school international business communication course is most likely to occur in the context of a well-developed international business concentration or program because of its highly specialized nature. As more school districts, especially in metropolitan areas where international business already flourishes, develop integrated programs to prepare workers for business in the increasingly global marketplace, one of those program components is likely to develop the international business communication competencies of entry-level workers.

Such courses will emphasize the development of basic international business communication knowledge, skills, and attitudes that can serve as foundations for not only launching careers in international business but also for more advanced study in international business-related fields at a later date.

A secondary school international business communication course curriculum could be structured around the relevant portions of the Level 3 national standards for communications and international business with particular emphases on the more specific international business communications standards detailed on pages 103 and 104 of the *National Standards for Business Education: What America's Students Should Know and Be Able to Do in Business* (1995).

These specialized standards are designed to apply the essential communication strategies to achieve effective and financially rewarding international business relationships. The standards focus attention on oral and written, nonverbal, and technological aspects of international business communication at a level appropriate for secondary school students.

Some of the specified performance expectations appropriate for international business communications students at Level 3 include the following:

- "Discuss complications involved when speaking or interpreting a language incorrectly abroad."

- "Explain usage of names, titles, and ranks in different cultures and countries."
- "Compose effective business communications based on an understanding of the relevant environments and differences in tone, style, and format."
- "Recognize gift giving in business relationships in several cultures and give examples of appropriate and inappropriate gifts for persons in a given country."
- "Relate cultural attitudes toward time, silence, space, and body/eye contact for successful international business relationships."
- "Evaluate which telecommunication methods are most appropriate for given international business situations" (*National Standards*, 1995, p. 104).

While secondary-level teachers of international business communication courses will want to rely extensively on the relevant national standards, they should feel free to add other topics that they perceive to be appropriate based on their own perceptions, those of international business communication experts, and those of members of the local international business community.

The undergraduate-level international business communication course is usually offered as an upper-division course, often with the basic or core business communication course as a prerequisite. Among the more common names for the course are International Business Communication, Intercultural Business Communication, and Cross-Cultural Business Communication (Green and Scott, 1996).

Typical subject matter for the course include the following, which are ordered from heavy to light emphasis:

- Accepting cultural differences and appreciating cultural similarities;
- Communication patterns–verbal and nonverbal;
- Comparative cultural perspectives;
- Culture- or country-specific information;
- Functioning effectively in multiple cultures;
- Communication strategies and systems;
- Understanding cultural constructs;
- Language(s) and communication;
- Negotiation;
- Understanding the global business environment;
- Differences within one culture;
- Managing global business communication;
- Worldwide social organization and systems;
- Communication ethics; and
- Technology (Green and Scott, 1996).

Teachers often integrate these types of topics into the structural framework of the selected primary course textbook. Among the varied textbooks selected for the undergraduate-level international business communication course are three basic types: (a) international business textbooks, such as *Managing Cultural Differences* (Harris and Moran, 1996), *The Cultural Environment of International Business* (Terpstra and David, 1991), and *Cultural Dimensions of International Business* (Ferraro, 1998); (b) intercultural communication textbooks, such as *Communication Between Cultures* (Samovar, Porter, and Stefani, 1998); and (c) international business communication textbooks, such as *Intercultural Communication in the Global Workplace* (Varner and Beamer, 1995) and *Intercultural Business Communication* (Chaney and Martin, 1995) (Green and Scott, 1996). As more textbooks devoted exclusively to international business communication like the last two become available, it is likely that they will become the dominant course textbooks in the future.

Although the upper-division international business communication course is the most common one, perhaps in part because many people entering the international business field do not pursue graduate-level course work before joining the workforce, the graduate-level international business communication course is available at a number of educational institutions. The best available evidence suggests that at influential business schools accredited by the American Assembly of Collegiate Schools of Business, about 16 percent offer a graduate-level international business communication course and an additional 19 percent offer a dual-level international business-communication course that can be taken for either upper-division or graduate credit depending on the needs of students (Green and Scott, 1996).

The typical graduate-level international business communication course either develops or reviews the basic content of the undergraduate-level international business communication course for the benefit of those with little or no prior subject matter exposure and/or relevant communication experiences and explores those and related topics in depth.

Some highly specialized topics that might be included in a graduate-level course, for example, include the following:

- Self-assessment of cross-cultural adaptability using a psychological instrument and development of an action plan to enhance cross-cultural flexibility and openness;

- Exploration of the consequences of using the English language, especially the American and British varieties, for international business communication purposes, including reactions of nonnative English speakers;

- Communicating with limited English proficient and nonEnglish proficient audiences for business purposes;

- Printing of business-related materials in foreign languages;

- Production of business-related videotapes in multiple languages;

- Application of contexting and face-saving concepts to advertising in the global marketplace;
- Assessment of exhibited communicative behaviors in international business communication settings;
- Ensuring of personal safety while engaging in international business communication activities abroad; and
- Coping with culture shock and reverse culture shock (Scott, 1998).

As with the undergraduate-level international business communication course, the graduate-level course content is often incorporated into the structural framework of the selected primary course textbook. Although any textbook suitable for an undergraduate-level course can be used as the primary textbook for a graduate-level course, *International Business Communication* (Victor, 1992) is a popular choice because it incorporates scholarly literature from the diverse disciplines of the international business communication field.

Business and industry level. Potential opportunities for creating specialized international business communication courses also occur within business and industry. As businesses increasingly participate in the global marketplace, more of them are recognizing the economic and other benefits of offering education and training that develops international business communication knowledge, skills, and attitudes. Such education and training are either delivered by such outside units as nearby educational institutions or private-sector consultants or by such inside units as the in-house training and development department.

Who delivers the desired international business communication instruction is often determined by such factors as where the needed expertise is found, how the needed instruction can be provided, when the needed instruction can be provided, and the number of employees needing the instruction.

Companies that have tuition reimbursement schemes for employee development activities may choose to rely on existing undergraduate- or graduate-level international business communication courses provided such courses have useful content delivered within a time frame that is compatible with the needs of the workplace. When the time frame is shorter than three or four months, in-house instruction offered by the training and development department or out-of-house instruction offered by a private-sector consultant is often available. Since the latter two options offer considerable direct control over both the instructional content and the timing, they may be selected in part or in whole for those reasons.

Another factor, sometimes of great significance to business and industry, is whether the offered instruction has a culture-general or culture-specific orientation. Instruction from the culture-general perspective uses a generalist approach to teaching international business communication content, with the supporting examples coming from many diverse cultures. This approach is ideally suited to the needs of those who want to learn the principles so that they can be generalized to a wide variety of cultures. In contrast, instruction from the culture-specific perspective uses a specialist approach to teaching international business communication content, with all of the supporting examples coming from one specific culture. This is ideally suited to the needs of those who want to learn the specific applications in one culture (Scott, 1996).

Because most enrollees in international business communication courses offered by educational institutions do not know in advance the specific cultural contexts in which they will engage in international business communication, they need to be exposed to many different cultures as the instruction progresses. As a result, most educational institutions offer primarily culture-general international business communication instruction.

Sometimes employees of business and industry do know in advance the specific cultural context(s) in which they will engage in international business communication. In this case, their needs are best met by custom-tailored instruction that focuses on one or a very limited number of specific cultures. Thus, much company- or consultant-delivered international business communication instruction has a culture-specific orientation that meets the immediate workplace needs of both employees and employers.

Often the international business communication education and training provided within business and industry is delivered in a content- and time-intensive format. Those who offer such instruction will have to carefully select the most relevant content for inclusion and then deliver that content in a very efficient, time-sensitive manner.

The basic principles of international business communication taught at the educational institution level are useful not only to employees of business and industry but also to their family members, especially if they are being transferred abroad in the near future. Instructors should be prepared to impart the identified content to such diverse audiences as employees, their spouses, and their accompanying children—sometimes at the same time. As business and industry increasingly acknowledge that spouse and family adjustment to the international environment are critical for employee success outside the United States, they are increasingly likely to invest in basic international business communication education and training for the entire family.

Summary

Since globalization is the watchword of business, business communication instruction must be internationalized. It is essential that people be well prepared for the complex international business communication tasks they will encounter in their professional and personal lives in the 21st century. International business communication instruction can be provided through the infusion approach, which enriches existing courses with relevant international business communication content, or the separate course approach, which creates new subject-specific international business communication courses. Relevant international business communication instruction should be offered within educational institutions at the secondary, undergraduate, and graduate levels and within business and industry using in-house and outside-of-house providers.

Since international business communication instruction is a powerful force that can give the United States business community a competitive advantage in the increasingly important global marketplace, business educators must actively engage themselves in delivering international business communication instruction in all of its varied forms. For both personal and societal well-being, business educators must make providing high quality international business communication instruction a top priority for the new millennium.

References

Andrews, M. (1990, April 9). ESL Proves a Boon to Boston Hotels, Others. *Boston Business Journal,* Sec. 1, p. 9.

Chaney, L. H., and Martin, J. S. (1995). *Intercultural Business Communication.* Englewood Cliffs, NJ: Prentice Hall.

Deutschman, A. (1991, July 29). The Trouble With MBAs. *Fortune,* 67-78.

Ferraro, G. P. (1998). *Cultural Dimension of International Business.* Upper Saddle River, NJ: Prentice Hall.

Green, D. J., and Scott, J. C. (1996). The Status of International Business Communication Courses in Schools Accredited by the American Assembly of Collegiate Schools of Business. *The Delta Pi Epsilon Journal,* 37 (1), 43-62.

Harris, P. R., and Moran, R. T. (1996). *Managing Cultural Differences.* Houston, TX: Gulf.

Johnson, B. S. (1997). Communication in a Changing Environment. In C. P. Brantley and B. J. Davis (Eds.), *The Changing Dimensions of Business Education, 1997 NBEA Yearbook , no. 35 (*pp. 112-118). Reston, VA: National Business Education Association.

Martin, J. S., and Chaney, L. H. (1992). Determination of Content for a Collegiate Course in Intercultural Business Communication by Three Delphi Panels. *The Journal of Business Communication,* 29 (3), 267-283.

National Business Education Association. (1995). *National Standards for Business Education: What America's Students Should Know and Be Able to Do in Business.* Reston, VA: National Business Education Association.

Nolan, C. A., Hayden, C. K., and Malsbary, D. R. (1967). *Principles and Problems of Business Education* (3ʳᵈ ed.). Cincinnati, OH: South-Western.

Popham, E. L., Schrag, A. F., and Blockhus, W. (1975). *A Teaching-Learning System for Business Education.* New York, NY: Gregg Division, McGraw-Hill.

Samovar, L. A., Porter, R. E., and Stefani, L. A. (1998). *Communication Between Cultures.* Belmont, CA: Wadsworth.

Scott, J. C. (1993). Preparing Business Correspondence the British Way. *The Bulletin of the Association for Business Communication,* 56 (2), 10-17.

Scott, J. C. (1996). *Facilitating International Business Communication: A Global Perspective.* Little Rock, AR: Delta Pi Epsilon.

Scott, J. C. (1998). *BIS 6550 International Business Communication* [Tentative course syllabus, fall semester, 1998]. (Available from Dr. James Calvert Scott, Department of

Business Information Systems and Education, College of Business, Utah State University, Logan, UT 84322-3515)

Scott, J. C. (1999). Developing Cultural Fluency: The Goal of International Business-Communication Instruction in the Twenty-First Century. *Journal of Education for Business,* 74 (3), 140-143.

Terpstra, V., and David, K. (1991). *The Cultural Environment of International Business.* Cincinnati, OH: South-Western.

Varner, I., and Beamer, L. (1995). *Intercultural Communication in the Global Work-place*. Chicago, IL: Irwin.

Victor, D. A. (1992). *International Business Communication.* New York, NY: HarperCollins.

Chapter 4 — Curriculum Integration: Optimized Learning for High School Students

Jim Mansfield
University of Missouri-St. Louis
St. Louis, Missouri

Lonnie Echternacht
University of Missouri-Columbia
Columbia, Missouri

The new millennium with increasing globalization, expanding technology, and a growing need to improve employment opportunities for youth will require changes in high school education. In response to such challenges, school districts are experimenting with different curriculum approaches and time frames, developing new programs which are more relevant to students, evaluating the uses of their shrinking financial resources, and involving the business community in curriculum decisions. Curriculum integration has captured the interest of educators, employers, and politicians, each of whom sees it as a potential solution to different problems.

The concept of integrating business education course work and academic curricula is still in the formative stages of development in many school districts. While integration seems like a sound educational idea, many questions such as the following need to be answered.

- What curriculum resources and instructional strategies should business teachers use?
- What business education content should be integrated within the academic areas?
- What academic areas should be integrated within the business education curriculum?
- What scheduling pattern best facilitates and encourages curriculum integration as well as promotes quality individual programs?
- Which instructional/learning practices have to change, and how will these changes be initiated and supported by the school administration?

Despite these challenges, curriculum integration has the potential to enable students to achieve higher levels of both academic and occupational competencies.

The major thrust of current integration efforts at the high school level typically combines the best curricular and pedagogical processes and practices of both the academic and the business education curricula. This combining of curricula helps reinforce and ensure that students learn both the theory and the application of the specific content areas involved. Thus, integration is typically viewed as a type of curriculum reform, justified by the need to better prepare students in the overall development of skills, knowledge, and attitudes. This intensified learning strengthens students' workplace readiness, furthers their post-secondary educational opportunities, and ultimately enhances their quality of life.

Models of Integration

The fundamental processes and components of curriculum integration can be configured in a variety of ways; curriculum integration may look different in individual school districts because of their unique characteristics, needs, and goals. Grubb, Davis, Lum, Philal, and Morgaine (1991) identified eight different integration models that business teachers might consider:

1. Incorporating more academic content into business courses. This model is probably the simplest form of integration. Efforts are made to incorporate additional academic material into the existing business education courses. This usually happens on a very informal basis. The school administration may simply encourage all business teachers to include additional writing assignments or essay type tests. These assignments encourage teachers to assess student writing deficiencies and take steps to remedy them.

Most business teachers will not find this approach a dramatic change. They may have already been incorporating academic instruction into their curriculum as a way of enhancing the development of workplace and technical skills that today's employers expect. However, this approach may be limited by the curriculum resources and support provided by the school district. There is a need to develop, adapt, and/or obtain integrated instructional/learning materials that can be used easily by teachers regardless of their abilities or their commitment to integrating academic content into existing business education courses.

2. Combining business and academic teachers to enhance academic content in business programs. This approach to integration is very different as it gives the responsibility of enhancing the teaching of academic content in business education courses to the academic teachers. At times, the academic teacher may teach small modules and units or present academic content relevant to a particular unit or learning activity within a business course. This model encourages the academic and business education teachers to interact and develop additional integration activities together.

The real strength of this model is the potential it creates for extensive collaboration between teachers in the two disciplines. This collaboration focuses on the presence of academic teachers and highlights the important contribution of their curriculum to the preparation of today's workforce. The major disadvantage of this model is the need for additional resources—both planning and instructional time—to enable collaboration to occur between the faculties and their respective departments.

3. Making the academic curriculum more relevant to the workplace. This model modifies the standard academic curriculum and makes it more relevant to the students who are also enrolled in business education courses. A common approach is for the school administration to urge academic teachers to incorporate basic skills and workplace competencies and applications into their course assignments. Academic teachers can then describe such courses as more "hands-on" and interdisciplinary than conventional academic courses. However, such practices must be done positively, because a general academic course is replaced with one that relates academic material to the workplace. This particular approach alters the academic course, while the business education course remains unchanged. Thus, cooperation and collaboration among teachers may tend to suffer or become nonexistent.

4. Curricular "alignment": modify both business and academic courses. Another approach to integration is to change the content of both the academic and the business education courses. This model integrates additional workplace competencies into an academic course and additional academic content into a business education course; the two courses are then combined into one. This model is highly flexible and encourages the infusion of content, as well as the skills and attitudes needed in today's workplace. To the faculty involved, flexibility is a positive aspect as the materials may be reviewed, modified, and updated when needed.

This curriculum alignment process can be simple and informal, when initiated on a small scale, or can involve much larger groups of educators. The crucial element of this model is that all teachers must work together to coordinate their offerings. Thus, students experience courses that are consistent and mutually reinforcing. A limitation of this approach is that, in most cases, the business education courses are modified while the academic courses remain largely unchanged.

5. The senior project as a form of integration. This particular model of integration involves organizing the curriculum around a project, usually a senior-level project, instead of changing existing courses. When properly implemented, this model provides an exciting alternative to traditional course work. Business teachers tend to be a step ahead with this model because they often utilize a series of small projects throughout their curriculum. Business teachers are well aware of and accustomed to assigning projects that provide students opportunities to apply multiple skills and abilities and demonstrate their competence.

The senior project method is an excellent alternative to other forms of integration because it allows students to use information from previous course work as they develop their specific, individualized projects. The major potential drawback of this model is faculty who allow the senior project to get out of hand and become the means for addressing and correcting all the deficiencies students may have in the basic skills areas.

6. The academy model. The academy model is the most defined and organized of all the integration models. It is usually designed to motivate students who might otherwise be high school dropouts. Often this model operates as a school-within-a-school. Each teacher is expected to teach the same students through an entire course or series of courses. Opportunities for teachers to coordinate their courses are excellent; they all work independently of their regular course load. Teachers can also incorporate special projects that provide students opportunities to use their existing course work in the completion of the projects. Open communication and close working relationships among teachers are encouraged. The major limitation of the academy model is that it tends to segregate students into those courses taught by a small number of individual teachers.

7. Occupational high schools. Occupational high schools are very similar to the schools in the academy model with all faculty members preparing students for a single broad occupational area. Most occupational high schools were established several years ago and were opened as a mechanism of racial desegregation. The incentives for teachers to mix academic instruction and occupational skills are evident in this model. This type of academic culture readily supports the integration of courses.

8. Occupational clusters, "career paths," and occupational majors. Occupational high schools generally emphasize preparation for clusters of related occupations. Occupational clusters can also be used in academic high schools to facilitate the integration of business education and academics. Specific course sequences can be offered which are closely related to a particular occupation or occupational cluster and help prepare students for today's workplace. One noticeable drawback of this model is that it will not work well unless schools have a well-developed business education program that provides numerous offerings related to each occupational cluster. This model, therefore, is probably best suited for vocational rather than comprehensive high schools.

It is often challenging for school administrators to initiate and support appropriate communication and collaboration among faculty as well as to encourage the development and implementation of curriculum changes necessary for fostering the various models of integration. As schools continue to experiment with integrated curricula, different processes and procedures will be developed, new models will be formulated, and authentic assessment strategies will be initiated. As business teachers consider curriculum integration, they need to examine the following benefits and challenges.

Benefits of Integration
Increases teacher involvement and enthusiasm for teaching. Teachers

are at the core of curriculum integration. Providing opportunities for academic and business teachers to work together to plan instructional strategies, develop and adapt resource materials, and coordinate course content reduces the isolation of individual departments and teachers. Collaboration among teachers fosters improved communication and cooperation among departments. These professional alliances can generate renewed enthusiasm for teaching because teachers gain new insights and perspectives relative to their individual disciplines.

Adds new life to existing programs by improving student preparation for the workforce. Teacher boredom can be a major factor of educational burnout. When teachers and departments work closely together to formulate new units and courses from existing course work, new life and energy are added both to the course work and to the teaching staff. By encouraging the teaching of occupational information in all classes, more teachers have opportunities to feel a sense of accomplishment when their students enter and succeed in the workplace.

Raises expectations that all students can achieve at a higher academic level. By combining the teaching of both academic and occupational competencies, integration can lead to increased course enrollments and student achievement. Integration makes academic courses more relevant to today's workplace and to students' adult roles; thus, higher levels of academic achievement can be expected from, and realized by, all students.

Enhances student participation by being part of an innovative and win-win group. The integration of business education and academics encourages greater student participation through contextual learning. Because students are involved in an active, applied learning process, they tend to sense that they are responsible for their own learning. They also recognize that their teachers are facilitators who are interested in enhancing this learning process. Active learning strategies result in a win-win opportunity for both students and teachers.

Develops student interests and self-fulfillment. Students are more interested in school when they can see the value of their learning and how it relates not only to their current but to their future lives. Integrating academic and business education course work brings greater relevance and context to the instructional/learning process. Thus, students' motivation to learn is enhanced, and this results in better course attendance, more active classroom participation, and a greater sense of accomplishment.

Encourages relevant learning and student achievement. Integrated courses enable students to see the relevance of both the academic and business education content to the workplace and make the appropriate connections as they transition from high school to career or college. Understanding the need for workplace basics as well as technical skills in today's high performance, technology-oriented workplace is critical. Because of this perceived relevancy, higher student achievement in integrated courses should translate into more successful experiences for students following graduation.

Creates professional development opportunities and recognition for faculty. Some of the most innovative methods of curriculum integration are not bound by the traditional discipline-related structure of courses. Teachers should be encouraged to attend workshops, symposia, and other professional development activities that focus on integrating course work. Providing in-service training to practicing teachers and preparing prospective teachers with instructional strategies that focus on how to integrate content should help make teachers more receptive to interdisciplinary instructional methods and techniques.

Increases the diversity of students in both academic and business courses. The integration of courses increases the number of students receiving both academic and occupational content. Some students only enroll in the traditional academic, college-preparatory courses; therefore, they may not receive hands-on information concerning possible occupational choices. Other students receiving only job-related vocational course content may feel that they do not have the necessary basic skills and knowledge to enter and succeed in their chosen occupational fields. Integrated courses help prepare high performance individuals who understand the basics and have the technical skills needed in today's complex, fast-paced workplace.

Reduces competition among departments for student enrollment. The integration of courses may be used to reduce competition among departments for student enrollments in their respective courses. All teachers need to be encouraged to collaborate and participate in professional development activities concerning integration. The school curriculum cannot be static, but must continually evolve to meet the needs of current and future students. Curriculum integration requires teachers to explore and collaborate in order to devise new strategies, materials, content, and structures.

The benefits of integrating a business education and an academic course are numerous. Students will increase both their academic and technical knowledge and skills, while teachers will develop a greater sense of accomplishment when more of their students achieve success. Administrators will be able to lead and facilitate in the development of integrated curricula, and schools will benefit by increasing their communication with the business community. In addition, the number of students who can successfully transition upon graduation from school to career or college will increase. Increased communication and cooperation among the faculty, staff, administration, and business community as well as an increasing number of students who achieve success are positive results of a successfully integrated curriculum.

Challenges of Integration

Although the following challenges or barriers to integration may exist, it is important to keep in mind that they can be overcome.

Requires administrative and financial support. If only limited resources for training and technical support are available, administrators may need to target a small number of receptive teachers at first. As this small group achieves success and their achievements are publicized, other teachers will become interested. When new teachers are hired, they should be receptive to offering and supporting integration projects in their courses. In addition, support should be provided to faculty for attendance at workshops and seminars and for acquisition of innovative, up-to-date curriculum resources.

Creates a scheduling need for time to meet, plan, and work together. As artificial barriers among departments and subject matter disciplines are broken down, teachers involved in integration activities may recognize that they all share a common purpose as facilitators of learning. Adequate planning and preparation time during the school day is vital, however. By meeting and working together, cooperation and open communication among teachers is fostered.

Establishes a need to communicate with parents, faculty, and the business community. Garnering support from the parents and the local community's businesses is fundamental for achieving success. Maintaining open communication regarding the successes and challenges of integration activities is critical. As students, parents, teachers, staff, administrators, and the business community begin to witness the motivating nature of integrated courses and curricula, support for the activity will grow.

Requires authentic assessment strategies and collaborative input on grades. Both learner and teacher expectations should help define the criteria for assessing student performance. In order to receive high school credit, students must be able to demonstrate their knowledge and skills at a defined level of performance. Authentic performance-based assessments bring integrity to the learning process and should be flexible enough to encourage student creativity. The collaborative assignment of student grades encourages open communication among the teachers and outside experts who are involved both in the instructional/learning process and the student assessment process.

Establishes a need to rethink teacher certification and college admissions requirements. State department personnel, school administrators and faculty, and college admissions personnel must work together to see that appropriate credit is awarded for integrated courses and establish equitable procedures for recognizing this credit. When students graduate and either attend college or join the workforce, they do not generally concentrate on just one particular subject or work area. We all live in a world that is "overlapping." Indeed, it often takes more than one skill to accomplish real-world tasks. Postsecondary institutions must be open to awarding credit for integrated or applied courses when general education requirements are satisfied through the overlapping and enrichment of academic and business education course work.

Examples of Business Education Integration

With the variety of approaches involved in the different models of integration presented above, it is important to remember that various processes or procedures can be implemented in high school business education classrooms. The following four examples of curriculum integration in business education are representative of the numerous strategies used in Missouri during the 1998–99 school year.

Office technology, English, and advanced earth science. A business educator (Robinson, 1999) in a small rural high school in Fair Grove took part in an integrated project that involved her office technology students with students from two other courses, English and advanced earth science. Initially, the earth science students took several field trips to the Lake of the Ozarks, gathering topography data and samples of various types of plant life. The earth science students then analyzed the data gathered during their field trips and passed their findings on to the English class.

The project for the English students was to formulate and write the findings as given to them by the earth science class. There was a tremendous amount of information; therefore, the English students had to review and condense the findings, being careful not to eliminate any necessary or useful information. The English and earth science teachers noticed that a considerable amount of student attention was given to communicating precisely and writing the information correctly before sending it to the office technology class.

The office technology students took digital pictures of the samples gathered by the earth science students as well as the information written by the English students and entered it all on three CD-ROMs. Additional, related scientific information was downloaded from the Internet by the office technology students and incorporated into the curriculum integration project.

All three teachers reported that the project was well-received by all students and that they were excited to see their individual work displayed on the CD-ROMs. The challenges indicated by the teachers were the lack of organization and preparation time and the need for additional computer equipment for students. Grading was completed using a rubric designed by the three teachers; however, each individual teacher graded the projects and incorporated their individual grades into the students' quarter grades.

Computer applications, government, mathematics, and media. Another example of a curriculum integration project (Reese, 1999) at a small high school in Bloomfield involved four different courses—computer applications, government, mathematics, and media. The government students were assigned to conduct mock elections. Students had to choose their political party and the office for which they would become a candidate. In-class time was provided for the students as they gathered information and prepared their speeches.

Each political candidate then presented a speech and other political information to the media class, which used a camcorder to videotape the entire activity. The computer applications students, using the information from the camcorder, prepared fliers, pamphlets, brochures, business cards, and campaign buttons for each of the political candidates. The computer applications students also downloaded additional information from the Internet to help the government students prepare appropriate political materials. The mathematics class calculated all the voter statistics and, following the election, displayed the results using spreadsheet and graphics software. The total time for the integrated project was approximately four to six weeks.

The integrated project was highly successful. Teachers indicated that it helped improve student self-esteem, demonstrated the need for teamwork, and promoted a better understanding of all the subject areas. The teachers noted that even though the four integrated courses did not have the same students enrolled, this did not create a problem. Grades were calculated by each teacher and incorporated into the students' quarter grades. The school administration was highly supportive of the integrated project and provided the teachers funds for the extra supplies necessary to complete the course assignments. The two greatest challenges noted by the teachers were the need for additional preparation time and more computer equipment.

Communication 2000, team taught. A business educator (Holbrook, 1999) at a vocational-technical school and an English teacher at a large high school in Cape Girardeau integrated academic content and vocational content into a course called Communication 2000. Now offered every year, the course is a senior-level, hands-on English class and is team taught by both teachers. The course content is applicable to college-bound students as well as those students choosing to enter the workplace immediately following graduation. Table 1 details the course project requirements. Students are required to become proficient in word processing and desktop publishing skills in order to complete all the assigned projects.

The administrators from both schools have been highly supportive and often refer to the course as one that has satisfied the unique needs of all the students. The course is designed for one year, and the enrollment often exceeds the number of classroom computers available.

The two teachers follow their respective districts' grading scales. The projects related to business are graded by the business education teacher, while those related to English are graded by the high school English teacher. However, both teachers work together closely and often consult with each other prior to assigning individual student grades.

Table 1. Course Project Requirements
Exploring career choices.
Collecting information relative to the challenges and barriers of communication.
Completing a job search.
Writing a letter of application.
Constructing a resume.
Conducting mock interviews.
Designing advertising brochures.
Writing television advertising.
Using the telephone to conduct business.
Composing memorandums.
Presenting oral business reports.

Integration of character traits development across the curriculum.
Pattonville Senior High School, a large suburban high school, uses a unique
approach to initiate character traits development activities across the total curriculum. During the summers, teachers meet to formulate curriculum revisions for the
approaching school year. Teachers from each grade level share ideas and provide
input as the updated curriculum and activities are developed. This high school
character traits program is known as Personal Responsibility Education Process
(PREP)—a school, business, and community partnership. Ready-made materials
are provided to the entire high school staff to encourage implementation and
participation in the PREP program. PREP is designed to help students develop
positive character traits, which include understanding, caring about, and acting
upon core ethical values. PREP encourages an infusion of positive character traits
into the total curriculum, regardless of the subject area being taught.

Some of the major PREP components are:

- All staff members are encouraged to model the character traits of the PREP
  curriculum.

- The PREP character words are visible throughout the school building.
  Banners are displayed prominently in key areas of the building, and
  teachers are provided monthly posters to display in their individual classrooms.

- Monthly lesson plans are provided for each staff member. These lesson
  plans are cross-curricular in content and include related quotations and
  discussion activities. Teachers are encouraged to use these lessons in their
  own classrooms.

- During the 1998–99 school year, the following nine PREP character traits
  were used:

  - September — Reliability
  - October — Cooperation
  - November — Respect
  - December — Compassion
  - January — Responsibility
  - February — Self-Control
  - March — Commitment
  - April — Service
  - May — Honesty

Funding for the PREP program was received from the corporate business
community, federal grants, and the local school district. Because the entire
community was involved in the decision-making process, the PREP initiative has
received an overwhelmingly positive reaction from students, parents, faculty,
staff, and administrators.

Elements of Successful Integration

The appropriate model(s) of curriculum integration for each school must be determined by giving consideration to the current curriculum and programs being offered; the teacher's interest; the administrative support; the students' characteristics, needs, and abilities; and the nature and needs of the local business community. Different aspects of the various models may be combined or adapted to create a unique integration model or process for a particular school. However, several common elements of successful curriculum integration activities have been identified in the literature (Stasz and Grubb, 1991; Pritz, 1989):

1. Vision and commitment from all levels;

2. Consistent support from district administrators and state officials;

3. New resources for funding;

4. Autonomy for teachers;

5. Teacher training and retraining;

6. Evaluation of efforts; and

7. Adequate time for implementation.

Recommendations for Business Educators

Based upon the review of the related literature and research, the identified benefits and challenges, and the current practices and procedures of curriculum integration, the following recommendations are presented:

1. Business educators should initiate efforts to collaborate with academic teachers for the purpose of integrating business education content into academic courses. Creating applied academic courses and/or activities will improve and expand students' skills and enhance their preparation for today's workplace.

2. Business educators should encourage and support the infusion of academic content and related materials into business education courses to improve and reinforce learning.

3. Business educators need to increase their involvement in statewide curriculum integration activities. This will encourage them to collaborate with other teachers and participate in local, state, regional, and national conferences that focus on curriculum integration. This increased involvement will provide opportunities for exchanging information regarding successful integration activities and materials and for promoting business education as a viable discipline for providing contextual learning.

4. Business educators should continue to develop and monitor instructional/learning strategies and authentic assessment methods used to integrate business education and other curriculum areas.

5. Business educators should encourage state supervisors, department

chairpersons, and teacher educators to promote implementation of integration strategies and/or curricula at the local level.

6. State directors of business education should assume a leadership role in helping business teachers develop and disseminate integration strategies and materials that can be implemented in their local schools.

Summary

Academic and business education content can be integrated in a variety of ways. By integrating academic and business education curricula, teachers can reinforce oral and written communication skills, develop problem-solving and decision-making skills, apply technology to real-world problems, provide a context for student learning, and improve student motivation and understanding. All of these skills are vital for achieving success in today's workplace.

In addition, instructional/learning activities which involve teamwork, problem solving, analyzing, and reasoning will strengthen both academic and workplace competencies and better prepare students for the transition from high school to college or career. Instead of just being providers of information, teachers must become mentors, facilitators, and coaches who encourage students to explore and apply subject matter content. Societal and workplace problems are generally not confined to just one subject matter area. They are often multifaceted, complex, and unique. An integrated approach to curriculum planning, development, and implementation can help prepare students for these challenges. While curriculum integration activities require time, planning, collaboration, and training, the future success of our students and our profession may well depend upon it.

References

Grubb, W. N., Davis, G., Lum, J., Philal, J., and Morgaine, C. (1991, July). *The Cunning Hand, the Cultured Mind: Models for Integrating Vocational and Academic Education.* Berkeley, CA: National Center for Research in Vocational Education. (ERIC Document Reproduction Service No. ED 334 421).

Holbrook, C., et. al. (1999). Integrated Business Education Curriculum Project. Cape Area Vocational School, Cape Girardeau, MO.

Pattonville Senior High School, Maryland Heights, MO (1998). Personal Responsibility Education Process, PREP.

Pritz, S. G. (1989). *The Role of Vocational Education in the Development of Students' Academic Skills: An Implementation Guide. Information Series No. 340.* Columbus, OH. (ERIC Document Reproduction Service No. ED 326 692).

Reese, K., et al. (1999). Integrated Business Education Curriculum Project. Bloomfield High School, Bloomfield, MO.

Robinson, S., et al. (1999). Integrated Business Education Curriculum Project. Fair Grove High School, Fair Grove, MO.

Stasz, C., and Grubb, W. N. (1991, July). *Integrating Academic and Vocational Education: Guidelines for Assessing a Fuzzy Reform.* Berkeley, CA: National Center for Research in Vocational Education. (ERIC Document Reproduction Service No. ED 334 420).

Chapter 5 — The Promise of Technology

Rodney G. Jurist
Rider University
Lawrenceville, New Jersey

In the 1990s, progress and options in technology dazzled the public, the educational community, and the government. All individuals use some form of technology, whether they watch television, send a fax, or interact with others around the world via satellite and the World Wide Web (WWW). Advances in technology—together with the globalization of the marketplace, the downsizing of the workforce, the accountability movement in education, and affirmative action—have had major impacts on society and education (Austin and Willis, 1997).

How is education changing as a result of these trends and their interactions? What are the implications for business teachers? This chapter addresses these questions and attempts to define where technology will lead business education in the 21ˢᵗ century.

How Is Education Changing?

Government, businesses, educational institutions, and the population at large are supporting definite shifts in educational emphases as people continue to discover how technology can be applied to everyday living, working, and learning. These shifts are, for the most part, influenced by the demands of the workplace, the complexities of society, and by advances in technology itself.

Technology use is more widespread. The use of technology for instruction and learning is relatively widespread throughout the public schools in the United States (see Table 1). The data indicate that educational technology associated with televised communications, multimedia computers, network access, and teacher certification are becoming increasingly common.

Table 1. Status of Technology and Instruction in the United States	
Technologies	**Percentage of schools that have and use the technology**
Videodisc players	55%
Cable TV	74%
Local Area Networks (LANs)	65%
Wide Area Networks (WANs)	30%
Satellite access	28%
Internet access	70%

Average number of students per multimedia computer is 21.

Number of states (N=50) that require technology training as part of teacher licensing (certification) requirements for elementary and secondary teachers is 33.

Source: Editorial Projects in Education. Technology and Instruction. (1997). *Education Week,* 17 (11), 20.

Computers themselves have evolved from the "automated drill sheets" used in the 1970s to tools for discovery, exploration, and collaboration (Jones, 1990). Statistics collected by the U.S. Department of Education demonstrate changes in the method and frequency of computer use between 1984 and 1996. For example, the percentage of 11ᵗʰ graders who reported using a computer to learn (as opposed to using the computer to play games) rose from 54.6 percent in 1984 to 80.2 percent in 1996; and 12.1 percent of 11ᵗʰ graders said they used a computer every day in 1984 compared to 18.1 percent in 1996 (U.S. Department of Education, 1998).

Technology is used to further education reform. *Education Week* (1998) reports that many teachers and educational establishments have been using technology to support educational reform and lists 10 ways that technology advances reform goals, including the following:

1. Teaching the basics in a way that extends beyond drill and practice.

2. Training students to think by using technology as teacher aides.

3. Preparing students for a digital world by permitting them to learn through projects involving the use of technology.

4. Making learning authentic through field experiences and "real-life" simulations.

5. Changing the way educators teach by moving from a lecture format toward active inquiry.

6. Building a better teaching force by networking with businesses, other educational institutions, and colleagues from other disciplines.

7. Strengthening the home-school connection by providing information services for parents and the community.

8. Enhancing student interest in class work through the excitement of technology.

9. Making the most of assessments through the use of interactive multimedia and portfolios.

10. Opening the classroom to the entire world through the Internet.

Technology is viewed as more than the sum of its components. Means (1994) found widespread agreement among psychologists and educators that the skills of comprehension, reasoning, composition, and experimentation are acquired not through the transmission of facts but through the interaction with content. She recommends that educational technologies not be classified by their root technology (microprocessors, fiber optics, etc.) but according to the way they are used. She suggests the following use categories: (1) as a tutor; (2) for exploration; (3) as a tool; and (4) for communication.

Tutoring (to compensate for absenteeism, differences in learning styles or special interests, physical disabilities, and cultural and language differences) has long been a serious issue for many teachers. Online tutorial resources can help teachers meet the needs of an increasingly diverse student body and let students progress at their own pace.

Using technology for exploration expands one's knowledge and opens new avenues of thinking not limited by geography or the resources in a particular school library. Exploration of a simple topic such as money via one of the compact disk encyclopedias can lead to further investigation on the Internet and WWW.

Information dissemination and retrieval, online shopping and banking, and recording and storing information are some of the ways technology can be used as a practical, everyday tool. Homes, schools, libraries, banks, shopping malls, and even small businesses offer various access channels for applying these tools.

Using technology for communication has become more prevalent over the last few years. It is not unusual for an individual to own or have access to a cellular telephone, pager, e-mail software, telephone answering machine, fax machine, several television sets, and a personal computer. Interactive Web and digital television appear to be the next wave of technological innovation. Tube-type television screens and computer monitors are being replaced by "flat" screens that can produce incredibly clear three-dimensional images. Sound quality has also improved.

Classifying technologies by how they are used rather than by what they are made of can benefit not only the mainstream population, but also those who have different physical or mental abilities. Such a shift in classification allows for individualized instruction and learning as well as interaction and collaboration with others in a multidisciplinary environment. Classifying technology in this way also suggests not only the availability of information and services, but also access to information and services through various routes at numerous times.

Workshops that deal with technology topics are increasingly offered at educational conventions, in-service programs, and board of education meetings. Technology topics also appear on state and federal education department agendas. In his 1998 State of the Union Address, for instance, President Clinton predicted that in the 21st century every student will be only a keystroke away from all the literature, art, science, and communication in the world.

Funding for technology is more available. Financial support has been a continuing problem for schools that want to implement the latest technology. Current literature, however, indicates that this is changing. Trotter (1997), for example, stated that unprecedented support for school technology has led government, industry, and foundations to invest billions of dollars in this endeavor. In addition, White (1997) reported that a number of sources are providing technology funds to schools: the U.S. Departments of Education, Commerce, and Agriculture; the National Science Foundation; and the National Endowment for the Humanities. Funding is also available from a variety of telecommunications companies, such as AT&T, Bell Atlantic, Sprint, MCI, and their affiliates.

Zehr (1998) cites state policies for planning, funding, standards, and best practices that enhance technological modifications for educational establish- ments, providing credible evidence that each state's schools are devoting more attention to educational technology (see Table 2). Her findings indicate that all states have technology plans and that nearly every state considers its plan up-to- date. Most states schedule revisions of their plans based upon data they collect.

Technology changes teacher beliefs and practices. Only a few years ago, David (1994) reported shifts in teacher beliefs and practices brought about by diverse populations and technological influences. These shifts include the following:

- Classroom activity has become more student- than teacher-centered. Strategies include more cooperative learning and problem-solving activities designed to teach concepts through experience.

- The teacher role has moved from fact teller and expert to collaborator and occasional learner. With the amount of knowledge increasing so quickly and becoming so complex, teachers must collaborate with students, col- leagues, and professionals in other disciplines. The classroom is an educational forum in which everyone learns from each other.

- The student role has changed from passive listener to collaborator and occasional expert. Students today possess more knowledge in certain catego- ries than do their teachers. This is particularly true in computer applications. Students learn a great deal from their peers, and teachers often state that they frequently learn more from their students than from other sources.

Table 2. State Policies for Planning and Funding to Enhance Technological Modifications for Their Schools*	
Types of Funds	**Number of States**
States targeting technology funds to disadvantaged schools or districts	22
States supplying special funds to upgrade infrastructure to support technology	12
States implementing standards or graduation requirements pertaining to technology	38
States requiring teaching candidates to take courses in technological literacy	38
States providing teachers with professional development opportunities in technological literacy	Almost all
Source: Zehr, M. A. (1998). The State of the States: Technology Counts. *Education Week,* 18 (5), 71–101.	
*(For fiscal year 1998, 42 of 50 states provided funds for educational technology.)	

- Instructional goals have shifted from memorization of facts to inquiry, invention, and the study of relationships. Inquiry stimulates interest in and excitement about learning. The study of relationships stimulates the mind to look for creative and innovative ways to solve problems. For example, students may investigate and create the best possible business letter for explaining the advantages of a product they have selected.

- The concept of knowledge has changed from the accumulation of facts to the transformation of facts. For example, students might participate in a problem-solving situation, working in small, cooperative learning groups. Each group is given a set of objects, directed to gather facts about them, and then determine how they can be used to illustrate business management concepts.

- Success is no longer demonstrated by the memorization of facts but by the quality of understanding. Many teachers believe that understanding can best be measured by some sort of culminating performance represented by a student product. For example, students demonstrate their understanding of the employment-seeking process by choosing an occupation, compiling a list of employers seeking employees in that occupation, developing a resumé, arranging and completing an interview, and then obtaining a promise of employment.

- Assessment has shifted from norm-referenced, multiple-choice instruments to criterion-referenced portfolios. Portfolios documenting student performances and achievement are now becoming commonplace in many school districts. Some school districts maintain special student portfolios that contain the best samples of student work in all the subject areas covered from kindergarten through grade 12. The portfolio practice is also in vogue for some teacher education and business administration programs in colleges and universities. Portfolio assessment appears to be a better indicator of what an individual can do than norm-referenced tests.

Assumptions: Teaching and Learning in the 21ˢᵗ Century

The changes discussed above herald an environment in which education may be reinvented. According to Bartholome (1997), the 21ˢᵗ century will emphasize innovations in learning rather than in teaching. Students will assume more responsibility for their education, and the role of the teacher will shift from a dispenser of knowledge to a manager or coordinator of learning. Educational establishments themselves will provide wider access to learning via technology that extends far beyond the physical plant, teaching staff, or library. Education will be available to anyone, anywhere, any time.

Matthews (1997, p. 1) notes that these "new technologies will create major changes in education. Students will become immersed in curricular scenarios where they will learn through actual participation rather than direct instruction (by a teacher in a traditional classroom)."

The educational environment of the 21st century will evolve as technology continues to penetrate educational settings and may be characterized as follows:

Student populations and needs will become increasingly diverse. Differences in academic attainment, cultures, languages, interests, occupations, ages, and physical and mental abilities will, through various pressure groups, continue to dramatically influence government and education providers. It is becoming increasingly difficult to meet these differences through traditional classrooms and traditional instruction. Advances in technology appear to have made inroads for addressing these complex issues.

Gifted and talented students, for example, can use computers to apply complex thinking skills by working with real problems and computer simulations, even participating in programming applications that allow them to invent their own syntax, integrate knowledge, and share ideas (Jones, 1990). ESL (English as a Second Language) students can use word processing software to focus on the content of their communications and stretch their writing skills.

All students will have opportunities to explore and practice advanced skills. Students are often placed in categories based on standardized tests associated with intelligence or aptitude. As a result of placement in these categories, students have been prejudged in regard to what they can or cannot accomplish without having the opportunity to experience what they can really learn. Through technology, however, students will be limited only by how far they want to progress in their learning.

Teachers can provide CAI (Computer-Assisted Instruction) for students with learning disabilities or help them use alternative keyboard technology to overcome their cognitive or physical limitations. Special needs students who might be overwhelmed by research and data collection assignments if they were to do them alone can be placed in project teams that use CD-ROM encyclopedias, spreadsheets, and databases to discover, capture, and manipulate information on a particular research topic (Fisher, 1997). Teachers can supplement lessons with multimedia presentations that allow more than one channel of sensory input. Closed circuit television and LCD (liquid crystal display) allows students with low vision or auditory difficulties to enlarge reading materials or print embossed pictures, diagrams, or maps (North Central Regional Educational Consortium, 1997).

Teachers will become facilitators or coordinators of learning rather than expert knowledge dispensers. In the past, teachers adhered to a prescribed curriculum in which they dispensed their expertise to a group of students. The teacher and what he or she brought to class was considered to be the universe of learning. The evolution in today's society suggests that teachers now and in the future monitor students, keep them focused on their learning goals, and provide channels for inquiry.

Teachers, for example, could collaborate with local businesses and national trade associations to help students investigate and write a research paper related to their trade area (Wagner, 1995). University or public librarians can provide instruction in research and use of online databases and list serves to help students collect needed information.

Instruction will become more interactive, collaborative, and multidisciplinary. Education has reached such complexity that it is difficult to learn anything that is not related to something else. Both the magnitude of knowledge available through technology and the diversity of learners will require interaction and collaboration with others from many disciplines. Also, the specificity and volume of the information available will require collaboration, as it will be impossible for one person to know everything required to solve any one problem. Since students learn best by experiencing and actually doing things, interacting individually and in groups in "real-life" situations will be expected.

The international trade and marketing students of a Charlotte, North Carolina, teacher, for example, have participated in real-time conferences with schools in Finland, Israel, and the United States. The class made plans to export and import products from classes in other countries (Wagner, 1995).

Another collaborative learning activity that involves coordinating information from various experts is that of developing and implementing a business plan. Students must integrate elements of marketing, demographics, sales, and product knowledge to create the plan. As an extension, project teams can be developed that would decide where to locate the business, based on specific geographic, environmental, and legal constraints, using a Geographic Information System (Dorhout, 1997).

Learning will be pursued well beyond the four walls of a classroom.
Technology is providing a more convenient means of learning at home and other places via interactive television, the Internet, and WWW. Distance learning courses and seminars are increasingly being offered by educational institutions, businesses, and special interest organizations. Further developments in technology will improve interactive learning to the point where it can be used to teach practically any topic, at any time, from any place.

Education on any subject will be available on demand. Homes, schools, libraries, and workplaces are acquiring satellite receiving systems at a rapid rate. These systems provide 24-hour access to educational programs. The television set has become a fixture in most households and advances in its configuration and use will contribute to its importance in providing education on demand.

Education will be available to everyone regardless of any special challenges. Regardless of physical, mental, cultural, social, economic, or other challenges, all individuals will be able to participate in the classroom and workplace. Improvements in voice and sight activation, Braille sound systems, note-taking devices and personal assistants, input technologies accessible via simple muscle movements or limited keystroking, advanced mouse developments, and combinations of adaptive computer hardware and software such as DiscoverKenx (T.H.E. Journal, 1998) will continue. Also, advances in various foreign language conversions and translations can provide instantaneous communication among people who speak different languages. Educators will need to learn how to facilitate, coordinate, monitor, and evaluate new and different styles and methods of learning.

"Education in a box" (Auerbach, 1998) whereby a virtual classroom is created through multimedia computers will become widespread early in the 21st century. Students and instructors will collaborate and interact in real time via the Web. Later, education will move "out of the box," and voice, sight, and movement-actuated virtual reality learning environments will become commonplace. Students will be able to enter a virtual learning environment and call into existence any situation. The setting will appear in hologram, and the student will be able to interact with it.

For example, students may be able to call into existence a notable business entrepreneur such as J. C. Penney and converse with him in English, Spanish, or sign language. Students can explore his retailing strategies, employee relations, personal life, and home environment through the interaction. Other examples of what a student might call into existence include a consultation with the director of the Federal Reserve, a session on how to create a report, a seminar on applying and interviewing for employment, or an interview with the president or prime minister of any country.

Students will be assessed through actual performance quality rather than quantitative test results. Quantitative, norm-referenced tests will disappear as a measure of evaluating student achievement. Simulations via virtual reality technology will enable students to experience actual situations in which they can demonstrate their learning. Immediate feedback will be provided to monitor progress and keep the students on track. Individual performance portfolios rather than cumulative records of test scores, grades, and disciplinary actions will be developed to document student accomplishments.

Business education teachers can require students to create specific workplace-related portfolios to demonstrate their understanding of the principles of business and commerce. Charles Lawrence, Business Department Chair at T. C. Williams High School in Alexandria, for example, says that the economics students develop stockholders' portfolios that reflect their understanding of investment principles.

Implications for Teaching Business Education

Teachers who want to successfully educate business students for the future may keep in mind the following considerations, which are based on assumptions about teaching and learning in the 21ˢᵗ century.

Business educators must teach students how to learn rather than what to learn. The employment environment is changing at a dramatic rate. Comparing employment advertisements that appeared in major newspapers 10 years ago to those in current issues reveals that most of today's employment positions, particularly those involving technology, did not exist a decade ago. Similarly, considering how rapidly technology advances, one can almost certainly predict that employment positions for the next 10 years will be in occupations that do not exist today. Preparing students for future careers has thus been receiving more attention.

How can teachers prepare students for the unknown? Given that students just now entering school will eventually take jobs that do not currently exist, many teachers believe that education should therefore emphasize capabilities for learning and ways of acquiring, sorting through, and using information (Roblyer, 1997). Fostering higher-order thinking skills, including creativity; strengthening competence in applied communication and computation; and developing some dexterity in integrating information via multimedia can help prepare students for tomorrow's jobs (Lawrence, 1999).

Teachers must prepare students for jobs that substitute communication technology for travel to a work location (telecommuting). Just as technology made it possible for learning to occur beyond the four walls of the classroom, so, too, has it allowed business to be conducted anywhere at any time. Though most telecommuters work at home, some work at their companies' satellite offices or are "hoteled" in shared office space. Since 1991, telecommuting has become mainstream. Given its documented advantages (increased productivity, greater accommodation for workers with disabilities, reduced illness and stress, decreases in real estate expenses), telecommuting is likely to become even more prevalent in the 21ˢᵗ century (Klayton-Mi, 1999).

To work as a telecommuter requires training in issues such as managing work remotely and managing remote workers. Management by objectives is more common in companies that practice telecommuting; information available through the "office grapevine" is less common or even nonexistent. To succeed as telecommuters, workers must develop and finely hone the following skills: self- and time-management, organization, and proactive communication (both written and face-to-face).

Teachers of students who will likely be telecommuters need to address and provide opportunities for students to practice such skills. They also must raise students' awareness of employer-employee rights and responsibilities unique to telecommuting, help them understand team and career management strategies for a virtual workplace, and introduce them to Occupational Safety and Health Administration (OSHA) and ergonomics issues specific to working "off site." Developing ethical standards for telecommuting scenarios, such as the appropriate use of computer data and employer equipment, or the viability and justice of "daylighting" (similar to "moonlighting," but in this case working a day job in addition to telecommuting), may be relevant jumping-off points.

Teachers must become even more technologically literate themselves or rely more heavily on the services of school-employed technology specialists. To meet the needs of a more diverse student population and simultaneously succeed in the role of learning facilitator, teachers must be intimately comfortable with new hardware and software. The greater availability of funding for technology has had an unfortunate consequence: many teachers receive new technological devices without any direction about how to integrate them into their curriculum. Particularly in situations where advanced, adaptive, or assistive technology is needed for students with different physical or mental abilities, teachers must become familiar with many different programs and understand the time required to use these programs and equipment (Fisher, 1997).

Schools that receive public funding must, by law, provide assistive technologies and services to eligible students with disabilities. Yet, as Marcia James, professor in the Department of Business Education and Office Systems, University of Wisconsin-Whitewater, states, "You're relying on schools to know the technology and the law."

Districts such as Fairfax County, Virginia, have begun to employ specialists to help teachers keep pace with advances in educational technology. In fact, "special education technology specialist" is one of the newest professions in U.S. education and through 2005 is expected to grow faster than the average for all occupations (National Clearinghouse for Professions in Special Education, 1996). In addition to aiding teachers who need to manage adaptive technology, this profession is an obvious example of a career choice for the 21ˢᵗ century business technology student.

Summary

Technology applications have been found to increase mastery of vocational and workforce skills, significantly improve the problem-solving skills of learning-handicapped students, benefit at-risk students, and encourage 21ˢᵗ century work values such as collaboration, leadership, and effective communication (Cradler, 1994). Today's business educator is challenged to embrace technology in order to prepare our future workforce to succeed in the workplace of the 21ˢᵗ century.

Many teachers tend to use new technology in the same capacity as the traditional technology it replaces, such as using a multimedia personal computer exclusively as a typewriter, dedicated word processor, or calculator. Instead, they will need to take full advantage of technology's uses as tutor, search engine, tool, and communicator. By taking a more involved role in educational technologies such as interactive multimedia, distance learning, adaptive/assistive technology, and Internet communications, teachers will find more creative and meaningful ways to incorporate technology and real-world learning into their own and their students' lives.

Current changes in teacher beliefs and practices indicate that business educators are finding more creative ways of using technology to meet students' educational needs. Widespread use of technology allows students to explore and practice advanced skills; work and learn in more interactive, collaborative, and multidisciplinary ways; and demonstrate their learning through performance-based projects. Increased funding for technology, professional development in technological literacy, and the assistance of technology specialists will allow teachers to grow in their roles as learning facilitators and ensure that all students are well educated regardless of special learning challenges.

Changes in employment practices suggest that educators emphasize knowledge acquisition, analysis, and application and help students master the learning process itself. Teachers must prepare students for the challenges of a virtual work environment and become intimate not only with the technologies of learning but also of the world of commerce. This can be accomplished by attending and participating in professional meetings focusing on technology, serving on various educational technology committees, associating with business professionals and colleagues concerned with technology, adopting a personal reading program in technology, and developing and implementing their own technology strategies. The following are resources for business educators who are planning or implementing technology in their schools:

- **Educational Technology Literature Review** (subscription); http://www.eschoolnews.org/newsletters/ETLR/

- **North Central Regional Technology in Education Consortium;** 630-571-4710; http://www.ncrtec.org/

- **Northeast Regional Technology in Education Consortia;** 212-541-0972; http://www.nettech.org/

- **Northwest Educational Technology Consortium**; 800-211-9435; http://www.netc.org/

- **Pacific and Southwest Regional Technology in Education Consortium**; 562-985-5806; http://psrtec.clmer.csulb.edu/

- **South Central Regional Technology in Education Consortium**; 888-TEC-2001; http://scrtec.org/

- **Southeast and Islands Regional Technology in Education Consortium**; 800-659-3204; http://www.serve.org/seir-tec/

- **Ten Best Web Sites for Educational Technology** (links to Armadillo; Classroom Connect; Institute for Learning Technologies (ILT); Mid Continent Regional Educational Laboratory (MCREL); North Central Regional Educational Laboratory (NCREL); North West Regional Educational Laboratory (NWREL); Reinventing Schools: The Technology Is Now; TERC-The Regional Alliance Hub; U.S. Department of Education; WEB 66); http://www.fromnowon.org/techtopten.html

Technology in business education for the 21ˢᵗ century presents more challenges and opportunities than ever before. To master these challenges, business educators must embrace technology as an integral component of the educational delivery system.

References

Auerbach, S. (1998, January). Classroom in a Box. *Inside Technology Training*, 2 (10), 38–40.

Austin, L. J., and Willis, C. L. (1997). Future Work. In C.P. Brantley and B.J. Davis (eds.), *The Changing Dimensions of Business Education: 1997 NBEA Yearbook, No. 35* (pp. 160–70). Reston, VA: National Business Education Association.

Bartholome, L. W. (1997). Historical Perspectives: Basis for Change in Business Education. In C.P. Brantley and B.J. Davis (eds.), *The Changing Dimensions of Business Education: 1997 NBEA Yearbook, No. 35* (pp. 1–16). Reston, VA: National Business Education Association.

Breaking Into High-Tech. (1998, January 11). *Sunday Newark Star-Ledger*, pp. 35–46.

Clinton, W. J. (1998, January). State of the Union Address. Washington, DC.

Cradler, J. (1994). Summary of Current Research and Evaluation Findings on Technology in Education. [Online]. Available: http://www.princeton.edu/~edutech/reports/findings.html.

David, J. L. (1994). Realizing the Promise of Technology: A Policy Perspective. *Technology and Education Reform*. San Francisco, CA: Jossey Bass.

Dorhout, M. (1997). Where Should I Put This Business? A GIS Simulation and How It Can Work for You. [Online]. Available: http://www.ncrtec.org/tools/camp/gis/gis1.htm.

Editorial Projects in Education. Technology and Instruction. (1997). *Education Week*, 17 (11), 20.

Editorial Projects in Education. Technology Counts '98. High-Tech Pathways to Better Schools. (1998). *Education Week*, 18 (5), 25–65.

Fisher, D. M. (1997, December). Computer Technology in the Instruction of Special Needs Students. [Online.] Available: http://boisdarc.tamu-commerce.edu/www/f/fisherd/spneeds.html.

James, M. (1999, January 25). [Telephone interview].

Jones, G. (1990). Personal Computers Help Gifted Students Work Smart. The ERIC Clearinghouse on Disabilities and Gifted Education, Digest #E483. [Online]. Available: http://www.cec.sped.org/digests/e483.htm.

Klayton-Mi, M. (1999, January 19). Telecommuting. Presentation at the meeting of the Potomac Chapter of the International Society for Performance Improvement, NOVA Community College, Annandale, VA.

Lawrence, C. (1999, January 25). [Telephone interview].

Matthews, L. (1997). Business Education to Run the World. *NJBEA Newsletter*, 32 (2), 1.

Means, B. (1994). Using Technology to Advance Educational Goals. *Technology and Education Reform*. San Francisco, CA: Jossey Bass.

National Clearinghouse for Professions in Special Education. (1996, Fall). Careers in Special Education and Related Services: Special Education Technology Specialist. NCPSE Product #118.96. [Online]. Available: http://www.cec.sped.org/cl/11896.htm.

North Central Regional Technology in Education Consortium. (1997). Closing the Gap 1997 Conference. [Online]. Available: http://www.ncrtec.org/tools/digi/adaptive/index.html.

Roblyer, M. D., Edwards, J., and Havriluk, M. A. (1997). *Integrating Educational Technology Into Teaching*. Upper Saddle River, NJ: Prentice-Hall.

T.H.E. Journal. (1998, December). Applications: Assistive Technology Helps Students Overcome Physical Limitations, p. 43.

Technological and Scientific Careers. *(1998, November 1). Sunday Newark Star-Ledger*, pp. 36–50.

Trotter, A. (1997). Taking Technology's Measure: Technology Counts. *Education Week*, 17 (11), 6.

U.S. Department of Education National Center for Education Statistics. (1998). The Condition of Education 1998. [Online]. Available: http://nces.ed.gov/pubs98/condition98/c9803a01.html.

Wagner, J. (1995). Using the Internet in Vocational Education. ERIC Digest No. 160, ED385777 95. Columbus, OH: ERIC Clearinghouse on Adult, Career, and Vocational Education. [Online]. Available: http://www.ed.gov.databases/ERIC_Digests/ed385777.html.

White, K. (1997). A Matter of Policy: Technology Counts. *Education Week*, 17 (11), 29, 42.

Zehr, M. A (1998). The State of the States: Technology Counts. *Education Week,* 18 (5), 71–101.

Chapter 6 — The Building Blocks of Multimedia Authoring

Carole A. Holden
County College of Morris
Randolph, New Jersey

Authoring software tools enable business educators to develop interactive multimedia courseware. More and more instructors are creating simple application programs that combine text, graphics, video, sound, and animation to accomplish learning objectives and enhance the classroom environment. This chapter includes a development model that describes the building blocks of multimedia authoring and illustrates the process to follow when producing computer-based training materials.

Instructional Technology

Now that 45 percent of schools use CD-ROMS and 24 percent of classrooms have Internet access, educators are realizing the importance of acquiring the skills to develop their own courseware (Five Trends Your Job Depends On, 1997). If this technology continues to transform the classroom, teachers will be expected to create the instructional materials—CD-ROMs, CBTs (computer-based training), or WBTs (Web-based training)—that will be used by their students. Currently, technology pioneers are taking the lead in authoring interactive multimedia courseware and in creating Web pages. Additional educators will join the ranks as authoring software becomes easier to use and sophisticated hardware and peripherals become more readily available.

Reasons to use multimedia in the classroom. Educators and administrators often have to be persuaded to commit the resources for instructional technology and to incorporate interactive multimedia courseware into the teaching and learning process. What may help secure their support is Perreault's suggestion (1995) that multimedia presentations reduce learning time because students interact with the material in a variety of ways. Research shows that people remember 10 percent of what they read, 20 percent of what they hear, 30 percent of what they see, and 70 percent of what they see and hear.

When interactive multimedia is employed in the learning process, the student can expect the following benefits: a high level of involvement and interaction, increased interest, concurrent engagement of multiple senses, hands-on experience using technology, access to otherwise unavailable experiences, and just-in-time learning. Interactive multimedia courseware empowers learners so they can "do more, with less, in a shorter time" (McGloughlin, 1997).

Provide educator training. A report by Scholastic, Inc. found that "a growing number of states and districts are recognizing the priority importance of training teachers to use technology" (1997). Business educators have an advantage over other teachers because of their skills in business communication, word processing, presentation software, and desktop publishing. Their knowledge of layout components and design elements assists them in understanding the concepts needed to create visually appealing training materials.

Often business educators are asked to provide technology development training to teachers in their districts. A recent *NEA Technology Brief* (1997) suggests that "it takes four to seven years of education, experimentation, reflection, and revision to turn classroom teachers into true education technology innovators." If educators are to embrace instructional technology and to author their own multimedia programs, they must be trained on specific software packages and taught how to operate peripherals such as scanners, CD-ROMs, laserdiscs, microphones, and projection devices.

Authoring Software and Hardware Options

Today's authoring software allows the user to prepare simple application programs for the computer in a structured approach without formal programming training. An extensive group of authoring programs is available to aid in the development of multimedia courseware. The selection depends on budget, hardware, goals, personal preference, and experience level. An analysis of the intended application often determines the software selection. Perreault (1995) notes that authoring packages have similar basic features; the user must determine the strengths and weaknesses of each package when deciding which program to select.

Metaphor categories. Fred Hofstetter states that "a *metaphor* is a way of thinking about new media in terms of something the user already knows" (1997). Each authoring tool employs what the user already knows to reveal how the program organizes elements, sequences events, and delivers a multimedia presentation. These authoring metaphors for creating multimedia presentations include time-based applications, card- or page-based relational databases, icon-based programs, and theatre-based applications.

Gold Disk's Astound is an example of a time-based metaphor where the multimedia events are synchronized along a time line. The text, graphics, audio, video, and animation elements are sequenced by the speed and length of time each plays or remains on the screen. The author coordinates each event via this time line. Other time-based software authoring packages include Macromedia Action, Animation Works Interactive, Media Blitz!, and Cinemation, to name just a few (Villamil and Molina, 1997).

SuperCard and Asymetrix ToolBook are systems using the card- or page-based metaphor. Each stack or card contains information that is in fact a relational database. Moving from page to page is easily accomplished because all pages are interrelated and connected (Villamil and Molina, 1997).

The icon-based metaphor provides a very visual, logical approach to the authoring process. "When using an object oriented, icon-based authoring system such as Authorware, the user drags icons onto a flowline and then assigns properties to each event" (Holden, 1997). Both IconAuthor and Macromedia Authorware are popular systems using this approach.

Finally, Macromedia Director is probably one of the best-known authoring systems using a theatrical metaphor. With this authoring package, media sequences are displayed as cast members that enter and exit on cue according to the score. The program allows the author to develop sophisticated and elaborate visual effects with its full-featured scripting language, Lingo.

Selecting Software. With so many authoring systems on the market, making a selection may not be easy. Several factors enter into the decision-making process: author knowledge level, resource availability, multimedia project goal, time element, budget, and product sophistication.

Educators should assess the capabilities of several authoring systems to determine which software meets their needs. They should also look at the Internet sites for the various software products, meet with courseware developers, discuss options with instructional designers, compare the features, test drive the software, enroll in a class, and attend multimedia conferences. All of these activities will assist educators in making a sound decision.

Hardware options. Probably the easiest part of the multimedia authoring project is obtaining the software. More challenging are the hardware obstacles that must be overcome at this stage of development. Planning for the necessary hardware to develop and play back the multimedia project is essential.

A minimum configuration for development on a PC would include the following: a multimedia PC with a Pentium processor, Windows 95 or higher, 16 MB RAM or higher, 300 MB hard drive or higher, a CD-ROM drive, and a Zip drive. Optional hardware would include a scanner, microphone, digital camera, and a CD-ROM burner. Similar configurations would be required for Macintosh or UNIX development. Distribution of the final product is a major consideration as well. Will the finished product be distributed via networked computers, CD-ROM, the Internet, or an Intranet?

The Roles of the Multimedia Development Team

Typically, a team of people works together to build a high-quality, professional multimedia presentation. The team often consists of the following specialists: production manager, content specialist, instructional designer, script writer, text editor, program author, computer graphic artist, audio and video specialists, computer programmer, and Web master. This section examines the roles of these team members.

Production manager. Keeping the project on time, on budget, and on track is the role of the production manager. He or she supports the other team members in the business and financial aspects of the multimedia project; delegates responsibilities to the team members; and guarantees that all equipment and software are in working order to bring the project in on time.

Content specialist. The content specialist is the subject matter expert for the multimedia project. He or she researches the topic carefully and summarizes and reports the content to the other team members.

Instructional designer. The instructional designer must make sure that the multimedia project adheres to sound pedagogical principles. The learning process, student learning styles, interactivity, organization and structure of the content, feedback, and evaluation methods are just a few areas of responsibility of the instructional designer. Subsequent learning activities must evolve around solid learning goals and objectives and should never take a backseat to the technical details of the project.

Script writer. When creating interactive multimedia applications, the script writer must think and create in a nonlinear way. The user of an interactive application has the ability to branch or link to any topic within the program through the navigation scheme developed by the author. Therefore, the script writer must envision the content as it might be used by the student and create the storyboard to communicate everything that will be present in the project. Storyboards assist the script writer in determining the structure that will work best for the content.

Text editor. Since much of a multimedia project is text-based, the text editor must possess excellent writing and editing skills. This team member has the responsibility of overseeing the narration for the project and maintaining the flow of the content in a meaningful way. He or she also directs the development of the accompanying documentation as well as the packaging material for the end product.

Program authoring specialist. A solid knowledge of the multimedia authoring software is essential to the program authoring specialist. This person integrates the graphics, text, audio, music, video, photos, and animation through the use of the authoring software. He or she communicates routinely with the content specialist, instructional designer, script writer, text editor, graphic artist, audio/video specialists, and computer programmer to guarantee the accuracy of all the project's elements.

Computer graphic artist. The graphical elements of the project are created by the computer graphic artist. These elements include the color scheme, backgrounds, navigation panel, buttons, logos, 3-D objects, animations, and renderings. The entire look and feel of the finished product must be in harmony and balance.

Audio/video specialists. The music and sound effects can be used from a library of music and sounds or custom developed by the audio specialist. The text narration files must be edited and then integrated with other elements of the project. The video producer shoots, digitizes, and edits the movies or videos used in the multimedia project. A strong background in digital sound or video is essential for this team member.

Computer programmer. Usually each authoring system includes its own high-level scripting language used to control the sequencing of the content and the animation, video, and sound files (Holden, 1997). Special lines of code or scripts are often required when producing quality, professional multimedia projects. An educational background in computer programming and a knowledge of the scripting language are important qualifications for the computer programmer team member.

Web master. Finally, the Web master position on the multimedia development team is especially important if the finished product is to be delivered over the Internet. The individual must possess skills in Java, Hypertext Markup Language (HTML), Web authoring software, C++, and other programming languages. Although multimedia courseware is currently under development for the Web, much of the learning on the Internet is still through text and illustrations (Horton, 1997). The Web master must transform the multimedia production into Web-based training.

Most business educators will probably not have a multimedia development team of this size to call upon. As Flanigan (1997) states, "What is the individual teacher or trainer who wants to develop multimedia applications to do…?" Educators can rely upon their own skills and talents to accomplish their goals.

Multimedia Development Model

The following multimedia development model provides the framework for a business educator who wishes to undertake the presumably daunting task of authoring interactive multimedia courseware. Gary Powell of Wayne State University recommends that an activity log be used to chronicle the steps undertaken to produce a multimedia project (1997). The components of this multimedia development model will be reviewed in the next section.

Goals and objectives defined. The anticipated outcome of the project should be clearly defined at the beginning. A list of measurable objectives should be developed, along with the activities and tasks required to meet the project goals. Defining the target audience is an important step at this point of the development model.

Project time line and budget. A production schedule will aid in the management of the goals and objectives previously outlined. Tracking the progress of the tasks to be accomplished, the amount of time to complete the task, as well as the identification of the team member responsible for each task is easily achieved with project management software.

Along with setting up the production schedule, a project budget should be developed. An understanding of the potential production costs will help the multimedia author develop a realistic budget. Villamil and Molina (1997) suggest the following guidelines related to personnel production costs: scanning one picture and performing minor maneuvers usually takes approximately 10 minutes at an average rate of $8 per hour; developing one minute of computer animation usually takes approximately 10 hours at an average rate of $20 per hour.

If the project requires video production, the costs to outsource the project will also need to be considered. Attention may have to be given to writing a grant or to identifying investors to fund the project.

Content analysis. The subject matter expert or content specialist gathers the data, facts, and information that become the knowledge base for the multimedia project. This content is organized in an outline format that can be shared with other team members. The content contains the facts, figures, graphics, videos, narration, text, bullets, charts, and tables that will be used in the intended project. Villamil and Molina (1997) propose that a variety of multimedia elements be applied to the content so as to appeal to different learning styles.

Production design planning. To ensure that the multimedia project facilitates the learning process, it is necessary to design an outline. A *flowchart* is a complex diagram of the entire program structure and sequence that specifies every possible choice the end user might make (Powell, 1997). At the heart of the multimedia production process is the *storyboard*: an outline of everything that is to be presented in the multimedia project. Wadley states that everything in a project includes "images, audio, links, text, animation, and other functions of the product" (1997).

Storyboards graphically present the flow and branching sequence of the project and provide a page by page description of the buttons, transitions, animations, video, graphics, and audio. Although storyboarding requires a tremendous amount of work, Adams (1997) considers storyboards "the blueprints of the interactive courseware design and development process." The more production design planning that is done through the use of outlines, flowcharts, storyboards, and scripts, the less likely the chance for delays, confusion, and revision down the road.

Copyright and fair use issues. Multimedia producers should be aware of the copyright and fair use issues when developing a project. The exclusive right to make and dispose of original works in the following categories has been granted by Public Law 94-553: literary, musical, and dramatic works; pictorial, graphic, and sculptural works; motion pictures and other audiovisual works; and sound recordings (Villamil and Molina, 1997).

Certain works with expired copyrights, as well as those issued by the United States government, are considered part of the public domain and may be used. Multimedia producers must get permission for the use of works that are protected by copyright laws. The fair use of copyrighted work for educational purposes is not always clear, and guidelines have recently been developed to help educators in determining their use. It is also important to register the completed multimedia project with the U.S. Copyright Office to guarantee its protection under the law.

According to Villamil and Molina (1997), using preexisting content is the most advisable way of acquiring content for a multimedia production. "The importance of these sources is that *usually* they grant you unlimited use and allow you to edit or manipulate these elements to create versions tailored to the needs of your project" (Villamil and Molina, 1997). Before using any clip art, video, or audio collections, it is important to read the license agreement to determine how the collection may or may not be used.

Evaluation methods. Evaluation of the multimedia project should be frequent and ongoing. Involving the end user is particularly important as the project reaches milestones on the time line. Evaluation and testing should include:

- Application design: does the product take into consideration educational psychology and pedagogy?
- Content: are all elements of the product accurate and correct?
- Text and narration: does the narration follow the prepared script and does it match the text on the screen?
- Graphical elements: are graphical elements appropriately placed and in balance with text, navigation scheme, and background?
- Audio: has sound editing been completed effectively with little variation in level or quality of sound files?
- Navigation: is it working properly? Does the navigation branch or link to the right place?
- Code or script: is the product performing calculations and other actions as programmed?
- Permissions: have all licenses, permissions, and releases been obtained for copyrighted material (Villamil and Molina, 1997)?

The ability to accept criticism and to make necessary changes regardless of the project's point on the time line is critical to the success of the multimedia production process. Testing and evaluation cannot begin too early or with too many people. Once a working model is available for field testing, educators should select a number of individuals to test it. Bugs and glitches will invariably be found at this point. It is important for educators to keep an open mind and be flexible regarding constructive criticism. Feedback can be used to make adjustments to the multimedia project and will contribute to its success.

Package, distribute, and deliver. The method of packaging the finished multimedia project depends on the application's file size and the computers to be operated by the end user. If the file size is under 1.44M and contains limited animation, no digitized movies, and few audio files, then a floppy disk may be the storage media of choice. Compressing the files is another alternative although this process may degrade the file quality unless AfterBurner and Shockwave software are used (Villamil and Molina, 1997). A Zip disk (100M) is a removable storage solution for those end users with a Zip drive, but the access time is very slow and satisfactory playback is not produced.

Recording or burning a CD-ROM with the application is a storage solution if end users have a CD-ROM drive on their computers. Before an application is recorded to a CD-ROM, it is important to make sure the application is stable and that audio, video, and graphic image files are located in the same directory or folder as the multimedia application.

Another distribution option for a large audience is through a network system. Decreased performance may be experienced with large graphic or audio files, but the advantages far outweigh the disadvantages. Finally, the World Wide Web may be used to distribute the finished multimedia application. "The good news is that the technology is now in place for networked delivery of video and audio files," state Horton and Lynch (1997).

One multimedia strategy is to use only digital audio on the Web since optimizing the sound quality and volume is much easier with audio than video. Apple's QuickTime movies allow cross-platform viewing and permit the user to start watching the movie before it is completely downloaded. Horton and Lynch (1997) recommend chunking the movies to allow the user to watch one segment at a time. Upgrades of QuickTime software will undoubtedly improve upon this situation. Technology is changing rapidly and developers looking to the future may not have to wait very long for the limitations of Web multimedia to all but disappear.

Implications for Educators

Over one million students now take courses via cybercolleges, compared to the 13 million attending the more traditional bricks and mortar colleges, notes Augustine Gallego (1997). With the Internet, videoconferencing, and other distance learning opportunities capturing seven percent of all college and university students, teachers need to respond to the changing educational environment. Online courses via the Internet are a reality, and the technology is available to implement the learning objectives for courses. Although this mode of instruction is not for everyone, educators should rise to the challenge of developing multimedia courseware for this new delivery method. However, it is important not to lose sight of teaching objectives as the new technology is mastered.

Summary

Technology tools, such as multimedia authoring software, can enhance the teaching and learning environment in the business education classroom. The availability of course materials that combine text, graphics, video, sound, and animation to accomplish learning objectives will increase as business educators join the ranks of technology developers.

References

Adams, D. L. (1997, May/June). What's the Story? Creating and Using Storyboards. *CBT Solutions*, 36-40.

Five Trends Your Job Depends On. (1997, October 29). *Electronic Learning*. [Online]. Available: http://scholastic.com.

Flanigan, E. J. (1997). Multimedia Toolchest. *NJBEA Observer*, 1-11.

Gallego, A. (1997, August/September). Tackling Technology Issues. *Community College Journal*, 3-4.

Hofstetter, F. T. (1997). *Multimedia Literacy.* (2nd ed.). New York, NY: The McGraw-Hill Companies.

Holden, C. A. (1997). Authoring Interactive Multimedia Courseware. *NJBEA Observer*, 23-29.

Horton, S. and Lynch, P. J. (1997, November/December). Web Multimedia: Turning the Corner. *Syllabus*, 16, 18, 20.

McGloughlin, S. (1997). *Multimedia on the Web.* Indianapolis, IN: Que Education and Training.

Perreault, H. R. (1995). Multimedia: An Educational Tool. In N. Groneman (Ed.), *Technology in the Classroom: 1995 NBEA Yearbook, No. 33*, (pp. 62-72). Reston, VA: National Business Education Association.

Powell, G. (1997, May). Documenting Multimedia: Well-Taken Steps for Educational Developers. *Syllabus*, 16, 18.

Technology: The Training of Staff. (1997). *NEA: Technology Brief No. 11*. [Online]. Available: http://www.nea.org/cet/BRIEFS/brief11.html.

Villamil-Casanova, J. and Molina, L. (1997). *Multimedia: An Introduction.* Indianapolis, IN: Que Education and Training.

Villamil-Casanova, J. and Molina, L. (1997). *Multimedia Production, Planning, and Delivery.* Indianapolis, IN: Que Education and Training.

Wadley, E. R. (1997, October). Storyboarding Your Educational Multimedia Project. *Syllabus*, 22-23.

Chapter 7 — Business Education Integration: Interactive Broadcast Media Technology

William R. Johnson and Linda I. Howard
Mechanicsburg Area Senior High School
Mechanicsburg, Pennsylvania

Blockbuster movies like *Star Wars* and *Jurassic Park* relied heavily on computer technology to enhance their visual presentation and heighten the impact of their story. While we may not all be as creative as Steven Spielberg, business educators have been at the forefront of using and teaching computer technology since the early 1980s. We are familiar with common applications like spreadsheets and databases; however, it is time to move beyond the familiar and into an area that gives us and our students opportunities to learn cutting-edge skills like those needed for video and broadcast media.

Some questions, of course, come to mind. How do we incorporate new applications into the current computer curriculum? How technologically sophisticated are our students? Can we integrate a video technology class across curricula? These are important questions, all of which must be answered before a course can be successfully developed and launched.

Background: Why Broadcast Media?

The computer applications courses we teach have been and will continue to be the mainstay of future business: spreadsheets, databases, word processing, desktop publishing, and most currently, the use of the Internet. Any computer application that was more innovative usually created conflict—or the fear of conflict—with another discipline. For example, consider the inclusion of desktop publishing as a business education class. The printing and graphic design teacher resists. "We already do that down here," he emphasizes. It is difficult to innovate: "turf wars" are sure to flare.

Yet how else do we challenge our already technologically sophisticated students and develop the thinking skills—application, analysis, synthesis, and evaluation—they are certain to need in tomorrow's economy? While not all students have the same level of technological expertise, technology is a part of their world, particularly the world of the so-called Net Generation (see Chapter 2, "Promoting the Work Ethic Among Generation X and N-Gen Students"). They not only need, but require innovative learning strategies. A cross-curricular course can meet this need and pave the way for a well-constructed experience in a technology application.

First Steps: Integrating Curricula at Mechanicsburg Area Senior High School

A few years ago, the business education and English departments at Mechanicsburg Area Senior High School each asked a teacher in their respective disciplines to help create a live television show, to be broadcast each morning with school announcements. As confidence in production of the show mounted and hardware was added to create a more professional presentation, these two teachers began to think of additional possibilities. What if the investment in equipment and peripheral support technology were more extensively utilized in a classroom setting? What if writing and speaking techniques were incorporated into a class dealing with technology? What if a video/television production class were added to the curriculum—how would it enhance the total school program? Would a video/television production class benefit and appeal to a wide range of students?

Problems and possibilities. The teachers began to discuss designing a course that might allow their two respective disciplines—business education and English—to combine. The possibilities were appealing. First, the teachers thought a video/TV production class would optimize student creativity: students would take an idea, write a script, videotape a story, edit video footage, and evaluate the final product. Even better, the combination of these activities would let students enhance their skills in English, technology, and higher-level thinking, regardless of their ability level. Also, the teachers believed their own enthusiasm, interest, and background would allow them to cooperate in creating and developing a solid course with appropriate learning criteria.

The more the teachers talked, the more benefits they saw to offering this kind of a course. However, potential problems also surfaced. The need to share facilities with school district media personnel, for example, might curtail what was available, in terms of equipment and class time, for student use. They also worried about schedule conflicts, which are always a concern with new courses. Finally, they hoped appropriate equipment and hardware would be available as the course evolved.

Getting started: views of curriculum integration. Several curriculum philosophies and models were examined for guidance. Among them were the following, which seemed best suited for integration across disciplines (Jacobs, 1989):

- Sequenced—Topics are rearranged to and sequenced to coincide with one another.

- Shared—Shared planning and teaching take place in two disciplines in which overlapping concepts or ideas emerge as organizing elements.

- Webbed—The teacher presents a simple topical theme and webs it to the subject matter.

- Threaded—The meta-curricular approach threads identified skills through the various disciplines.

- Integrated—This interdisciplinary approach matches subjects for overlaps in topics and concepts with some team teaching in an authentic integrated model.

After some study, the integrated model was chosen to develop a course that would combine strengths from both departments. A course would be created for students interested in advanced technology, which would combine television production, video, and computer technology with writing and speaking skills.

Case Study: Strategy and Technology for the Course "Interactive Broadcast Media Technology"

In this course, students would create and complete a video program. The video would have a "message" and, if all went as planned, the video would function as a learning and teaching tool and as a creative outlet. The students would learn about broadcast technology "from the ground up," working in teams as they experienced the writing, directing, producing, studio work, and postproduction phases of this medium. They would have to master creative and technical components, and the teachers would have to gather resources and add enhancements to make it all work.

Creative components. Perhaps the greatest challenge involved in making a video is learning to think in terms of images rather than words to communicate a message. Effective visual communication relies on pictures that tell a story, explain an idea, or sell a product. Pictures must be sequenced well and the creator of the piece must understand the possibilities for using scenery, background, lighting, and special effects to enhance the presentation.

Video is an auditory as well as visual medium; it includes a sound track as well as pictures. This aspect challenged students to conceptualize how they could incorporate appropriate dialogue, sound effects, and possibly music to effectively communicate their message.

Messages are verbalized through scripts. A script provides a road map for the concept or story and helps communicate the creative team's vision into film-based reality. Done well, scripts present a smooth, attention-getting beginning and an effective wrap-up or conclusion. They orchestrate accurate, precise timing of narrative events, and finally, they provide the technical staff with the information they need so that the right pictures and sounds come together at the right time. Scripts (and the storyboards developed from them) can be produced with computers and specialized software. Possible formats include interviews, play-by-play sportscasts, game shows, newsbreaks, commercials, documentaries, and dramas.

Technical components. In video, certain basic principles apply regardless of the type and sophistication of the camera and related equipment. Function is foremost: students must become familiar with how the camera works; how to use its lenses, ranging from a wide angle lens for shots of large groups, a long close-up lens for faraway shots, and a zoom lens (often called a variable-focal-length lens) to create "movement" or to change perspectives; and how to direct or interpret related vocabulary. For example, camera movements may include dollying, panning, and tilting. Picture composition can include two- or three-dimensional visuals, graphics, and props.

Second, because videos are shot on "sets," students must understand how the camera "sees" and how scenery, set design, and lighting combine to create a three-dimensional world on a two-dimensional medium. Floor plans can help specify the design of the set (scenery and background) as well as create the best plan (lighting and camera angles) for the shots. Lighting is critical in getting the best pictures and inspires the entire mood of the production. Sets—and the story they highlight—can be enhanced by special effects, which can be generated by computers with video input/output capabilities. Dissolves, fades, corner wipes, and split screens are just a few of the special effects that can be achieved. Even though special effects are generally added in the postproduction phase, it is important to consider their possibilities for adding to the video's impact so that any necessary footage can be shot or obtained beforehand.

In video, sound consists of speech, music, and sound effects. Various types of microphones, mounted on a floor stand or clamped to the lapel of a shirt, are used to obtain suitable acoustical conditions. An audio mixer or console is used to mix various microphones as well as other sound sources, such as cassette tape and compact disk players—a must for the production studio.

An understanding of the postproduction phase, particularly editing, can help focus the preproduction stages of scripting, storyboarding, and shooting. Students must think linearly so that a story can be appropriately sequenced, and then use "mind-mapping" strategies so that a shooting schedule can be devel-oped. For instance, scenes are shot out of order to make efficient use of the camera crew's time and to minimize the number of times equipment must be moved to different sets. Students use planning and organizing skills as they develop a shooting schedule—for example, all exterior shots, then all interior shots. They learn how to determine which scenes they need—including raw footage from other sources—to give their video maximum impact. They decide whether or not to acquire such footage from other sources—and arrange for it in advance so that it is available for editing later.

Working in teams. Effectively transmitting the message from the communicator in the studio to the viewers is a team responsibility. The production team consists of the following individuals:

- The director who orchestrates the human and technical elements into a harmonious whole;

- The studio crew, such as camera operators and audio technicians, who control the equipment in the studio; and

- The floor manager, who relays the director's instructions to the performer, who transmits an idea, a musical selection, a dance, or an act to a camera and microphone.

Any member of this team can create a distraction that prevents the message from getting across to the viewer. All need to work together to ensure a smooth production.

Postproduction. The footage shot during the production phase is not final. To ensure that students produce the best possible product that communicates their intended message, they enter the almost magical world of video editing.

Although regular VCRs may be used for direct machine-to-machine editing, special editing hardware is by far the best. It is in the "edit suite" that students arrange scenes in their best narrative sequence, add special effects and raw footage as needed, and massage the story message to pinpoint exactly what the videographer wants the audience to see and hear.

Course Enhancements

Aside from using the word processor for scriptwriting, the course in broadcast technology started with little or no actual computer use. The teachers incorporated enhancements as the course proved its mettle, adding digital multimedia hardware and software. Systems designed to manage and manipulate multimedia have followed the trend of other computer hardware and software: the cost to purchase and update such systems has dropped to accommodate even the home user. This puts that cost very much in the range of most school budgets.

Over the past decade, the video industry has been moving toward digital editing devices. To allow students to work with digital video technology is to allow them access to the same tools that created the lifelike animated dinosaurs of *Jurassic Park* and the destructive spaceships of *Star Wars*—the potential and the power to draw the viewer/learner into a real world (Azarmsa, 1998). High-quality video usually includes sound; combining the two media more powerfully represents reality.

Combining text, images, sound, and animation through video technology allows students to plan, create, and design the reality they want to present. They then assess how the audience that views the product learns from that presentation.

As the students plan their production, work with the members of their production team, and learn techniques such as digital editing, animation, and morphing, they also learn to apply higher-order thinking skills to a project that is meaningful, creative, and holds future career opportunities.

Field Trips and Other Professional Resources

The teachers at Mechanicsburg Area Senior High School use field trips to expand the course's depth. For example, students are taken to WGAL-TV, Channel 8, an NBC affiliate, each semester. The station conducts a tour of the studio, and students become the audience for a live broadcast show. Students witness all behind-the-scenes production activities for such a broadcast. In addition, the hosts meet with the students before and after the show to discuss production and answer questions concerning jobs in the television broadcast field.

Each semester the class also travels to NBC studios in New York for a tour of its facility. Students not only get a historical perspective of broadcast media, but also become part of a broadcast team simulating a live news show. They use professional quality video equipment, including a "blue screen" and teleprompters.

A similar learning opportunity exists at the Newseum in Rosslyn, Virginia (outside Washington, DC). The Newseum provides interactive experiences that allow students to see and participate in how and why news programming is made.

Guest speakers are another feature of the class, and several anchor personalities from local television and radio stations have shared their experiences and expertise with the students. Additionally, a partnership has been established with a local video production facility. The partnership originated as a result of a local grant for innovative and emerging district-wide programs. Through the grant, the class gained the services of a professional videographer who works with the students and teachers to hasten the transition to the use of digital video.

An alliance was also formed with a local television station, WHTM-TV, Channel 27, an ABC affiliate. The news director of the station provided a "News 101" (the TV station's name for their alliance) packet for class use, which included a detailed description and handouts of the video knowledge needed to produce a quality product. The class used a video and several handouts as an integral part of the course and produced several two-minute videos during the year, which the station aired as a weekly part of programming, showing viewers the station's involvement with local schools in the area.

Outlets for Completed Creativity

The first avenue for showing completed videos is during daily morning and special announcements featuring school group activities such as the National

Honor Society, yearbook sales, musical concerts and achievements, and sports events and awards.

Students enter contests such as the Scholastic Art Awards, sponsored locally by the *Patriot News*, and area winners then qualify for national competition. Video magazines also offer contests and Channel 1, the school communications network, encourages schools to send in pieces that can be aired nationally. The class produced one special sign-off, which was aired last year, featuring the school's award-winning marching band.

Students also create an end-of-the-year video that the entire student body enjoys. This video highlights the year's events, including sports, homecoming, prom, plays, musical events, pep assemblies, and special group activities.

This end-of-the-year show encompasses many of the activities that one would expect in a professional video studio. Footage must be filed, classified, and evaluated to augment the process of scriptwriting. Narration and background music must then be mixed to ensure a perfect blend.

Last year, the class was instrumental in writing, taping, and editing a presentation that aired during the Middle States High School Accreditation Evaluation. The video was given special attention in the visiting committee report, and students received special recognition at a school board meeting for their achievement and performance.

Because of the success of the video broadcast class, all teachers in the high school and district want to tape their classroom activities for future presentations and review. Science teachers have taped laboratory experiments for end-of-semester review, English teachers have taped speeches for student self-evaluation, and metal technology teachers have taped the steps for building intricate projects for student observation and analysis.

Community groups have also solicited the help of the class. The first in a series of historical documentaries for the local historical society was taped recently. A cooperative effort with this community group will continue with collaborative scriptwriting, taping, and editing. This series may be offered for sale to the public at some future date, with proceeds going to the historical society.

Creative outlets for a student's video work can be found in most communities. Any business educator can contact local cable companies about community access channels and available broadcast opportunities through the local cable operator. Likewise, business, fraternal, and other service groups in a community may be looking for video documentation of their events and meetings. This would be a great opportunity for a video class to work in a "real-world" setting.

Beyond the Multimedia Classroom: Video Applications in Other Business Departments

Business departments in other high schools throughout the country use video in various ways. The most popular applications involve presentation graphics programs, such as Microsoft Powerpoint or Lotus Freelance Graphics. Video insertion into presentations is a great way for students to learn how video adds "dimension" to this application. Many schools have purchased CD-ROMs that include royalty-free video clips that are easily inserted into presentations. Most schools also have camcorders and VCRs capable of editing and video dubbing. This equipment can be used to develop video presentations for student and class activities. Adding a video capture card to an existing Windows 95/98 or Macintosh computer allows students to take their own recorded video and insert it into any presentation.

One school in southwestern Pennsylvania has recently purchased a complete video studio. The hardware includes everything from edit VCRs and titlemakers to videotapes. A business department teacher at that school will be directly involved in its implementation and use. This is a great opportunity to expand the business department and to ensure that students continue to have outlets for exhibiting their work. Business teachers who want to add a video-based course to the curriculum can begin by expanding current course content to include video presentations.

Benefits: How Video Enables Teacher-Student-Community Interaction

Adding a video course or video application to current courses in the business curriculum should be a great incentive to teacher and student alike. Students like learning this visual medium, and business teachers must take advantage of any application that gets students excited about business subjects. Video provides that opportunity.

Career exploration lends itself well to the use of video. Accounting classes could videotape various accounting professionals on the job to compare accounting opportunities. Business law classes could use video much like Court TV. Computer application students can use video to develop software training modules for other students or faculty; developing corporate training videos is a large industry in the United States, and this kind of project provides practical experience.

Business teachers and students would be well advised to look at video as not only an extension of their classroom but as a delivery system for educational and career opportunities in the next century. These opportunities are a great way to develop business partnerships and to take advantage of a burgeoning technology that will continue to grow in the next decade.

As video and computer technologies mature, educators will rely more on compelling video to convey course content, both in the classroom and on the Internet. This compelling video will include all of the things that digital video software, combined with a 32-bit operating system on a compatible computer, can give us.

Summary

Computer applications are the mainstay of secondary business education offerings. These classes continue to be useful for the majority of students in all areas of interest and aspiration; however, new career paths and technology demand that computer application classes bridge expanding technology areas.

In this regard, innovation and creativity are a must. A correct first step for the business education department at Mechanicsburg Area Senior High School was to develop an alliance with another academic department that had similar educational ideas and concepts. When developing an idea for a cross-curricular course of study, it is useful to think about what will work best in a particular school and in the context of its needs, administrative support, available resources, and budget concerns. Furthermore, teachers must research and consider different views of curriculum integration to find the proper model for their unique situation.

An "Interactive Broadcast Media Technology" course combining business education and English is one way to bring cutting-edge technology and computer applications to students who are looking for an outlet to develop and hone advanced skills. The course content gives students opportunities to create, organize, visualize, analyze, and evaluate. While a course in media technology could be started in most schools using equipment they already have, teachers should allow room for expansion into video technology as it changes and becomes cost-effective. Digital video, for example, is an expanding field that will give students experience in using up-to-date computer applications skills and opportunities to practice and apply higher-order thinking.

Many resources may supplement this course's activities. Partnerships with local television stations, professional video studios, and community organizations enhance the course's quality and appeal. Many creative outlets, such as contests in which students can have their work critiqued and appreciated by professionals, are available.

At Mechanicsburg Area Senior High School, the integration of business education and English into an interactive video broadcast media course has been a success for the students and the school. The students' final products have helped them develop skills that will enhance their lifelong learning, while the faculty and administration have accepted and benefited from this new and different approach to the overall curriculum.

References

Azarmsa, R. (1998, January). Digital Video: In the Classroom and on the Net. *Syllabus*, 11 (5), 18.

Jacobs, H. H. (1989). *Interdisciplinary Curriculum: Design and Implementation*. Alexandria, VA: Association for Supervision and Curriculum Development.

Chapter 8 — Distance Education: Learning for the 21ˢᵗ Century

Jack E. Johnson
State University of West Georgia
Carrollton, Georgia

A mainstay of the educational environment since the turn of the century has been the traditional classroom, which consists of an instructor lecturing to his or her students within the confines of four walls. Only since the 1980s has technology transformed how information is transmitted from instructor to student. Computers are undeniably the primary reason for this change.

Distance learning (DL) can be defined as a medium used to provide instructional programs to students separated by physical location from the instructor. Moore and Kearsley (1996) expand on this definition by describing it as

> ...planned learning that normally occurs in a different place from teaching and as a result requires special techniques of course design, special instructional design, special instructional techniques, special methods of communication by electronic and other technology, as well as special organizational and administrative arrangements. (p. 2)

In the years of its early development, distance education was viewed as a technology that could provide little or no interaction among students and faculty. Today's classrooms, however, prove this view false. DL in the late '90s provides a choice of both synchronous and asynchronous activity. Recent advancements in technology, such as fiber optics, have resulted in an experience that minimizes the differences between classroom instruction and distance education.

DL instruction is growing dramatically at all levels of education. It is extremely popular with the following individuals:

- Adults interested in finishing high school;

- Students with scheduling conflicts at their place of employment or with other classes;
- Graduates who need to upgrade their certification; and
- Employees who want to upgrade their job-related skills.

Most adult learners work and, therefore, are not able to attend classes in the traditional sense. An increasing number of these adults are seeking access to both secondary and postsecondary education and are demanding an increased array of educational options. These options include distance education in a technology-based support system.

Nontraditional adults are rapidly becoming the new majority in classrooms today, and policymakers must recognize the educational expectations voiced by this majority. Learning in the 21st century will focus on a more personalized, accessible venue that relies more on convenience than on the traditional classroom.

The popularity of distance education has grown exponentially in the past five years. Today, it is not unrealistic to estimate that nearly 30 percent of all schools use the World Wide Web (WWW) for instructional purposes and that nearly 50 percent of all schools use resources such as online encyclopedias and Web sites to enhance classroom instruction, instructional methodology, and research.

In 1997 alone, approximately 400,000 students enrolled in DL classes nationwide. The proportion of adult learners in higher education has increased from approximately 40 percent in 1980 to over 50 percent in 1990; and by the millennium the majority of students will be in this category.

Definitions

As with any new technology, distance education has coined several terms that are unique to its operation. Although their precise meaning may vary from school to school, in general they carry similar definitions and include the following terms.

Distance education/learning. A medium used to provide instructional programs to students separated in space from the instructor. Some authorities differentiate between "distance education" and "distance learning" by suggesting that "distance education" is what takes place from the viewpoint of the provider of instruction (the instructor), whereas "distance learning" is what takes place from the viewpoint of the recipient of instruction (the student). This chapter, however, uses these terms interchangeably because of the similarity of the two.

Distance education mode. Any one of three modes is used within a DL environment: audio, video, or data exchange (e-mail, online chats, discussion groups)—all of which can be combined.

Distance education transmission. The transmission of information from the base (originating) site to one of several receiving sites. This transmission can take place via satellite, cable, telephone lines, local area networks, wide-area networks, the Internet, T-1 lines, or ISDN lines.

Synchronous. A learning style that allows participants to interact immediately and simultaneously with their classmates and/or the instructor. The traditional classroom allows this kind of immediate interaction between teacher and student. In a DL environment, a synchronous classroom requires both a two-way audio and video connection to allow for simultaneous classroom interaction.

Asynchronous. A learning style that delays the interaction between students and the instructor or other students. In the traditional classroom, if the instructor asks for feedback at a later date, the interaction would be asynchronous. In the DL classroom, asynchronous learning takes place when students are reacting to questions or discussion topics posted in a chat room or on a bulletin board to be viewed later by other students or the instructor.

Videoconferencing. A combination of audio, video, and networking technology that allows groups of people to engage in synchronous (real-time) interaction with each other.

Facilitator. A person assigned to a DL classroom to provide technical assistance in the operation of DL hardware. This person may be assigned to activate and deactivate the system for each class, to run the cameras, to change the presentation mode, or to send faxed materials to the remote-site students.

Teaching Strategies for Distance Education

Teaching in a distance education classroom requires the instructor to employ some of the methods and strategies used in the traditional classroom. These include preplanning time, lecture preparation, motivational stimuli, and audio/visual aids. The DL instructor, however, teaches in an environment where many of the students are physically detached from the classroom at a remote site. This separation presents unique challenges for the instructor and requires some of the strategies listed below to ensure success.

Attend special DL training. Educators should attend as many distance education training sessions as possible before teaching a DL class. It would also be helpful to observe a colleague already teaching a class via distance education. Before the first class session, DL teachers should videotape the presentation and analyze its strengths and weaknesses. Colleagues should be invited to critique the teaching style or method; their feedback can be used to improve the presentation.

Conduct an orientation session. Before the first class, the instructor should prepare a handout and/or conduct a technology orientation session with the students. All facets of the course must be reviewed. The teacher should explain how attendance will be recorded. The students will also need to know how the class will be conducted, e.g. the manner in which material will be presented and how they will respond to questions and communicate with one another. They will need to know the specifics of their roles: how their assignments will be transmitted to the instructor and how they will take examinations.

Finally, they will need to know how they will be evaluated. Courses taught online, using the Internet and WWW, have special requirements. Students must know which hardware and browsers will be compatible. They will need to know how to login to the class and what to do if their connection is lost. If a chat room or discussion group is part of the course, protocol must be clearly outlined. For example, access procedures must be delineated, especially if they are to be used simultaneously since a chat room differs from normal conversation.

A good suggestion for the instructor to follow when interacting with students in a chat room conversation is to have students use upper and lower case letters when replying but for the instructor to use all caps when responding. Students will then know immediately when the instructor is responding, giving directions, or questioning the students. Proper "netiquette" suggests that all caps should be used sparingly to avoid the impression that the instructor is "yelling" at the students; but in this case, the all caps technique is quite acceptable.

Use the Internet. The WWW offers an abundance of information on teaching in a distance education classroom. Although it would be impossible to list all the sites that could help an instructor become effective in a DL classroom, a brief selection follows:

- http://www.uidaho.edu/evo/dist1.html. This site offers 13 guides—plus a glossary—that can be found at the same URL (the "dist1" portion of the Web site address should simply be changed to "dist2," "dist3," etc.). The guide is entitled "Distance Education at a Glance" and covers such topics as an overview, strategies for teaching, evaluation, print, strategies for learning, and other content.

- http://www.pbs.org/learn/als/gtd/project/distlearn.html. This site provides several links to different schools that use distance education in their curriculum.

- http://www.yahoo.com/education/distance_learning. A wide variety of distance education resources and information is available at this site.

- http://www.fwl.org/edtech/distance.html. This URL gives a basic introduction to distance education.

- http://uwex.edu:80/disted/index.html. This site provides links to resources available from the Distance Education Clearinghouse at the University of Wisconsin.

- http://www.cde.psu.edu/ACSDE. This is the Web site for the American Center for the Study of Distance Education at Penn State University. It contains several links to a variety of publications on the topic of distance education.

Prepare visuals. Because DL students will view all presentations on a television screen, the instructor must pay close attention to the type size used to prepare these visuals. The minimum type size should be no less than 28 to 32 points. With a 32-point font, seven or eight lines of text will fit nicely on each screen. A smaller point size will make it difficult for students in the back of the room to read the print.

Color is also an important consideration when preparing visuals for DL transmission. Good contrast is essential, and color combinations such as black and white (black print on white background) or yellow print on a dark blue background are the best choices. Instructors should be careful not to use the same color for both background and type (i.e., dark blue on light blue).

Elaborate backgrounds or textures should not be used. A consistent shade or color is the best background for displaying text.

Visuals should be prepared in a 4-to-3 ratio, similar to that of a computer screen. Margins of no less than 1.5 inches should be used so that none of the text or visuals is cut off at the sides of the screen.

Instructors should make copies of all visuals and be prepared to send or fax them to the remote sites, or to transmit an electronic file of the visuals to each site. If students have the visuals, they can spend more time listening to the instructor's presentation.

Revise questioning techniques. DL classrooms, in contrast to traditional classrooms, do not permit the instructor to have visual contact with all students simultaneously. Therefore, all questions posed should be directed to individual students at specific remote sites. Doing so will minimize the wait time between the question and the response.

Many DL classrooms operate in a real-time mode where students can respond after hearing the instructor's question. However, there may be a slight transmission delay between the time the question is stated and when it is actually received at the remote sites. Instructors should expect transmission delays of a few seconds and resist the temptation to keep talking after the question has been asked. Finally, it is a good idea to restate a question to make certain that students at the remote sites have received it correctly.

Approach distance education enthusiastically. Several studies on distance education have concluded that students will often display the same attitude their instructors show toward this new technology. Instructors should therefore always approach this experience with enthusiasm. The distance education classroom is not designed for straight lecturing from the podium, and DL students do not appreciate an instructor who is nothing more than a "talking head." Distance education instructors must be motivated, spontaneous, and inspired; and they must be able to convey this attitude to the students.

Evaluate the course. Instructors should use both formative and summative methods of evaluating the distance education class. Student input should be obtained for all areas that may impact the success of a distance education class. These may include the instructor's use of technology; the clarity of visuals; the interaction between teacher and student as well as among students at different sites; the instructor's organizational skills; the instructor's ability to motivate students; and the effectiveness of support services such as the facilitator and the library.

Advantages and Disadvantages of Distance Education

Some of the advantages and disadvantages of distance education are highlighted below.

Advantages:

- Enables an instructor to transmit and/or receive instruction from a considerable distance.
- Is a fiscally sound method of providing instruction to students who are physically located a great distance from the originating site.
- Encourages students to be involved in discussion-related activities with students at numerous locations.
- An excellent medium to encourage nontraditional students to continue learning.
- Promotes the use of the WWW as a resource.
- Is convenient for students to "stay at home" and take a course.
- Easy for shy or timid students to "speak out" when they are not involved in face-to-face conversations.
- Promotes the blending of technology and education.
- Offers students the opportunity to think about their answers before responding (in online courses).
- Is a more relaxing and less stressful environment.

Disadvantages:

- No personal contact when online instruction is used.
- Students may not have access to the Internet or may not have the necessary computer configuration to take the class.
- Interaction is difficult with large groups at multiple sites.
- Computers and/or technology may "freeze-up" or disconnect.
- In online instruction, poor keyboarding skills may limit the student's ability to communicate with other students.
- Online instruction hinders spontaneity.
- Students cannot see or hear what is taking place in online instruction.
- Online instruction does not promote detailed discussions.

Distance Education Models

In the early 1990s, distance education was in the beginning stages of development. Those implementing this concept into their instructional presentations were fortunate to be affiliated with a school system or university that could support the expensive hardware requirements or satellite connect time.

Less than 10 years later, it is truly the exception for schools not to offer some type of distance education in their curriculum. In an informal investigative study, graduate students at the State University of West Georgia surveyed all states through the use of the Web to determine the prevalence of distance education courses. Results indicated that all states are now participating through some form of synchronous or asynchronous distance education.

Some of the distance education activity taking place in this nation is highlighted below. Certainly, it would not be possible to list all programs that are currently active; and, even if this were possible, it would change on a day-to-day basis. Therefore, the following examples are provided as illustrations of the effort to initiate distance education programs in selected states.

California. Distance education at California State University (CSU) at Chico takes an international flavor with its instruction via a satellite feed to a sister institution in Tokyo, Japan. The classrooms have video cameras, microphones, and television screens enabling teacher and student communication across the Pacific.

Today, CSU-Chico is using distance education to deliver its instructional programs to thousands of students in California and across the nation via its Satellite Education Network. As with most distance education classes, the Chico experiment was successful largely because of the availability of numerous telecommunication mediums being used simultaneously in the classroom: television, satellite transmission, and e-mail connections.

Delaware, New Jersey, and Pennsylvania. The Delaware Valley Distance Learning Consortium (DVDLC) uses a local television station to broadcast credit courses to students between the hours of 1 a.m. and 6 a.m., at which time students can tape the lesson on a video recorder and play it back at their convenience. The DVDLC is an alliance of 47 area colleges and universities organized by WHYY (a local television station) in 1995 with the purpose of making education available to more people.

After viewing the taped programs, students read the appropriate sections in their textbook and do other course work facilitated by the instructor. Students must participate in a few on-campus visits, but they complete all course work on their own schedule. DVDLC offers 42 telecourses in such areas as the liberal arts, science, business, history, social studies, and health. Most of the telecourses are run for either 13 weeks or as seven-week accelerated sessions.

Georgia. Distance education in Georgia is multifaceted, and its success is primarily due to the capabilities of GSAMS (Georgia Statewide Academic and Medical System). GSAMS is a distance education network that links nearly 400 interactive audio and video teleconferencing classrooms throughout the state. Classrooms are located at colleges and universities, K-12 schools, technical institutes, and correctional institutions as well as Zoo Atlanta and the University of Georgia Marine Extensive Service. Students at up to eight remote sites can participate simultaneously in course instruction, regardless of geographical location.

As reported by Johnson et al. (1998), each GSAMS classroom contains four, 46-inch televisions, two cameras, a computer system, a document camera, a scan converter, a VCR recorder, and a fax machine. A facilitator assists the instructor with hardware operation. GSAMS instruction covers all disciplines, from business to education to arts and sciences.

At the State University of West Georgia, WebCT courseware is used in an asynchronous environment to offer courses on the WWW. In 1998, the WebCT courseware was used to conduct a class on the methodology of teaching keyboarding. In the course, the Internet linked 38 instructors from 27 states with 25 students. E-mail was used to communicate with the instructors, and four online chat rooms were used to invite a number of the "visiting experts" to discuss methodologies of teaching with the students.

Illinois. Ehrhard and Schroeder (1997) described videoconferencing that is being used at Northern Illinois University in DeKalb, Illinois. The classroom is equipped with two, 35-inch television sets, a computer, a document camera, and a video camera. One of the television sets is used to project the classroom at the main campus, and the other is used to show the remote site classroom. Both sites have identical hardware. Although the class is presented via distance education, instructors travel to the remote sites to interact with students and establish a student-teacher relationship.

Indiana. Many students at Indiana University have never set foot on campus while taking courses at this university. The Indiana Higher Education Telecommunications System (IHETS) transmits courses to more than 250 sites over a two-way audio, one-way video system. Austin (1997) reports that recently the IHETS system was converted to satellite transmission, thus opening the door for distance education from the Indiana campus to as far away as Washington, D.C., Alaska, and Puerto Rico. Although all courses are taught at the Indiana campus, negotiations are underway to develop a joint program with some of the local community colleges. The lower division courses would be taught by the community college faculty and the upper division courses would be taught by Indiana University.

Iowa. At an Iowa community college, an origination site worked with four remote sites to broadcast a social science class via a fiber-optic system. The hardware components were similar to those found in the Georgia example described above. A secondary purpose of this experiment was to determine how students at remote sites perceived distance education. McHenry and Bozik (1995) summarized their findings by concluding that: (1) DL had a positive influence on classroom interaction; (2) students viewed DL positively and adapted fairly well to this technology; (3) teaching in this environment required special skills by the teacher; and (4) distribution of materials and working with deadlines was a challenge to the teacher.

Maryland. One of the most aggressive distance education initiatives is found at Howard Community College (HCC) in Columbia, Maryland. The project used at HCC is entitled Going the Distance (GTD) and is a nationwide effort transmitted over 60 public television stations and 175 colleges and universities in 37 states. Most of the courses in GTD are telecourses, supported by television and supplemented by textbooks and study guides. The goal of GTD is to be able to offer degree programs in every state by the year 2000.

Another popular distance education effort in Maryland is found at Prince George's Community College (PGCC). In addition to the GTD program, PGCC also offers online courses through its on-campus bulletin board system (BBS). Through this telecommunications system, students complete homework and send it to their instructors, receive course information from their instructors, participate in chat room conversations with fellow students, and conduct research online. Finally, PGCC incorporates technology similar to the GSAMS network in Georgia, where the teacher and students located at several remote sites are connected via two-way video and audio conferencing.

New Jersey. The New Jersey Institute of Technology uses a DL system called the Virtual Classroom to provide asynchronous instruction in two degree programs, information systems and computer science. Hiltz (1995) reports that students in the class interact via the Virtual Classroom in small discussion groups that promote collaborative learning. Students can participate in the class any hour of the day, at any location via the Internet. Also included as part of the class structure are face-to-face meetings, interviews, videotapes, and observations of online activities during the course.

Oklahoma. Parents, teachers, and students in the Western Heights School District in western Oklahoma are using JetNet, a telecommunications network for bringing desktop videoconferencing capability to its more than 200 classrooms. Teachers use the technology to share teaching methods and develop lesson plans. Students are involved in interactive sessions between classrooms and schools; they also interact with schoolchildren around the globe. Parents use the technology to participate in meetings with their child's teachers and administrators.

The district also uses programs such as the Mars Base Project and the Iowa Communications Network (ICN) to support its distance education activities. The ICN network is similar to the GSAMS network used in Georgia.

Wisconsin. Students at Lakeland College in Sheboygan, Wisconsin, use an asynchronous software package called Convene. The menu bar of Convene provides a number of options available to the students and the instructor. For example, the instructor can send all students daily assignments that may contain graphics, photographs, charts, or text. If necessary, students can be directed to a related page on the WWW. They can also receive private messages from other students or the instructor and can be invited to join in discussion groups. Completed homework assignments are sent in before the students log off.

The Convene system is used in a number of states under the name of The University of Phoenix, a distance education consortium offering course work and degrees in business and management, the humanities, computer information systems, and math and science.

Western Governor's University. The Western Governor's University (WGU) is a consortium of 16 western states and one territory that have joined forces to share distance education resources. A combination of Internet and satellite connections, videotapes, and advanced telecommunications and net-working technologies are used to provide educational opportunities for students throughout the western states. The "nerve center" of WGU's program is a smart catalog, an Internet-based collection of all courses offered through the consortium. The catalog also maps the courses students need to complete to receive a WGU credential as well as provides career and assessment information.

Summary

In the new millennium, classrooms and instructional methodology will experience a dramatic transformation in regard to the Internet and its related technologies. Business educators must approach these technologies with all possible enthusiasm and dedication to guarantee that instructional leadership will continue to flourish in business education.

As technology changes the classroom of tomorrow, so must attitudes toward the manner in which the basic concepts and structure of education are defined. In decades past, the view of an educational environment was limited to four walls, an instructor, and students. The instructor and students are still present, but technology has redefined the "walls" to include the global community. Business educators must be sensitive to the needs of students who require an increased array of options to pursue their educational goals.

References

Austin, D. R. (1997, June). Teaching Over Television: Indiana University's Distance Learning Program. *Parks & Recreation*, 32 (6), 22-23.

Ehrhard, B. J. and Schroeder, B. L. (1997, April/May). Videoconferencing...What Is It and How Is It Being Used? *Techtrends*, 32-34.

Hiltz, S. R. (1995, October 3). Impacts of College-Level Courses via Asynchronous Learning Networks: Focus on Students. Sloan Conference on Asynchronous Learning Networks, Philadelphia, Pennsylvania.

Johnson, J. E., Hill, M., and Lankford, W. (1998, February). Teaching Computers via Distance Learning. *Business Education Forum*, 52 (3), 39-42

McHenry, L. and Bozik, M. (1995, October). Communicating at a Distance: A Study of Interaction in a Distance Education Classroom. *Communication Education*, 44 (4), 362-371.

Moore, M. G. and Kearsley, G. (1996). *Distance Education—A Systems View*. Belmont, CA: Wadsworth.

Chapter 9 — Organizational Leadership in the 21ˢᵗ Century

Kenneth L. Gorman
Winona State University
Winona, Minnesota

In the past two decades, unprecedented national and international social, political, and economic changes have challenged long-established paradigms of business management. Shifts in the world economic order, growth in global competition, and phenomenal advances in information and communication technologies are among the forces that have instigated these changes.

Other trends that have affected business culture include the movement from industrial to service and information industries; the shift from large multinational, Fortune 500 companies to small entrepreneurial businesses; the development of corporate visions and strategic plans; and the increase in consumer demand for quality products. Because of these evolutionary and revolutionary transformations, old ways of managing business have become ineffective.

Leadership and Management

To address these challenges, organizations are shifting from authoritarian, autocratic management models to paradigms in which managers must also be leaders who can empower employees and enable their participation in setting and achieving organizational goals. Crandall (McFarland, Senn, and Childress, 1993, p. 183) stated:

> *The ideal leader for the 21ˢᵗ century will be one who creates an environment that encourages everyone in the organization to stretch their capabilities and achieve a shared vision; who gives people the confidence to run farther and faster than they ever have before; and who establishes the conditions for people to be more productive, more innovative, more creative, and feel more in charge of their own lives than they ever dreamed possible.*

Keeton (McFarland et al., p. 194) indicated that "the most important quality that a 21ˢᵗ century leader needs is the ability to inspire other people, first to pull together in the direction of the vision, and second to do their very best in producing excellent results."

These newer management philosophies are often a stark contrast to hierarchical architectures in which top management drove the organizations, using power to control employees and the environment. For organizations to thrive in the 21ˢᵗ century, they must cultivate the leadership function of management.

Whereas management is "the process of working with and through people to achieve objectives by means of effective decision making and coordination of valuable resources" (Mosley, Meggison, and Pietri, 1993, p. 8), leadership is "the process of influencing others to achieve organizational goals" (Bartol and Martin, 1998, p. 415).

Based on these definitions, all managers may not be leaders, and all leaders may not be managers. Managers are appointed to management positions and have legitimate power; they may not have the leadership capabilities to influence people beyond the power inherent in their positions. Leaders may be able to influence others to achieve levels beyond those dictated by formal authority; they may not, however, have the capabilities to carry out other essential management functions.

Many contemporary definitions of management include a leadership component, but this has not always been the case. Although it appears that the basic management functions have been similarly identified and defined during the 20ᵗʰ century, leadership has emerged as one of the distinct management functions only in more recent years.

In the early part of the 20ᵗʰ century, Fayol (cited in Robbins, 1991) identified five functions he believed all managers performed: planning, organizing, commanding, coordinating, and controlling. During the 1950s and 1960s, Koontz and O'Donnell (cited in Robbins) identified the management functions as planning, organizing, staffing, directing, and controlling. By the latter part of the 20th century, leadership became more commonly identified as one of the major management functions. In 1998, Bartol and Martin identified the four major functions of management as planning, organizing, leading, and controlling.

As we move into the 21ˢᵗ century, all of the commonly identified functions of management will be important; however, a greater emphasis will be placed on the leadership function (see Table 1).

Forces Driving Change in Organizational Structure

Classical organizational hierarchies with command-and-control management styles are simply no longer effective. "In simpler times, when the market was far more predictable, customers were not as knowledgeable and demanding, and employees were more accepting of the traditional command-and-control model, effective management was often all that was required" (McFarland et al., p. 200).

Today, corporate hierarchies are flattening, and some are collapsing. "Effectiveness can no longer be centered in positions with a rigid hierarchical structure, but must be centered in interdependent relationships in which leadership and power are shared broadly" (McFarland et al., p. 53).

During the 1980s and 1990s, many organizations reduced

Table 1. Qualities of Leadership

Leaders achieve organizational goals through their ability to influence others. Effective leaders share the following characteristics:

- Confidence and self-knowledge
- Vision and the ability to inspire it in others
- Good communication skills
- Collaborative work styles
- Inclusivity/appreciation for diversity
- Self-discipline
- Strong problem-solving and decision-making skills
- Flexibility
- Desire to serve
- Respect for lifelong learning
- Ethics and integrity

Sources:
Covey, S. R. Characteristics of Principle-Centered Leaders. *Principle-Centered Leadership.* New York, NY: Simon and Schuster, 1991.
Remp, A. M. Workplace Privacy, Confidentiality, and Surveillance. *The 21ˢᵗ Century: Meeting the Challenges to Business Education (1999 Yearbook).* Reston, VA: The National Business Education Association.

---

the number of managerial levels in their hierarchies, which reduced the bureaucratic levels of decision making and helped to facilitate communication. This reorganization has resulted in the empowerment of employees, the use of team decision making, and the need for many leaders—not just a few— at the top of the organizational chart.

What has caused such unprecedented restructuring of how businesses are managed and led? What forces have changed once-unquestioned rules, regulations, policies, and procedures that formerly prescribed the practices of the powerful hierarchy? The globalization of business, the emergence of the new world economies, and the advancements in communication technology have broken down barriers and have mandated organizational restructuring. These forces are discussed in detail below.

Globalization. Over the years, businesses have moved from self-contained and rather independent entities to organizations that have become increasingly interdependent and internationally focused. Kiernan (1996, p. 147) stated that "companies can and do now shop in a single global supermarket for capital, employees, customers, suppliers, raw materials, and strategic alliance partners." The globalization of markets, the opening up of free competition, and the development of trade agreements have accelerated the pace of international transformation.

The European Community, U.S.-Canadian Alliance, and the U.S.-Mexico Border Zones are late 20ᵗʰ century regional agreements between and among countries. These agreements have greatly impacted how and where business is conducted, how the workforce needs to be educated, and why strategic planning is needed to participate successfully in expanding and changing global markets. The next century will, undoubtedly, continue to see the establishment of similar agreements, which will further expand international opportunities.

Expanded international markets will provide many leadership opportunities and challenges. Operating successfully in an international environment will require management and leadership skills that are far more complex and sophisticated than those needed to operate only in a domestic marketplace. Global markets will require all managers to be well versed in environmental, economic, political, social, legal, ethical, and cultural aspects of the international marketplace.

Kiernan (p.147) stated that "of all of the potential beneficiaries of globalization, none face more exciting and unprecedented opportunities than small and medium-sized enterprises." Unlike large multinational organizations, "the small and medium-sized enterprises have lacked the opportunity, the necessity, and especially the wherewithal to attack international markets" (Kiernan, p. 147). In the next century, being a player in these international markets will be critically important for the competitiveness of organizations.

Shifting economic order. "By the year 2020, the World Bank predicts that nine of the world's top 15 economies will be what we patronizingly call today the industrialized world, including China, India, and Indonesia" (cited in Kiernan, p.146). Other developing countries emerging as major exporters of manufactured goods include Hong Kong, Taiwan, and South Korea. Rapidly growing third world countries are increasing both their exports and imports.

O'Sullivan and Sheffrin (1998) stated that the growth rates in real gross domestic product (a common measure of the total output of an economy) for the world in 1996 showed that developing countries demonstrated the greatest percent of change (6.3 percent) as compared to the industrial countries (2.3 percent) and the world as a whole (3.8 percent).

Also indicative of change in the economic environment is the increased membership in the Organization for Economic Co-operation and Development (OECD). "The purpose of the OECD is to boost prosperity by helping to knit a web of compatible policies and practices across countries that are part of an ever more globalized world" (About OECD: How the OECD Works, p. 1). Twenty countries, including Australia, Canada, United Kingdom, Germany, and the United States, became members in 1961, when OECD was created. Japan joined OECD in 1964, and New Zealand joined in the 1970s. Poland, Hungary, Korea, Mexico, and the Czech Republic joined in the 1990s.

International discussion and cooperation are becoming increasingly important because of the rapid growth of international interdependence. "Through globalization of the world economy, national borders are, in part, losing their economic meaning" (About OECD: The OECD and Its Origins, p. 1).

Continually changing world economies are having a tremendous impact on management and leadership skills. Thus, it is imperative for corporate managers and leaders to internationalize their competitive strategies in order to operate and thrive in this ever-changing world.

Information and communication technologies. Technology has transformed the world into an interdependent, international village. Global communication via readily available technologies has made instantaneous contact possible even in the remotest parts of the world, which once had impenetrable boundaries. The rate of technological advancements in the 21st century will increase more rapidly than ever before. Kiernan (p. 1) stated that the "newly converging technologies are shattering organizational and political barriers, empowering new players, and completely rewriting the rules of international business competition for both individual companies and entire countries."

Quantum leaps will be made in multimedia technologies, satellite systems, digital data, silicon brains, expert and voice systems, knowledge discovery, genetic algorithms, and fiber optics. Technological advances and communication power have dictated and will continue to dictate change for organizational structure, management, and leadership.

Foundations for Effective Leadership

Dealing with the revolutionary changes in the business environment will be a challenge for organizational leaders. Effective leaders will need to build on the knowledge, skills, characteristics, and traits learned from preceding generations, when the environment was relatively stable. They will then need to augment those leadership attributes with other concepts, principles, and tools that will help them face the uncertainties and insecurities of doing business in the future. Following are a few strategies that will help managers build a solid foundation for leadership.

Values, vision, and planning. Organizations that wish to grow and develop must establish and agree upon a solid foundation of values and guiding principles. These values and principles become the unifying force that shapes organizations and gives them purpose and direction. Organizations must identify and define those values that will propel them to success and achievement and inspire and compel employees to do their best work. Without sound values such as empowerment, ethics, integrity, and trust, and without employee support of and alignment with those values, organizations will be neither successful nor able to plan for the future.

Identifying, understanding, and committing to a vision are critical to strong leadership. Every organization needs to establish and communicate a clear vision, because it is this vision that guides goals, strategies, decisions, and activities (McFarland et al.). Bartol and Martin (pp. 361-62) stated that "to bring about change and innovation, it is important to be able to develop a picture of the future that is fairly easy to communicate and has appeal to those who must change or support change and innovation ... , and managers need to embolden employees to take actions on behalf of the vision." Thus, once a company has established and committed itself to a vision, leaders must remember that employee motivation and empowerment become crucial if the vision is to become a reality.

In addition to establishing values and vision, organizations must engage in strategic planning. Generally, organizations should create formal plans designed to reach strategic goals and objectives within a specific time period. They should make those plans available to everyone in the organization.

Empowerment. As organizational structures flatten, greater emphasis is placed on utilizing the knowledge, experience, expertise, and talents of all employees. Instead of leadership, responsibility, and accountability resting solely at the top of the organizational pyramid, empowering others throughout the organization provides the maximum opportunity to unleash the potential of all employees. This process will ultimately strengthen the organization. Empowering individuals allows them to become a significant part of the planning process and to become more innovative and creative in finding ways to advance the organization's goals.

Since empowerment allows employees to have greater input into their destinies, they are more likely to be positive, contributing members to the organization. Empowerment moves decision making downward in an organization, closer to the employees who are directly involved in the situation. As employees become more empowered, the workplace of the next decade will be characterized by a greater use of teamwork and self-directed work teams.

Education is a critical part of successful empowerment. Managers must learn to relinquish power and authority and to share essential corporate information with employees. Employees will be taking on greater responsibility, and they will need proper education and training to be successful. Empowerment takes a great deal of trust and confidence throughout the organization, and companies must develop strategies and a framework to help guide those who are to be empowered. Blanchard (1997, p.1) stated that "it is important that managers identify boundary areas, guidelines, or procedures within which employees can operate, including the company's purpose, corporate values and goals, and employee roles and measures and incentives on employee performance."

To feel truly empowered, employees must believe that their contributions will be recognized and seriously considered, and they must be able to see how their contributions keep the organization competitive.

Communication. Improving communication skills in the workplace has been a top organizational priority for years. Although millions of dollars have been spent on workshops, seminars, courses, consultants, and interactive multimedia, improving communication skills continues to top the list of what managers identify as most needed to enhance their job performance.

In the past, elaborate and complex organizational structures often dictated communication flow and direction. However, flattened organizational structures, increased use of electronic communication, and the emergence of the international environment have greatly impacted communication in the business world. Given the power of technology, the speed at which knowledge and information can be sent and received, and the rate at which decisions must be made, there probably has never been a time when learning how to communicate quickly and accurately has been more important.

Excellent oral, written, and interpersonal communication skills are vital in today's workplace. Without mastering communication skills and the appropriate electronic tools, organizations can fail.

Ethics and integrity. Ethical leadership in an organization is critical because leaders set the tone and establish the ethical culture. Ramsey (1996, p. 15) stated that "ethical supervisors send a powerful message about what's important, how people are to be treated, and how the organization does business." Individuals want to work for organizations that are ethical, and customers want to do business in an ethical environment. Ethical reform is a response to outside pressures from regulators, bad publicity, or stockholders. Indeed, improving business ethics has become so important to corporations that they are spending $1 billion a year on business ethics renewal (Krohe, 1997).

Business leaders must become aware of the ethical behavior that is expected, and they must develop strategies to bring their companies into alignment with those expectations. Ramsey identified 21 basic, ethical values that are readily agreed upon by the vast majority of business owners and CEOs in America. These include trust, integrity, altruism, honesty, justice, helpfulness, individual worth, excellence, service, hard work, fairness, mercy, tolerance, courage, authenticity, discipline, responsibility, loyalty, cooperation, truthfulness, and accountability.

According to Larimer (1997), business leaders must encourage ethical conduct in their companies by making a formal commitment to promote ethics and integrity throughout the organization, developing an ethical vision of responsible business conduct, demonstrating and modeling ethical conduct, rewarding ethical achievements, and conducting ethics training.

For ethical behavior to permeate an organization, high ethical standards must be established, communicated, and demanded.

Proactiveness, innovation, and speed. The future holds many uncertainties, but according to Hamel and Prahalad (1994, p. 29), "failure to anticipate and participate in the opportunities of the future impoverishes both firms and nations." Successful organizations will be those that can anticipate customer demand for goods and services, risk dealing with uncertainties, control the environment to the best of their advantage, and lead the change.

Hamel and Prahalad (p. 34) further note that "production life cycles are getting shorter, development times are getting tighter, and customers expect almost instantaneous service." Successful organizations will keep one step ahead of the competition. "In today's era of hypercompetition, you need to be better, cheaper, faster, flexible, responsive, and creative just to get into the game" (Kiernan, p. 35). However, just getting into "the game" will not be sufficient for survival in the next century; getting ahead of the competition will also be important.

Bartol and Martin (p. 352) stated that the "fierce domestic and foreign competition during the past decade has brought about a new emphasis on innovation and change in organizations." Changing creative ideas into productive, useful outcomes will be a delineating factor that will separate the winners from the losers. Corporate leaders will need to create a culture that will foster and stimulate creativity and innovation.

Collaborative advantage. Organizations around the world are learning that the ability to form alliances is a critical factor in creating opportunities and building business relationships in a global environment. In the global economy, the ability to initiate and sustain fruitful collaborations gives companies a significant competitive edge or collaborative advantage (Kantor, 1994). According to Kantor (p. 105), "active collaboration takes place when companies develop mechanisms—structures, processes, and skills—for bridging organizational and interpersonal differences and achieving real value from the partnership."

Working together to achieve mutually agreed-upon goals can give once independent organizations unlimited opportunities to grow and thrive. These collaborative efforts could range from one-time, short-lived partnerships created to complete a project or a task to a collaboration that could merge corporate technologies and capabilities to achieve specific objectives and advantages for the partnering companies. Additionally, collaborative partnerships and alliances also provide greater value to the marketplace. Without them, organizations might not be able to provide customers with the goods or services at the speed and the quality they demand.

Diversity. Organizations are facing changes in the demographics of their employees, customers, investors, clients, and other stakeholders. Diversity is not limited to race and ethnicity and can include perceived differences of geographic origin, lifestyle, nationality, sexual orientation, physical abilities, position in an organization, profession, socioeconomic status, or religion. "Customers/clients, investors, and other key stakeholders are all diverse, and there is an increasing expectation that their diversity will be reflected in the organizations that supply their products and services" (Bazile-Jones, 1996, p. 11).

Dobbs (1996, p. 351) stated that "managing diversity has become a new human resources mandate as organizations seek to maintain a competitive edge and compete successfully in a global economy." For several years, experts have predicted changes in the workforce composition. At the beginning of the 21ˢᵗ century, African-Americans, immigrants, and women will make up a larger share of new entrants into the workforce, with nearly one-half of the labor pool expected to be women. Managers must realize that all employees are strategic resources vital to achieving organizational objectives. "Managers must recognize and value the differences among members of the workforce and actively seek to create a working environment that enables each person to maximize his or her highest potential" (Dobbs, p. 351).

Organizations with success in implementing diversity education, enforcement, and exposure have several things in common. They changed their mission statements, received support and leadership from top management, involved employees in planning and implementing organizational strategies, used a variety of interventions, integrated changes into business practices, and evaluated the results against pre-established goals (Dobbs). How successfully management addresses diversity issues will be a key factor in how well organizations prosper in a global environment.

Culture of lifelong learning. Lifelong learning will become more important to professional growth and development than ever before. "Propelled by the competitive imperatives of speed, global responsiveness, and the need to innovate constantly or perish, learning will be the essential edge against corporate extinction" (Kiernan, p. 195). For individuals to become effective leaders, they will have to learn more quickly and acquire more skills in order to develop and sustain a competitive edge. In order to compete, survive, and prosper, corporations will have to evolve into learning organizations.

Marquardt (1996, p. 19) stated that a learning organization is "one that learns powerfully and collectively and is continually transforming itself to better collect, manage, and use knowledge for corporate success." O'Brien (1964) purports that successful learning organizations have woven a continuous and enhanced capacity to learn, adapt, and change into the fabric of their character; and they have values, policies, practices, programs, systems, and structures that support and accelerate organizational learning.

Kiernan (p. 197) stated that "a company's attitude to training must ... embrace lifelong learning for everyone and stress group-learning experiences in addition to individual ones." He also stated that the content of corporate training programs should place more emphasis on the "soft" process skills of managing change, innovation, and learning, and less on "hard" factual knowledge, which has an increasingly short shelf life.

Education for Leadership

Effective leadership will be essential to ensure the successful development and growth of 21ˢᵗ century organizations. Leadership development, therefore, should be a key component of business education.

The National Alliance of Business (1996) reported that, by a number of measures, the state of education is markedly better than it was a decade ago:

students are taking rigorous academic classes; achievement in math, science, and college entrance exams is up; and dropout rates are down. Although the data appear to be improving, many deficiencies still exist. Many students continue to fall short of the increasing expectations demanded by business.

McFarland (et al.) identified three educational priorities that are crucial to supporting successful organizations in the 21st century: (1) America needs to establish a world-class educational system that effectively prepares the future workforce; (2) educational institutions need to train future leaders; and (3) organizations must train and educate their own people, including the top leadership teams. Following are a few strategies that will help educators incorporate leadership education into their curriculum. (See Table 2 for additional resources.)

Paradigm shift. Just as business management paradigms have shifted from autocratic to empowering,

Table 2. Selected Resources for Leadership Development

- Business Professionals of America, Columbus, OH; 614-895-7277; http://www.bpa.org
- Center for Entrepreneurial Leadership; Kansas City, MO; 888-4-CELCEE; http://www.celcee.edu/
- Center for Visionary Leadership, Washington, DC; 202-237-2800; http://209.41.34.77/index.htm
- Center on Education and Work, Madison, WI; 608-263-3696; http://www.cew.wisc.edu/
- Future Business Leaders of America, Reston, VA; 800-325-2946; http://www.fbla-pbl.org
- HP E-Mail Mentor Program, Fort Collins, CO; 970-206-9352; http://www.telementor.org/hp/
- Hugh O'Brian Youth Leadership (H.O.B.Y.), Los Angeles, CA; 310-474-4370; http://www.hoby.org/
- Leadership, Education, and Athletics in Partnership (L.E.A.P.), New Haven, CT; 203-773-0770; http://www.leap@yale.edu
- National School-to-Work Learning and Information Center, Washington, DC; 800-251-7236; http://www.stw.ed.gov/
- National Service Learning Clearinghouse, St. Paul, MN; 800-808-7378; http://www.nicsl.coled.umn.edu/home.htm
- Project-Based Learning Network, Autodesk, Cupertino, CA; 408-517-1700; http://www.autodesk.com/foundation/pbl/pblnet.htm
- Public Education and Business Coalition, Denver, CO; 303-861-8661; http://www/pebc.org/business.htm
- Student Leadership Institute, Boulder, CO; 303-492-8342; http://www.colorado.edu/SLI/
- U.S. Dept. of Education (Four-Stage Plan for Beginning Business-Education Partnerships), Washington, DC; 800-USA-LEARN; http://pfie.ed.gov/txt_four.htm

classroom management paradigms must shift from teacher-centered to student-centered if significant progress is to be made. Learning must become interdisciplinary and collaborative so that students can experience and practice the leadership skills that will be required of them in business. To turn McFarland's phrase, "Effectiveness must be centered in interdependent relationships in which the roles of teaching and learning are shared broadly."

The fastest way to change a paradigm is to change a name (Covey, 1991). Thus, teachers must become facilitators and mentors, and students, partners and active participants in their own learning.

Sequential experiences. Leadership skills develop over time, through a series of experiences. Teachers can create a mission or vision statement for a leadership development program that includes the program's definition of leadership, specific short- and long-term goals, and specific skills, concepts or behaviors with which to equip the students (Blewett, 1997). Ideally, outcomes will be observable in behavior change; i.e., the participants will have changed in some way or acquired tools, skills, or a deeper knowledge of their abilities that will allow them to assume leadership roles.

As learning facilitators, teachers can select program activities that feature higher-order thinking skills, such as analysis, synthesis, and evaluation; set up multiple projects in which students assume different work roles, such as organizer, researcher, leader, or project engineer; and provide regular opportunities for self-assessment and reflection by encouraging students to keep journals about their work.

Real-world applications. Teachers can foster leadership development by working with students to select projects and resources that give students a real-life context in which to apply what they learn and to see what works in the real world. Teachers do not need to "reinvent the wheel": model programs already exist on national, regional, and local levels. For example, teachers could participate in programs such as School-to-Work (National School-to-Work Learning and Information; Washington, DC) or community-based initiatives such as L.E.A.P. (Leadership, Education, and Athletics in Partnership; New Haven, CT). Students could supplement information they get from textbooks with experience they accrue by participating in such programs and with research from the Internet or from magazines such as *Business Week* or *Fast Company*.

Teachers can also develop their own projects or work with organizations to design projects relevant to their own community. Eco-Educators, for instance, a nonprofit based in Columbus, Ohio, teaches students how to perform waste audits for local businesses.

Service learning credits, which many high schools and colleges now require for graduation, offer business education teachers yet another venue for students to practice leadership skills in a real-world context. In addition, by actively pursuing these opportunities and working with other individuals or groups to realize them, teachers model the leadership behaviors (vision, collaboration, inclusion, and service) they are trying to inculcate in their students.

Project-based learning. Problem solving and decision making are at the heart of project-based (also known as "authentic") learning. Students must draw from many sources of information and disciplines, usually working in teams to define a given problem and generate solutions. Because the problem is real, students "buy into" learning whatever will help them solve it and believe their contributions will be taken seriously.

Jeffrey Leaf, a teacher at Thomas Jefferson School for Science and Technology, Alexandria, Virginia, used project-based learning with his ninth-grade students when he launched his "disability" project. Students were placed into teams based on their assessments of which team role would best suit their talents and complement the roles of other team members. Each team had to design a product that would make life easier for a disabled person but also improve the quality of life for the able-bodied population. Students were required to:

- Experience a physical disability, such as wearing an arm in a sling, for a week, and note in a journal which activities became difficult to perform;

- Choose one problem to solve;

- Invent a product to solve that problem;

- Research material composition and properties, manufacturing and production issues, and environmental impacts;

- Design and produce a prototype;

- Develop and give a sales presentation for their product; and

- Present their product and their research to a group of professional design engineers for evaluation.

When the problem rather than the school subject becomes the learning focus, students are more likely to take the lead in their own education. As a consequence, students sharpen their skills in organization, time and resource management, communication, decision making, and the self-discipline necessary for lifelong learning.

Business and education partnerships. To enable the United States to become more globally competitive, a highly educated, skilled workforce is needed. To help educational systems prepare that workforce, strong collaborative partnerships between business and education must continue to be built.

Although businesses have always had an interest in education, never before have they been so willing to serve as partners in improving education. Across the country, business and academic communities have been working together to address common educational concerns and to strive toward mutually beneficial goals relating to the development of productive employees and well-educated citizens. Many of these successful partnerships are being formed because business and education are gaining greater respect for each other and because they agree on the importance of the educational issues and concerns that must be addressed.

Businesspeople are a valuable resource for the educational community. Not only are they taxpayers, parents, and former students, they are major employers and business experts. These individuals know what positions are currently available, what jobs will be needed for the future, and what knowledge and skills will be necessary to gain and maintain employment, as well as advance in companies. In addition, business leaders recognize the importance of leadership development and are looking to educational institutions to help prepare the next generation of leaders.

Business and education partnerships exist in many different forms and with varying levels of partner participation. For example, the Rochester Minnesota Area Chamber of Commerce sponsors a three-day interactive "School-to-Work" Institute that provides opportunities for educators to better understand their business community. Half of the first day of the workshop is devoted to discussing current workforce issues, and the other two-and-a-half days are devoted to interactive work site visits. During the visits, businesses talk about their products and services and related jobs and careers.

The Campbell County School District in Gillette, Wyoming, offers a "School-to-Careers" program that provides well-marked pathways that students can follow to move from school to good first jobs or from school to continued education. One such pathway is a mentoring class that consists of a three-week training course in the areas of ethics, goals, responsibility, and professionalism in the workplace. The students are then placed with employers and complete an unpaid internship.

Hewlett-Packard creates one-to-one e-mail mentor relationships between HP employees and 5th – 12th grade students and teachers and is launching pilot programs at the university level. Teachers design lesson plans for mentoring projects (for instance, "Create a Web site for a Community Nonprofit"), coordinate those projects with traditional class work, and guarantee that students have e-mail access. Mentors agree to "own" the relationship, responding to every e-mail message the students send.

Patuxent High School in Calvert County, Maryland, has adopted the "Academy of Finance," a nationwide program that operates as a school-within-a-school (Berselli, 1998). The program operates with an advisory board of local business professionals, many of whom provide paid internships to academy students.

Autodesk, Inc., sponsors an intern program in which students collaborate with corporate employees on software and engineering projects. The Mustang Project, for example, in which students designed parts for a convertible race car, let participating students not only learn but see the benefits of learning (Weil, 1997). The Autodesk Foundation has created the Project-Based Learning (PBL) Network, a year-round, on-demand convening of professionals with special emphasis on the important role of project-based learning in school reform.

Only by partnering can business and education identify the appropriate goals and set the priorities that are needed to prepare future leaders, and only by collaboration can strong, competent leaders emerge from our educational systems.

Summary

In the past few years, organizations have been faced with reorganization, shortages of skilled workers, global competition, technological advancements, and the knowledge explosion, along with other social, political, and economic changes. Dealing with these challenges and changes has been difficult for many organizations.

Nevertheless, transformation is essential for organizations to survive. With the certainty of continued change at an accelerating pace, organizations have no choice but to learn quickly how to adapt and move forward. "Almost every organization is trying to create leaders who are capable of helping the corporation shape a more positive future" (Fulmer, 1997, p. 59).

Acknowledging the importance of effective leaders and recognizing that leadership should be an evolving process starting early in life, business educators clearly have not only a responsibility but also tremendous opportunities to become actively involved in helping students build and enhance their leadership skills. Teachers can meet this responsibility by modeling and mentoring leadership skills for their students and by creating leadership programs founded on the principles of vision, collaboration, self-assessment and knowledge, communication, inclusion and empowerment, self-discipline, critical thinking, flexibility, ethics, integrity, and lifelong learning.

Leadership development must be an interactive process. To develop leadership skills successfully, students must be given numerous interactive opportunities in the learning process to apply what they have learned. Designing sequential leadership experiences; engaging in real-world, project-based learning; and creating opportunities for business-education partnerships are some strategies educators can use to teach leadership skills. Learner outcomes that will ultimately allow students to assume leadership roles in business should be of the utmost importance; and teachers must determine the best ways for students to achieve those outcomes.

Our country's success in the global marketplace will depend on educated leaders and a highly skilled workforce. Organizational leaders of the 21ˢᵗ century will be facing a new world with complex demands, and they will need to be innovative to manage these challenges.

References

Bartol, K. M., and Martin, D. C. (1998). *Management.* (3rd ed.). Boston, MA: Irwin McGraw-Hill.

Bazile-Jones, R. (1996). Diversity in the Workplace: Why We Should Care. *CAM—The Management Accounting Magazine*, 70, 9-12.

Berselli, B. (1998, November 4). In Business Education, Moguls in the Making? *The Washington Post*, C1.

Blanchard, K. (1997). The Blanchard Management Report. *Manage*, 48, 9-11.

Blewett, R. G. (1997, March). What We Know About Leadership Studies. *Leadership Studies Journal*. Boulder, CO: University of Colorado Student Leadership Institute. [Online]. Available: http://www.colorado.edu/SLI/LSJ/vault/marart1.html

Covey, S. R. (1991). Characteristics of Principle-Centered Leaders. *Principle-Centered Leadership*. New York, NY: Simon and Schuster.

Dobbs, M. F. (1996). Managing Diversity: Lessons From the Private Sector. *Public Personnel Management*, 25, 351-67.

Fulmer, R. M. (1997). The Evolving Paradigm of Leadership Development. *Organizational Dynamics*, 25, 59-72.

Hamel, G., and Prahalad, C. K. (1994). *Competing for the Future*. Boston, MA: Harvard Business School Press.

Kanter, R. M. (1994). Collaborative Advantage: The Art of Alliances; Successful Partnerships Manage the Relationship, Not Just the Deal. *Harvard Business Review*, 72, 96-108.

Kiernan, M. J. (1996). *The Eleven Commandments of 21st Century Management*. Englewood Cliffs, NJ: Prentice Hall.

Krohe, J. (1997). The Big Business of Business Ethics. *Across the Board*, 34, 23-29.

Larimer, L. V. (1997). Reflections on Ethics and Integrity. *HR Focus*, 74, 5.

Marquardt, M. J. (1996). *Building the Learning Organization*. New York, NY: McGraw-Hill.

McFarland, L. J., Senn, L. E., and Childress, J. R. (1993). *21ˢᵗ Century Leadership: Dialogues With 100 Top Leaders*. New York, NY: The Leadership Press.

Mosley, D. C., Meggison, L. C., and Pietri, P. H. (1993). *Supervisory Management: The Art of Empowering and Developing People*. (3rd ed.). Cincinnati, OH: South-Western Publishing Co.

National Alliance of Business. (1996). On the Road to Better Schools: Are We There Yet? *Work America*, 13, 1-6.

O'Brien, M. J. (1994). Learning Organization Practices Profile. San Francisco, CA: Pfeiffer & Company.

Organisation for Economic Co-Operation and Development (OECD). (1997, November). About OECD: The OECD and Its Origins. [Online]. Available: http://www/oecd.org/

O'Sullivan, A., and Sheffrin, S. M. (1998). *Economics: Principles and Tools*. Upper Saddle River, NJ: Prentice Hall.

Ramsey, R. L. (1996). Are Ethics Obsolete in the '90s? *Supervision*, 57, 14-16.

Robbins, S. P. (1991). *Management*. (3rd ed.). Englewood Cliffs, NJ: Prentice Hall.

Weil, E. (1997, April). Who's Teaching Whom? *Fast Company*. [Online]. Available: http://www.fastcompany.com/online/08/kidsautodesk.html

Chapter 10 — Workplace Privacy, Confidentiality, and Surveillance

Ann M. Remp
Eastern Michigan University
Ypsilanti, Michigan

More business education graduates than ever before will have responsibilities that relate to privacy in the workplace. Privacy and its related issues—surveillance, trust, confidentiality, and disclosure—may be as important as the concept of free enterprise. Because it is an integral component of electronic commerce and all trusted economic transactions, privacy is a major concern to business education and will be examined from the context of the Class of 2001.

A Workplace Privacy Survey

To start the discussion, the reader is asked to take the Workplace Privacy Survey in Table 1 about his or her attitudes or opinions. There are 10 scenarios with no right or wrong answers and with no added qualifications or clarifications upon which to determine legality or illegality. As each scenario is read, the reader should rate his or her immediate reaction to the acceptability of the action: "If this happened to me in the workplace, how acceptable would it be?"

Rate each scenario based on a scale from 1 to 5, with 1 for the low end (totally unacceptable or very unusual/atypical) and a 5 for totally acceptable and very usual/typical. These rating methods will give the reader some way to gauge his or her own sensitivity to workplace practices.

In reacting to these scenarios, readers will no doubt discover areas of discomfort or even conflict that are occasioned by considering workplace surveillance and the individual's sense of privacy. These areas of discomfort and conflict may be compounded when the employee is now the agent of surveillance, as many business education students will be upon entering the workplace.

Table 1. Workplace Privacy Survey

Scenario 1. Periodic credit checks on employees.
☐ 1 ☐ 2 ☐ 3 ☐ 4 ☐ 5

Scenario 2. Routine polygraphs on employee use of company resources.
☐ 1 ☐ 2 ☐ 3 ☐ 4 ☐ 5

Scenario 3. Unannounced monitoring of telephone conversations.
☐ 1 ☐ 2 ☐ 3 ☐ 4 ☐ 5

Scenario 4. Random reading of electronic mail (e-mail).
☐ 1 ☐ 2 ☐ 3 ☐ 4 ☐ 5

Scenario 5. Random, periodic background check for legal infractions.
☐ 1 ☐ 2 ☐ 3 ☐ 4 ☐ 5

Scenario 6. Wearing an electronic tracking device while at work
☐ 1 ☐ 2 ☐ 3 ☐ 4 ☐ 5

Scenario 7. Random drug testing.
☐ 1 ☐ 2 ☐ 3 ☐ 4 ☐ 5

Scenario 8. Periodic screening of electronic bulletin board or electronic conference discussions for employee participation
☐ 1 ☐ 2 ☐ 3 ☐ 4 ☐ 5

Scenario 9. Filing of DNA testing or other medical screening results
☐ 1 ☐ 2 ☐ 3 ☐ 4 ☐ 5

Scenario 10. Videotaping/viewing by cameras in work location
☐ 1 ☐ 2 ☐ 3 ☐ 4 ☐ 5

The Electronic Communication Privacy Act

Johnson (circa 1994), in discussing the 1986 Electronic Communication Privacy Act (ECPA), provides one illustration of what the Class of 2001 will deal with (and what current employees deal with):

> *[M]any employers are becoming electronic communication system operators whether they know it or not. Portions of ECPA apply to intra-company telephone and electronic message systems ... If 'internal' electronic mail messaging is carefully limited to business communications among employees then ECPA ... should not limit the employer's discretion to disclose those messages to others ... because they are the employer's own messages ... But what if employees begin to send personal messages over the system ... ? What if customers are given access to the network? What if a large number of non-employees have access?*

Note that, in the context of ECPA, employer disclosure of e-mail can occur in a closed network; this particular law does not prohibit surveillance. As the network becomes more and more public, subtle questions about the legal protections of privacy afforded by the legislation enter the picture.

Business education in the second millennium will prepare increasing numbers of information systems and resource managers and administrators, other information workers, entrepreneurs, managers, CEOs, government leaders, and others who will make policy decisions and establish practices for the global information society. These policies and practices will deal with problems of how to promote commerce; protect privacy; enforce intellectual property rights; provide security to employees, customers, and assets; prevent physical violence, industrial espionage, and electronic terrorism; and a host of other interrelated information problems.

Many of these problems will not initially be concerned with privacy and surveillance in the workplace. As solutions are tested, however, workplace and electronic privacy issues may arise.

The Faces of Privacy

Privacy is not well defined, yet it represents an important value for many people. Today, it is difficult to discuss workplace privacy without also address-ing concepts like trust, confidentiality, disclosure, or surveillance. It is also difficult to proceed without a few examples that illustrate the kinds of situations students will encounter and/or decisions they will make as leaders in the next millennium.

Leadership can be defined as a responsibility to engage in active, assertive, thoughtful decision making, and in this context, all individuals must be leaders. This section serves as a glossary with resources cited that provide potential teaching materials.

Privacy. The Office of Technology Assessment (OTA), in its 1994 Congressional report on privacy in networked environments, demonstrated the need for a definition of privacy, even though there is no commonly adopted one. OTA states, "Privacy refers to the social balance between an individual's right to keep information confidential and the societal benefit derived from sharing information, and how this balance is codified to give individuals the means to control personal information."

This is a useful definition because many individuals view privacy as a personal, individual matter. Privacy, however, is only at issue in social interac-tions and in organizational relationships.

Confidentiality (and disclosure). Confidentiality is control over disclo-sure of sensitive or private information. Individuals are themselves the sources of significant amounts of private, personal data, and acts of self-disclosure are often the basis for building relationships. No breach of confidentiality exists when the individual chooses to disclose this information voluntarily. In the workplace, disclosure of information by an unauthorized person or by an authorized person to unauthorized receivers is a breach of confidentiality.

What happens in the workplace when individuals disclose personal information about themselves voluntarily but without thought about unintended audiences has been the subject of much discussion. A useful exercise might be for students to consider the relationship of e-mail use to confidentiality. Policies do not always identify appropriate uses of e-mail, and even when they do, employees do not always follow those policies.

Surveillance. Surveillance, like confidentiality, represents control over the collection and storage of information and can be defined as "monitoring and supervision of populations for specific purposes" (Lyon and Zureik, 1996). The focus of workplace and worker surveillance has changed over time from a primary focus on work products and performance to an increasing interest in worker characteristics (Regan, 1996).

The grandparents of the Class of 2001 were concerned about what would be disclosed to prospective employers about past work performance. The parents of the Class of 2001 debated the uses of drug testing and polygraph testing for employment. The Class of 2001 will continue those debates and move on to form the policies over collection and use of DNA test results, or what some call "biological surveillance" (Lyon and Zureik, 1996).

They will continue to debate how widespread the use of video surveillance, e-mail and telephone monitoring, and electronic tracking in the workplace should be (ACLU, 1996). They will decide whether worker profiles constructed from electronic data collection technologies are legitimate tools for employment decisions. Surveillance is inherently part of the discussion of privacy, but it is also a necessary activity to prevent or limit intrusions into private data by hackers or agents of industrial espionage.

Trust. Confidence between parties to a relationship that no harm will be done defines trust. In today's networked environment, trust is a major concern. Electronic commerce and meaningful communication, for example, depend upon confidence that the author of a mail message, the host of a Web site, the interme-diate links in the transmission process, the electronic financial institution, or other party are all who they claim to be and engaged in legitimate business activities. How is trust established? There are technical, ethical, and sound business practice answers, but not easy ones.

Khare and Rifkin (1997) discuss the social contract nature of trust and the necessity of mechanizing certain elements of trust in building a society that has confidence in its information and communication systems. The idea that trust might be mechanized forces a shift in thinking about how technology affects a free society. Invariably, a trusted environment will require a test of that trust. That test will be a form of surveillance.

In late 1997, some U.S. airlines introduced a plan to profile potential terrorists in order to build consumer trust. Objections were raised that these profiles focused on certain ethnic and national groups and encouraged stereotyp-ing, discrimination, and fear of individuals. Is the attribution of traits to an individual because he or she resembles an electronically constructed profile a violation of privacy? In establishing the trust of a consumer, businesses must be increasingly wary of privacy issues, which will take on greater importance as new technologies continue to emerge.

Case Study: The Class of 2001

The attitudes and values of the high school Class of 2001 are likely to reflect their experiences, especially their history with information technology. Their college counterparts graduating in 2001 represent a much more diverse population relative to age and experiences, but those college students of traditional age (the 18- to 22-year-old group) will share many of the same experiences as the high school class. To prepare these graduates for the leadership roles they must play in developing privacy policies, practices, and legislation, business teachers might find it helpful to look at a collage of experiences these students have had during their short lives. The three periods are: early childhood (1984-1991), later childhood and early adolescence (1992-1997), and finally the high school years (1998-2001).

1984-1991. Members of the high school graduating class of 2001 were born just before or during 1984, a year made infamous by Orwell's prediction of worldwide government "super" surveillance and thought control of the population. In parts of the world, governments did practice considerable censorship.

Yet, in 1984 the information revolution was spreading throughout the free world, while information undergrounds existed in the nonfree world. As political and technological systems changed, political clashes over economic systems became discussions over economic problems. The children of the 1980s, during their visits to the world via television, saw a rise in international terrorism and violence in the workplace and school.

The Class of 2001 is probably the first generation with parents experienced in information, communication, and entertainment technologies, regardless of their levels of formal education. Many parents were computer literate because colleges and high schools had been offering computer courses since the 1960s, and PC courses had started in many high schools by the late 1970s. Workplaces were using computer technology in manufacturing, marketing, and research. Even parents who did not operate computers knew about them and their impact on work.

The PC revolution that began a few years prior to 1984 would change the quality and quantity of work accomplished by computers and broaden the base of employees working directly with the technology. Business was increasing its information work, in part because it faced global changes in competition. Although the parents of the Class of 2001 would have qualitatively different experiences in certain respects, students of the next millennium were born into the Information Age.

Computers in some form would be in the schools from the day these students arrived. They would be featured on television and would influence entertainment. Students would also have experiences with other information technologies. They would be videotaped by parents, as earlier generations had been photographed. Their teachers might videotape their class play. The children would play with video cameras. In their consumer experiences, they would perform for video cameras in stores set up to advertise the product. They would discover that video cameras tracked them in stores as they shopped. Information technology, in the form of computers, videos, or telecommunication, was a normal part of their everyday lives.

1992-1997. By the time our Class of 2001 was in third or fourth grade, another dimension would be added to the Information Age. Pressure for computer interfaces that were easier to learn, more graphic in nature, and more uniform across different environments altered available computer products. Concurrently, the demand for better tools to merge telecommunication and computers produced inexpensive means of connecting people around the world. The appearance of Internet services, thousands of hosts providing resources and services, and graphic interfaces changed the world.

At eight or nine years old, our Class of 2001 would scarcely be aware that the world had not always been this way. They would scarcely distinguish this new technology from the video games available to them almost everywhere. Unlike their grandparents who might remember the shift from radio to television and the years between the appearance of one technology and a newer one, these children would experience technological changes almost daily.

Their older brothers (and maybe their sisters) might even have tried hacking or other types of snooping around computers. The Internet had made tools available to accomplish simple break-ins by even novice computer users. Curiosity, which could be endlessly satisfied on the Net, was the primary credential, along with an absence of any strong moral imperative not to try out this adventure in cyberspace. The infamous hackers had been prosecuted by the late 1980s, but the ubiquitous lure and ready availability of tools would result in continued cyberspace adventures and later admissions of attempts at hacking by individuals who hardly seemed to fit the criminal type.

To raise the question of whether hacking was an invasion of privacy—of consumers or patients, of a business for its information assets —or a compromise to the security of the population was not a topic of discussion in most classes. Their teachers were dealing with the political fallout of whether schools could teach values and were just learning about the Internet themselves.

Business ethics was being added to the college and high school curriculum, but whether it would reach all students and make an impact remained doubtful. Guidance from the law was sketchy and incomplete. Only as the mid-1990s approached, did states begin to address computer crimes in the law. Bills on privacy were introduced at the federal level, but not enacted as legislation. The Class of 2001, not yet in high school, would have been largely unaware of these developments.

1998-2001. By the time the Class of 2001 entered high school or ninth grade, they had considerable experience with the information technologies.

Computer software (whether for games or other purposes) was readily available to them. They might have shared such software with their friends for years without much thought to copyright issues. Their parents might have brought home unlicensed software and said, "It can't hurt anyone—I'm just borrowing it." The students might have been asked to use the Internet to find information for school projects or term papers. How were they to distinguish who owns the information retrieved from this global library? Would the term plagiarism have the same emotional impact on this class as it had on earlier generations of students?

What, then, will be the primary source of values for the Class of 2001? How well formed will students' understanding of the information economy be versus their attitudes about "what's OK" and what is "not OK" relative to privacy?

There is a distinct possibility that students' practice of information literacy includes many activities that have ethical and legal implications. What will they view as risks to their privacy in general? Will they even be concerned about the workplace environment they are to enter in just a few years?

Graduation Day, 2001. During high school, the members of the Class of 2001 have made some decisions actively and others by default. Many students, however, know that information technology is a critical component of most professions and careers because their parents and teachers will have emphasized this. Their business teachers will also have opened doors to emerging careers. If a large percentage of the Class of 2001 becomes committed to continuous learning, many graduates will pursue their education concurrently with their careers.

These new graduates will still be 17 or 18 years old in 2001, but they will face a complex work environment requiring many important decisions. They have witnessed court debates about who really owns the intellectual property created by individuals while affiliated with employers. They have seen the first electronic malls, the birth of electronic commerce, and have heard someone advocate "slowing down" another employee's chance for promotion by electronically sabotaging a budget or stealing an idea. They know about electronic "identity theft." These graduates are the generation whose entertainment features war games started by computers, altered videos in commercials, and easy eavesdropping on others via the network. Now they will be the generation that will have the task of establishing the policies and practices for workplace surveillance and privacy.

Learning Objectives

Business educators must prepare this generation for its profound challenges. What should the Class of 2001 know and be able to do in business about privacy? The National Business Education Association (1995) provides guidance through a number of standards areas on privacy. This section will identify seven achievement standards and suggest how these standards relate to workplace privacy issues. The business student (all students, ideally) will:

1. "Analyze the relationship between ethics and the law and describe the sources of the law ... " (Business Law Standard I, p. 22). In addition, the student will "identify the basic freedoms guaranteed by the Bill of Rights and describe several key Constitutional amendments beyond the Bill of Rights" (Business Law Standard IB, Level 3, p. 22). In relationship to this standard, students should discuss the reasons that the Constitution and Bill of Rights do not identify an individual right to privacy. They should debate and take positions on whether privacy is an individual concept or inherently a social construct with value only as it relates to interrelationships among individuals and within organizations (See Lyon and Zureik, 1994).

2. "Design and implement security plans and procedures for information systems" (Information Systems Standard XI, p. 97) and "Establish and use a personal code of ethics for information systems use and management" (Information Systems Standard XII, p. 98). Students should pose examples that put these two standards in conflict; they should evaluate cases that demonstrate the conflicts that information systems and resource management personnel and others face in carrying out their responsibilities.

3. "Explain how the advances in computer technology impact upon such areas as property law, contract law, and international law" (Business Law Standard VII, p. 31). "Explain how common law, constitutional law, statutory law, and administrative regulations can be used to prevent the use of computers to invade privacy" and "Outline the various types of federal, state, territory, and province statutes designed to combat computer crime" (Criminal Law and Privacy Issues in Computer Law, p. 32). Not all computer crime is related to privacy; however, it is valuable to ask students to identify any possible links to privacy as they review federal and state laws.

   Intellectual property, which is specifically addressed in these standards, will become a privacy issue as individuals increasingly form virtual or electronic work groups using media that record their individual ideas and contributions. Perrole (1996) says, "If the purpose of CSCW [computer-supported cooperative work] is to support the actual activities of cooperative groups, some attention must be paid to the ways groups negotiate privacy. This involves ... the individual's privacy from the demands of the group and the organization, and the group's privacy from the organization" (p. 51). Students must be able to articulate the conflicting needs of the organization and the individual.

4. "Discuss the role of government in an economic system, especially the necessary and desirable role of government in the U.S. economy" (Economics and Personal Finance Standard XII, p. 73). In relationship to this, students should be able to debate and take positions on the extent to which regulation should solve privacy problems versus the extent to which

personal and social responsibility (ethics) should govern privacy as it relates to the electronic economic characteristics of society.

5. "Relate work ethic, workplace relationships, workplace diversity, and workplace communication skills to career development" (Career Development Standard III, p. 39). Among the specific objectives for this standard should be one that asks students to research the meaning of trust in an information society, including the limits of technical solutions to building trust (Khare and Rifkin,1997).

6. "Use technology to enhance the effectiveness of communications" (Communication Standard III, p. 51). Achieving this standard should require students to articulate the pros and cons of monitoring employee telephone, e-mail, electronic bulletin board/conference participation, and physical movement through electronic means from a privacy perspective and from a security perspective. Each student should be able to state what he or she will do if directed by an employer to conduct such surveillance especially if the student is concerned that an action is illegal. There is no "right or wrong" position to take, but resolving conflicts will require the individual to develop a position.

7. "Analyze the role and importance of agency and employment law as they relate to the conduct of business in the national and international marketplaces" (Business Law Standard III, p. 26). "Demonstrate an understanding of the basis on which employees or applicants may be asked to take tests, such as aptitude, psychological, polygraph, and drug tests." There is a specific element of agency that should be addressed in conjunction with this standard. Students who pursue technical and/or professional certifications may at some future time incur a greater professional liability as they carry out their positions. Students should be able to state what their liabilities may be, to the extent that information is available, when they add certifications to their employment credentials.

By achieving these standards and suggested objectives, the Class of 2001 will be better prepared for the next millennium. Business educators should continue to develop these future leaders in a broad-based fashion, as suggested by the Interrelationships of Business Functions standard.

It is impossible to predict what future technologies will emerge. Those that we anticipate for the Class of 2001 may not have the scope required for the Class of 2002, 2003, and for generations not yet born. There is no doubt that these future generations will face new challenges, conflicts, and paradoxes. They will find, as do their parents and teachers, that solutions to one problem create new ones and that what were expected to be problems are, in fact, not problems at all. They will also, as citizens of a global society made possible through communication technology, create new opportunities.

A recent discussion of "digital citizenship" (Katz, 1997) offers some data to support a very optimistic hypothesis: Those who are technologically "superconnected" are also most positive about democracy and free enterprise and most confident in the free market system. Prior to the survey, Katz had believed that highly "wired" individuals would be estranged in an electronic world; instead, "they are actually highly participatory and view our existing political system positively, even patriotically…" (1997, pp. 71-71).

No research is definitive for all time, but if this research indicates anything about the future, it is that business teachers can aid students by fostering discussion of the kind of world they want for themselves and their children. It matters little that we do not have a crystal ball for technology in 2010 or 2020 as long as we help students grow in their understanding of technology impacts. Some teaching approaches may help the teacher to develop this understanding.

Teaching Activities

What materials and approaches are available to teachers? Business teachers will need to integrate privacy issues with other learning objectives. There is little time to add new, dedicated content to most curricula, and decisions to delete content should be made carefully. Therefore, the suggestions in this section are designed to reinforce other learning outcomes.

The approaches to instruction should be diverse and fit with the ongoing major learning units in business law, economics, business communication, information systems, and technology. They should foster the major outcomes needed by future leaders: the ability to research source materials, to synthesize large volumes of materials and to analyze the issues, and to communicate the issues clearly orally and in writing. They should also encourage students to engage in problem solving and decision making, and, in short, to demonstrate all the abilities that the SCANS Commission calls for and that the NBEA standards encompass.

"The Privacy Game," published by Simile II in 1979, is an example of an activity that requires many of these skills. Funding by AT&T supported the development of the game and is an indication of the interest businesses have in introducing students to privacy issues. More a case analysis and group problem-solving approach than a game, "The Privacy Game" begins with a series of vignettes that concern workplace privacy. In spite of its age, the cases are still relevant today.

The student reads each vignette and attaches a marker to a summary board to indicate whether or not the employer should be able to exercise the surveillance identified. Students then divide into groups. Half the groups receive additional information on the individual's perspective, while the other half receive information on the employer's concerns.

Following discussion, each group formulates a decision. These decisions are then presented and debated by all the groups. The objective is for students, through their decision making, to achieve the "delicate balance [that] must be struck between the needs of the individual and the needs of organizations in society" (*Director's Guide of the Privacy Game*, p.3). It would be fairly straightforward to add a few contemporary workplace surveillance vignettes representing the technological environment of today.

Teachers can also make up new games and simulations. One might be called, "The Secret Will Out." The teacher may start with the basic birthday game of passing a secret from one individual to another to determine how much distortion of the communication will occur. The teacher may want to introduce a rumor (carefully) to determine how much elaboration and interest is expressed as it is passed from one individual to another. Part of understanding privacy is recognizing how much individuals like to know about everyone else.

Still another activity that teachers might want to introduce is a social engineering role play. Social engineering is the process of obtaining secrets from individuals by conventional social means. Often this means simply engaging in casual conversation that leads the innocent person into an area of confidentiality before he or she realizes that information has been revealed. There should be a script for the "social engineer" and "the victim." Without a script, real confidential information might be revealed, resulting in harm to a student. Follow-up discussion should focus on the potential harm that results from revealing confidences. Discussion can also focus on how to resist telling secrets in order to please someone else.

Research on workplace surveillance and privacy online can precede or follow an activity like "The Privacy Game" or prepare for still other activities. Sites on the Internet that provide discussions of privacy are numerous. A characteristic of the information world, however, is the dynamic nature of Internet sites.

Several organizations post information on the Web that is suitable for a variety of classroom discussions; among these are: the Electronic Privacy Information Center (EPIC); the Electronic Frontier Foundation, founded by one-time Grateful Dead member, Jerry Barlow; Privacy Times; and the American Civil Liberties Union (ACLU). The online or published *Wall Street Journal*, *New York Times*, *Forbes*, and an almost infinite variety of other publications continue to carry stories and articles on privacy in the workplace.

Students can learn to read the laws through sites like Findlaw that provide the actual text. Examining the 1986 Electronic Communication Privacy Act, the 1987 Computer Fraud and Abuse Act, the proposed 1993 Privacy for Consumers and Workers Act, and other federal and state laws and regulations can be a learning experience in itself.

While the teacher is focusing on search engines and basic and advanced search techniques, the students can use workplace surveillance and privacy as topics. As students download the text of files to change from ASCII to word processing format, they can also discuss whether authors are wise to post their ideas on a medium that provides so little protection from intellectual theft and whether such theft of ideas has any bearing on privacy. The number of stories, articles, privacy surveys, research studies, and other electronic publications on privacy to be found on the Internet precludes describing even a small portion of them.

With research in hand, the teacher may want to form student panels to present a particular topic, such as the pros and cons of video surveillance in the workplace. The panels may demonstrate simply the ability to summarize information orally, or they may be asked to take and defend positions. A panel has the added advantage of allowing students to demonstrate their ability to organize a formal team effort.

Speakers from the business community are more than willing to aid business teachers. The local chapter of the ACLU has business professionals among its membership. An ACLU or other privacy group panel presentation, discussion leader, or a presenter should result in a very positive experience for students.

Summary

The graduates of 2001 will enter an exciting, but challenging environment. Relative to privacy, surveillance, and trust, it will be a more complex world than their parents and teachers grew up in. They should be a generation full of great optimism and desirous of shaping their world.

Business teachers will make significant contributions to society by fostering those attitudes and by requiring the graduating class to think hard about privacy issues. Without policies on privacy, electronic commerce will not occur. Free enterprise will falter, for it is built on a premise of individual freedom, and privacy is part of that freedom. Privacy is essential for a workplace culture that fosters creative thinking. The graduate who steps into the workplace of the next millennium without the ability to think through such issues will be severely handicapped.

Science fiction writer, William Gibson, has been attributed with the creation of the term "cyberspace." His first book, published in 1984, was not an echo of George Orwell's prediction of surveillance. It was, however, a look at a complex future in which competitive industrial espionage figures prominently in business enterprise and requires contracted employees equipped with biotechnology to hack the highways of cyberspace. Without oversimplifying a tremendously thought-provoking glimpse at one type of future, business teachers must think about various futures. They need to help the Class of 2001 build a positive future. Privacy and workplace surveillance are issues that enable both teachers and students to think about which future will exist.

References

American Civil Liberties Union. (1996, September). Surveillance, Incorporated: American Workers Forfeit Privacy for a Paycheck. [Online]. Available: http://www.aclu.org/library/wrrpt96.html.

Gibson, W. (1984). *Neuromancer*. New York, NY: Ace Books. (See also *Count Zero* and other works by William Gibson.)

Johnson, D. R. (circa 1994). Barbed Wire Fences in Cyberspace: The Threat Posed by Calls for Ownership of Transactional Information. Washington, DC: Wilmer, Cutler, & Pickering. [Online]. Available: http\\www.com.

Johnson, D. R. (circa 1994). Electronic Communications Privacy: Good Sysops Should Build Good Fences. Washington, DC: Wilmer, Cutler, & Pickering. [Online]. Available: http\\www.com.

Katz, J. (1997, December). The Digital Citizen. *Wired*, 68-72, 76-82, 274-275.

Khare, R., and Rifkin, A. (1997). Weaving a Web of Trust. [Online]. Available: http://www.cs.caltec.edu/~adam/local.trust.htm.

Lyon, D., and Zureik, E. (1996). Surveillance, Privacy, and the New Technology. *Computers, Surveillance & Privacy*. Minneapolis, MN: University of Minnesota Press.

National Business Education Association. (1995). *National Standards for Business Education: What America's Students Should Know and Be Able to Do in Business.* Reston, VA: National Business Education Association.

Office of Technology Assessment. (1994, May). Information Security and Privacy in Network Environments. Washington, DC: U.S. Government Printing Office.

Perrole, J. S. (1996). Privacy and Surveillance in Computer Supported Cooperative Work. *Computers, Surveillance & Privacy*. Minneapolis, MN: University of Minnesota Press.

Privacy Game, The. (1979). Del Mar, CA: Simile II.

Regan, P. M. (1996). Genetic Testing and Workplace Surveillance. *Computers, Surveillance & Privacy*. Minneapolis, MN: University of Minnesota Press.

Chapter 11 — Fostering a Diverse Workforce for Today's Global Marketplace

Carol Larson Jones
California State Polytechnic University
Pomona, California

In our global marketplace, the corporate client base is changing even faster than the demographics of the workplace as companies take advantage of the economic opportunities that exist beyond traditional markets. The promotion and management of diversity in the workplace can make business practices more effective and contribute to customer satisfaction. Richard (1997) states that "as companies continue to globalize, obtaining the proper human resources becomes a business necessity to survive in a global economy."

Defining diversity. Diversity, broadly defined, is the condition of being different or having differences. All employees bring differences, including group identity differences, to the workplace. Accepting a broad definition of diversity moves differences beyond "us vs. them" polarization and allows companies to regard these differences as strengths that can accomplish both individual and organizational goals (Wentling, 1998). Nordstrom's, a successful retail chain, is an example of one company that promotes this broader interpretation. (See Table 1.)

Table 1. How Nordstrom's Defines Diversity

D = disability, different styles
I = individuals
V = varying, various, variety
E = education, economic status
R = race, religion
S = sexual orientation, social class, similarities
I = intelligence
T = thought processes, team effort, traits
Y = youth, years

Importance of understanding, valuing, and managing diversity.
Considerable attention is now devoted to managing diversity in the workplace because many organizations have become aware of the relationship between valuing diversity and how an organization performs. Specifically, managing diversity well enables companies to tap new markets or to increase their market share; operate more competitively on a global level; attract new ideas; and communicate better with a wider range of clients (Raisfeld, 1998).

Companies incorporate diversity to improve productivity and to remain competitive rather than because it is the "right" thing to do (Raisfeld, 1998). A diversity perspective allows companies to maximize the talents of its employees and, in turn, develop an organizational culture that facilitates superior performance in a global economy. Companies wishing to develop this competence will adopt such concepts as empowerment, continuous improvement, and total quality management. The common denominator among these prescriptions for improving organizational performance is the focus on workers' individual contributions.

Core Dimensions of Diversity

Despite the tendency to define diversity in its broadest sense, organizations working with diversity issues may define diversity narrowly, especially if they seek to correct company biases against particular groups (Wentling, 1998). "Core" dimensions of diversity are those that have been recognized as specific barriers to advancement.

The following core dimensions may be considered relatively immutable or inborn: age, ethnicity, gender, physical abilities, and race (Loden and Rosener, 1991). Sexual orientation is frequently considered a core dimension although research is inconclusive on whether or not this difference is genetic.

Age. One in five Americans is 55 or older, compared to one in 10 at the beginning of the century. By 2010, the U.S. Census Bureau projects that this number will be one in four.

Age discrimination has increased with the aging of the workforce. The Equal Employment Opportunity Commission (EEOC) reports a 20 percent increase in age discrimination claims since 1991.

Efforts are underway to promote the advantages of an age-diverse workforce. The American Association of Retired Persons (AARP), for example, has begun research, education, and advocacy programs to convince American companies to hire older workers. Like AARP, Stuart Silverstein (1997) believes an older workforce offers advantages to employers. He predicts that employers will overhaul their employment practices to find ways to hire and retain older workers and that "older workers often pushed out the door amid the corporate layoffs of the 1980s and 1990s are likely to emerge as hot prospects in the job market."

Gender. Approximately 68 percent of all women today are in the workplace. By the year 2000, it is projected that approximately 80 percent of women between the ages of 25 and 54 will work full-time (Jardim and Hennig, 1990).

A study by the U.S. Census Bureau noted that women who leave the workplace to stay at home full-time and raise families are no longer the majority. In its 1976 study, the U.S. Census Bureau reported that 31 percent of women returned to work within 12 months of giving birth; the 1995 study reported that 55 percent of women went back to work within the first 12 months. The 1995 study also indicated that 77 percent of college-educated women between the ages of 30 and 44 decided to juggle motherhood and an outside job (Fiore, 1997).

While many organizations have made significant progress in valuing and managing women in the workplace, many others have done very little. For example, even though the pay gap between male and female executives has shrunk, companies pay significantly higher salaries to their male executives (Dogar, 1998). In addition, according to a report in *Working Woman*, the national average for female representation on companies' boards of directors is only 10 percent.

Other issues besides compensation affect women in the workplace. Sexual harassment, for example, is a form of discrimination predominantly directed toward women (Jardim and Hennig, 1990). Communication styles also impact the work performance of women:

> *When business was almost exclusively the domain of the white male, styles of communication were a non-issue. Most white men under-stood what other white men meant not necessarily by what they said but by how they said it. That has changed on the factory floor and in the management suite. Minorities and women bring their own styles of communicating and this proliferation of styles introduces a potential for misunderstanding. Misunderstandings cost money. Business can ill afford breakdowns in communication* (Federal Glass Ceiling Commission, 1995).

Physical and mental abilities. Disabled individuals can be broadly defined as those with limitations in activities due to physical or mental impair-ments. The National Health Interview Survey (NHIS) estimates that the total number of Americans with disabilities living in households is 33.8 million or 13.7 percent of the U.S. population (LaPlante, 1992).

Individuals with disabilities are frequently patronized or prevented from obtaining employment opportunities available to the more able-bodied. A major step toward removing barriers to employment and advancement was the passage of the Public Law 101-336: The Americans With Disabilities Act (ADA). This legislation was intended to prevent companies from denying qualified individuals participation in equal employment opportunities, and to require employers to provide reasonable accommodations for qualified employees with physical or mental disabilities.

Under the Act, a disability is defined as (1) a physical or mental impairment that substantially limits one or more life activities; (2) a record of such impairment; or (3) being regarded as having such an impairment. Protected individuals include those who have physical limitations such as disease or chronic health conditions (AIDS, cerebral palsy, spinal cord injuries); impairments having to do with vision, speech, hearing, or mobility; cognitive limitations such as learning disabilities, attention deficit disorders, mental retardation, autism, and psychiatric conditions; and those diagnosed with head injuries or Down's syndrome.

Ethnicity and race. Diversity efforts received major attention with the publication of the Hudson Institute's "Workforce 2000" report, which predicted changes that would occur in the demographic composition of the United States population and workforce by the year 2000. This 1987 study, commissioned by the United States Department of Labor, made the following forecasts:

- White males will account for only 15 percent of the 25 million people who will join the workforce between the years 1985 and 2000.

- The remaining 85 percent joining the workforce will be white females, immigrants, and individuals (of both genders) of African-American, Hispanic, and Asian origins.

- The Hispanic and Asian populations will each grow by 48 percent; the African-American population will grow by 28 percent; the white population will grow by only 5.6 percent (Johnston and Packer, 1987).

The Hudson Report forecasts that the portion of the workforce consisting of minorities will edge up from 23 percent in 1994 to 26 percent in 2005 (Silverstein, 1997). The U.S. Census Bureau projects that by 2050 approximately 50 percent of the United States population will be composed of the following minorities: African-Americans, Hispanics, Asians, and Pacific Islanders (Minehan, 1997).

Sexual orientation. Homosexuals comprise three to 10 percent of the population (Gilmour, in Taylor, 1997). Undoubtedly, sexual orientation is the most controversial core dimension of diversity. Stereotypes about homosexuals include beliefs that they are sexual beings first and foremost, are sexually aggressive and hit on "straights," are unclean and unholy, and choose not to be "straight" (Loden and Rosener, 1991).

While other core dimensions of diversity are genetic in nature, the evidence concerning sexual orientation is inconclusive. Studies investigating homosexuality have ranged from the "nature" approach, in which sexual preference involves heredity and hormonal imbalance, to the "nurture" approach, in which sexual orientation is a result of psychological and environmental influences. Regardless of the explanations, homosexuality exists and, like individuals who represent other core dimensions of diversity, homosexuals want to be evaluated based on their abilities and motivation to perform. They do not want to be discriminated against because they differ from the dominant group.

A key issue involving gay and lesbian workers is domestic partner benefits. A recent survey by KMPG Peat Marwick indicates that only 25 percent of employers nationwide with more than 5,000 employees provide health benefits to domestic partners. As Allan Gilmour stated in an interview with *Fortune* magazine, the actual cost of these benefits is not high, because large numbers of gays and lesbians are concerned about public exposure and do not apply for them. Despite the cost of AIDS in the gay community, Gilmour said, the costs of other medical problems, such as complicated pregnancies, are higher in the traditional family (Taylor, 1997).

Managing Diversity in the Global Marketplace

Businesses and organizations that wish to serve an increasingly diverse marketplace are themselves becoming more diverse. The presence of diversity in these organizations can either add to or detract from company performance and competitiveness: the key is how well diversity is managed.

Guidelines. Companies may use various strategies to give employees the skills needed to operate in a multicultural environment. The most effective are training and education programs; organizational policies that mandate fairness and equity for all employees; mentoring programs for minority employees; more systematic career guidance and planning programs; performance appraisal systems that are nondiscriminatory; and outreach programs, such as internships, scholarships, community recruitment efforts, and school lectures (Wentling, 1998). Upper management support of these initiatives is crucial.

The one area in which discrimination is appropriate is individual performance. Performance is based on ability (what a person can do), motivation (what a person will do), clarity of expectations, and opportunity. It is the responsibility of the organization to provide this clarity through its policies, goals, and objectives and to provide opportunity subject to a person's ability and motivation to perform.

Leadership. The leadership function of management in accommodating diversity is especially critical. Managers must be able to motivate and inspire their employees to perform at their best. To put forth persistent effort in the direction of organizational goals, people must be wholly involved with and committed to their jobs. Therefore, employees must believe they are valued and understood by the organization regardless of their race, ethnicity, age, gender, abilities, or sexual orientation.

Managers must also be able to create an environment that fosters open and respectful communication. Diversity issues that are centered in team building—especially if they emphasize the value of viewing issues from all perspectives—will foster the collaboration that will help change the culture of the organization from one that only acknowledges diversity to one that understands and values it (O'Neil, Personal Interview, 1998).

The job of management has always been to achieve organizational goals and objectives in an effective and efficient manner through and with people. While the technical, conceptual, and administrative skills of managers continue to be important to the achievement of superior results, human skills will ultimately make or break an organization.

Training. Management's challenge—to recognize the need for tapping the potential of a diverse workforce in an increasingly global business environment—will require educating employees, through diversity training workshops, about the importance of understanding, valuing, and managing diversity. How well management accepts this challenge will determine whether the United States continues to be a world leader.

Training program success depends on many organizational aspects, especially commitment and support from top management (Wentling, 1998). Training can help build awareness of diversity issues, underscore the importance of valuing diversity in the workplace, educate employees on specific cultural differences, provide the skills necessary to work successfully in diverse work teams, and develop activities that will help diverse groups succeed at their jobs and create opportunities for advancement. Effective training programs are integrated with other organizational education and training systems, combined with other diversity initiatives within the organization, planned (to include accountability), and delivered to all employees.

A survey conducted by the Society for Human Resource Management/ Commerce Clearing House (SHRM/CCH) of public and private human resources specialists revealed that over 70 percent of diversity training programs are one day or less in length. The survey concluded that this strategy is insufficient and often results in failure (Riccucci, 1997). Therefore, organizations must plan, develop, and evaluate diversity training programs that focus on changing the actual culture of the organization, an effort that requires long-term commitment.

Programs must be assessed to ensure they are achieving the goals set for them; they can unwittingly backfire. Instead of creating harmony, they can have the opposite effect of polarizing the workplace and exacerbating rather than relieving problems (Raisfeld, 1998). Conducting ongoing training and evaluation can help revise and strengthen future program content and direction.

At the University of California Riverside branch of Bank of America, for example, diversity training is an ongoing process. Cara Bukowski, a student at California State Polytechnic University in Pomona, works as a personal banker at the bank's branch office and is involved in the diversity program. She notes that monthly meetings are held to review all facets of diversity and to discuss strategies for handling various situations. Indeed, the majority of larger companies are now beginning to offer regularly scheduled (and long-term) diversity programs.

Federal Express, based in Memphis, Tennessee, recently expanded and redefined its existing diversity training program. In contrast to initial training, which focused on awareness and targeted upper management, the new program is a course that addresses practical and fundamental issues and reaches all levels of the organization (Tri-Comm, Diversity in Education, 1997). The program is internal and integrated into all FedEx activities.

The curriculum is multilayered and includes both management and non-management issues. Leadership attributes such as lifelong learning (each employee must develop a personal learning curriculum) and effective communication get strong corporate support. No more than three levels of management separate any employee from the CEO. This policy is intended to enhance the organization's entrepreneurial spirit, moving ideas freely between employees and upper management and rewarding innovation with financial compensation (Tri-Comm, Diversity in Education, 1997).

At Motorola SPS (which has offices in Phoenix, Arizona, and Austin, Texas), diversity initiatives move beyond recruitment to focus on personal development. In 1991, Motorola established a diversity task force that explored diversity activities at other companies with the objective of improving its own. In 1994, the task force established the WellQuest program, a health maintenance program for employees. The Individual Dignity Entitlement (IDE) program, founded in 1995, provided a forum for steady, incremental career development. Other initiatives, such as individual training plans, mentoring efforts, and community outreach are all designed toward continual improvement and helping employees find their full path to productivity (Tri-Comm, Diversity in Action, 1997).

Legal requirements. A number of legislative mandates are spurring businesses to develop programs that support and nurture diversity and to incorporate them into their goals and mission statements.

Title VII of the 1964 Civil Rights Act prohibits discrimination on the basis of race, religion, gender, or national origin. The Age Discrimination in Employment Act (ADEA) prohibits employer discrimination against anyone over 40 years old. Unlike the Civil Rights Act, ADEA provides for a trial by jury and can lead to possible criminal penalty. Trial by jury is significant because juries do not typically react favorably to discrimination against older workers.

The Americans With Disabilities Act is a comprehensive statute designed to provide equal access to "qualified individuals with disabilities." Title I of the ADA, which became effective July 26, 1992, prohibits discrimination in employment. This legislation is of particular interest since it aims to make the workplace readily accessible to and usable by those who are differently abled.

Only the sexual orientation dimension of diversity is left unprotected by federal legislation from discriminatory practices. However, some state legislation on the subject has been passed. California, Connecticut, Hawaii, Massachusetts, New Jersey, Vermont, and Wisconsin have all enacted legislation prohibiting discrimination based on sexual preference. (Colorado, on the other hand, passed a bill permitting such discrimination.)

Recently, legal initiatives related to domestic partner benefits have begun to emerge. In a landmark move that took effect during June 1997, San Francisco is now requiring its contractors to offer domestic partner coverage to their employees (Boxall, 1997). Recently, California voted to provide domestic partner benefits for employees of the University of California system in order to remain competitive with other institutions of higher learning that offer such benefits.

Examples of Companies Operating Successfully in a Global Marketplace

At one time, the United States dominated the world economy; therefore, U.S. businesspersons largely ignored the rest of the world. Now that our national economy has become part of an integrated international economy characterized by global companies, distribution, and consumerism, businesspersons must learn to function efficiently and effectively in this new environment. A first step in preparing to operate in the new global marketplace is to recognize the importance of understanding, valuing, and managing diversity internally. The second step is to apply the same careful planning to understanding, valuing, and managing diversity externally. In the real world of business, however, these two facets of managing diversity—internal and external—may occur simultaneously and in a complementary fashion.

Coors Brewing Company. President Peter Coors appreciates the importance of diversity within the company and is turning that diversity into an advantage in the marketplace. Coors has instituted an Ethnic Marketing Council in an effort to come to terms with a changing marketplace—domestic and foreign competitors and consumers—and excel in the year 2000. The company has chosen to court these emerging markets (Rundles, 1997).

Lucent Technologies. Believing that diversity is necessary for both internal and external success, AT&T spinoff Lucent Technologies is increasing its focus on the individual employee. In an interview with *Colorado Business* magazine, Jeff Akers, Vice President of Lucent's Customer Care division, said, "We want Lucent Technologies to be a great place to work and to be an organization that mirrors our communities." Lucent seeks qualified minority interns and pairs them with members of the company's Global Leadership Development Program (GLDP). GLDP members mentor the interns in management skills (Tri-Comm, Diversity in Education, 1997). Akers further stated that "… since Lucent Technologies is a worldwide organization, we want it to be the best customer-service organization worldwide. We want people that speak Spanish, Chinese, Japanese, and more" (Rundles, 1997).

McDonald's Corporation. This organization knows how to grow in the global marketplace. The company presently operates 18,380 restaurants in 91 countries. Its strategy for global success is adapting its winning people and employment practices to many different cultural settings. The company carefully plans each restaurant location and demands flexibility and sensitivity to local cultural mores (Solomon, 1996). For example, in communities with lots of vegetarians, franchises don't cook french fries in lard (Kane, 1997).

McDonald's recently opened its first restaurant in India, which will serve no beef products out of respect for the culture of the country. Instead, the restaurant will offer vegi-, mutton-, and lamb-burgers. The company also recently opened a new restaurant in Saudi Arabia with two dining rooms. One dining room serves only men, and the other serves only women and children, to reflect the dining habits prevalent in Saudi culture.

Rita Johnson, staff director in Central Europe, states that McDonald's believes its restaurants should always reflect the communities it serves: not only the individuals employed and the culture and ethnicity of those communities, but also the employment practices (Solomon, 1996).

Lexis-Nexis. Starting as a grassroots movement to focus on and commit to full utilization of all employees throughout the organization, the diversity program at this online news and information service increased the talent pool of minorities (13.5 percent of its workers) and women (54 percent of its workers). The company added several work-life initiatives to its "diversity umbrella" (Tri-Comm, Diversity in Action, 1997). Telecommuting, for example, offers workers who need flexible work environments, such as employees with disabilities, the option to work from a home office. Lexis-Nexis negotiated discounted child care rates for employees with several child care providers. Parents who adopt may take advantage of "adoptive leave" policies.

Cherry Semiconductor. Because of its history of hiring international students, Cherry Semiconductor has a diverse technical workforce that brings a variety of backgrounds and perspectives to the company. Though it is small (975 employees), the company has tripled the number of female and minority engineers and increased its community outreach to encourage young people, especially minorities and women, to pursue technical careers.

Preparing Students for the Diverse Workplace

Companies face the same issues and problems public schools have been facing in understanding and utilizing the full range of human potential in a diverse population (Wentling, 1998). Since our students will be entering the new workplace, it is essential that they be exposed to diversity issues in school. One way of teaching students the importance of understanding, valuing, and managing diversity is to have them participate in diversity-related discussions, activities, and projects in class.

Instructors must set the climate for open and honest discussion well in advance of introducing diversity as a topic of study in the classroom. To avoid "canned" answers to problematic issues, teachers must excel at reading the meaning inherent in students' facial expressions and in their words, their silence, and their body language. They must give the "sensitivity issue" its due and at the same time be careful not to patronize students (O'Neil, Telephone Interview, 1998).

Teachers should acknowledge the diversity issues already inherent in their specific classroom or school environment, such as students with disabilities, students who speak English as a second language, and students who may be older than others, as can happen in the college setting. These in themselves may be a starting point for dealing with diversity. Below are examples of additional educational projects that students can undertake.

Global e-mail exchange. Teachers and students establish an e-mail partnership with a class of students of the same age level in another country.

They write about their stereotypes of life and business in that country, and with the guidance of the teacher differentiate between knowledge and stereotypes. For a detailed description of this project, see http://www.messalonskee.sad47. k12.me.us/auspapr.htm. To find classroom partners for e-mail exchanges, go to the Intercultural E-Mail Classroom Connections Web site (http://www.stolaf.edu/ network/iecc/) or the International WWW Schools Registry (http://web66.coled. umn.edu/schools.html) (Davis, 1996). This activity can be combined with the presentation activity listed below.

Interview and oral presentation. Students interview an individual from a foreign country and then make an oral presentation on the country, the culture, and the business environment of that country. Students should include information obtained from the interview and from their own research. A good source for the information can be found in the *Culturgrams* published by the David M. Kennedy Center for International Studies at Brigham Young University. Students may access the Center's Web site at http://ucs.byu.edu/kenncent/publications/ for a catalog of available books and *Culturgrams* for more than 150 countries.

Core dimensions discussion. Divide students into groups of two to three individuals and discuss each of the core dimensions of diversity. Ask students to recall an incident in which a problem arose due to a lack of understanding and respect for one of the core dimensions of diversity. Then require students to locate an article on each core dimension of diversity and present their findings to the class. This activity encourages open discussion.

International community map. Whether they know it or not, students are involved daily in the world of international trade and the global economics of business. In this activity, students read the labels in their clothing (and shoes) and note where the items were manufactured. They then trace the raw materials and production processes used to manufacture the clothing and annotate each part of the process on a world map (Keddington, 1994).

Consulate information memo. Have students assume that they are going to conduct business with the following countries: Australia, China, Ecuador, Mexico, and South Africa. Students can access *The Web of Culture* at http:// www.webofculture.com and locate the consulate closest to their home. (*The Web of Culture* considers itself a premier Web source for global business competency. The Web site seeks to inform business professionals on the topic of cross-cultural communications and on how to conduct business with a foreign counterpart.) Students then prepare a memo directed to the consulate nearest them and outline the nature of their business. Have students design a protocol describing how they will modify their own practices and train their employees so that their business venture will be successful.

Diversity pioneer inquest. Students select a company that has a recognized program of diversity management (for example, CIGNA, which received the Exemplary Voluntary Efforts Award from the U.S. Department of Labor for hiring, promoting, and advancing ethnic minorities) and interview key players in the program. Students can focus on the program's goals, obstacles to its success, solutions to obstacles, and future directions.

Case studies. Using case studies can accomplish several objectives: raising awareness of diversity issues, increasing understanding, and promoting the thinking and decision-making skills critical to the leadership function. Teachers can devise their own cases (short scenarios featuring diversity-related issues, including questions for discussion) or use examples they find in print (see Table 2).

Using role-play makes the case study come alive in the classroom, but teachers must be careful that students do not pit themselves against one another and that they are respectful of sensitive issues that may emerge. Educator Sharon Lund O'Neil (1998) suggests the following additional options for using case studies:

- Listen for meaning as the case is read aloud. Pay attention to inflections and pauses, as they may challenge participants to change some of the "hard facts" identified in the first reading.

- Differentiate essential facts from unimportant elements in the case. Point out the pitfalls of drawing conclusions from unsubstantiated information.

Table 2. Examples of Case Studies on Diversity Issues

The following cases may be suitable for use with business education students.

1. **Homeless girl denied admission to Guntersville High School.** Case: Penny Doe vs. Richardson. Diversity applications: homelessness, race. Legal: McKinney Act; Civil Rights Act. Source: Southern Poverty Law Center. (1998, December). School Enrolls Homeless Girl After Center Files Lawsuit. Montgomery, AL: *SPLC Report,* 28 (4), 4.

2. **Eviction of person with manic depression.** A woman who has repeatedly failed to pay her rent on time was evicted and her belongings placed on the street, where they were stolen. The woman sued the apartment owners claiming that management had failed to accommodate her mental handicap. Diversity applications: physical/mental abilities. Legal: ADA, Fair Housing Act. Source: National Apartment Association. (N.d.). Legal Issues. *Certified Apartment Manager Student Handbook.* Alexandria, VA: National Apartment Association.

3. **Race discrimination suit.** Texaco executives were caught on tape belittling blacks and plotting to destroy incriminating documents. Diversity applications: race. Legal: Civil Rights Act. Source: Associated Press. (1996, November 16). Texaco Settles Race Discrimination Suit for $176.1 Million. *The Detroit News.* [Online]. Available: http://detnews.com/1996/menu/stories/75179.htm.

- Outline the facts and sequence the events presented in the case.
- Compare and contrast viewpoints. Include the students' own reflections on the viewpoints as an additional perspective.
- Lead a discussion or debate on possible solutions to the case.
- Present the alternatives and the best solution to the case. Time-limit the discussion to challenge problem-solving skills.
- Write a summary or brief of the case to develop written communication skills.

Cultural Immersion. Cross school departmental boundaries to create a "school-within-a-school," as Hylton Senior High School did in Woodbridge, Virginia. In September 1998, Hylton launched the Center for International Studies and Languages (CISL). Its vision: to create an interdisciplinary curriculum that would graduate well-rounded students prepared for the challenges of an international society.

CISL students take the typical secondary courses; however, each course is taught with an international focus. A cornerstone of the CISL program is the exchange network that program director Margaret Holt set up between Hylton and schools in countries such as Germany, Mexico, France, and England. Hylton students travel abroad (for a limited time) to immerse themselves in a foreign culture; their host country in turn sends its students to the U.S.

The entire Hylton community—not just CISL participants—benefits from meeting the international students who have come to America. Holt says students, perhaps for the first time, see their own culture through another's eyes. They question assumptions and learn to appreciate what they have. "It enriches, not erases, the cultural traditions," she says.

Quoting from her county's five-year instructional plan, Holt said, "The ability for Prince William [County] students to compete with students on a national and international level cannot be just an option. It is a necessity."

Summary

Our workplace is changing, and diversity is no longer the exception, but the norm. Diversity is good for business, and businesses have discovered that employee satisfaction and organizational success are intertwined. Exploring diversity can help organizations understand how they can use human resources to gain a competitive advantage domestically and globally.

In the classroom, the challenge for students is to recognize the necessity of understanding and valuing members in our diverse workforce as the business environment becomes more global. As instructors, we can assist our students by providing opportunities for activities and projects that will help them learn about other cultures and explore various dimensions of diversity.

References

Boxall, B. (1997, July 7). A New Era Set to Begin in Benefits for Gay Couples. *Los Angeles Times*, A3.

Davis, S. (1996). Building Global Understanding Through E-Mail Exchanges: The Stereotypes Project. *Microsoft (MSN) Encarta Schoolhouse Lesson Plan*. [Online]. Available: http://encarta.msn.com/alexandria/templates/lessonFull.asp?page=454.

Dogar, R. (1998, February). Nineteenth Annual Salary Report [Sidebar: Bigger Is Better]. *Working Woman*, 25.

Federal Glass Ceiling Commission. (1995, March). *Good for Business: Making Use of the Nation's Human Capital: The Environmental Scan*. [Fact-Finding Report]. Washington, DC: Federal Glass Ceiling Commission.

Fiore, F. (1997, November 26). Full-Time Moms a Minority Now, Census Bureau Finds. *Los Angeles Times*, A1, 22.

Gallaher, J., and Bull, C. (1992, November 3). California Enacts Rights Legislation. *Advocate*, 18–19.

Holt, Margaret. (1998, December 30). [Telephone interview].

Jardim, A., and Hennig, M. (1990). The Last Barrier: Breaking Into the Boys' Club at the Top. *Working Woman*, 130–134.

Johnston, W. B., and Packer, A. H. (1987). *Workforce 2000*. Indianapolis, IN: Hudson Institute.

Kane, K. (1997, October). It's a Small World [Sidebar: Think Global, Market Local]. *Working Woman*, 22.

Katz, J. N. (1992). *Gay American History: Lesbians amd Gay Men in the USA: A Documentary History*. New York, NY: Plume.

Keddington, P. (1994, May). We Live in an International Community. *AskERIC Lesson Plan #AELP-GGR0037*. [Online]. Available: http://ericir.syr.edu/Virtual/Lessons/Social_St/Geography/GGR0037.html.

LaPlante, M.P. (1992, June). *How Many Americans Have a Disability? — Disability Statistics Abstract #5*. [Online]. Available: http://dsc.ucsf.edu/abs/ab5.html.

Loden, M., and Rosener, J. B. (1991). *Workforce American!* Homewood, IL: Business One Irwin.

Minehan, M. (1997, May). The Fastest-Growing U.S. Ethnic Groups. *HR Magazine*, 160-161.

Nordstrom. (1996). *Tapestry*. [Newsletter, first ed.]. Los Angeles, CA: Nordstrom.

O'Neil, S. L. (1998, April). An Empowered Attitude Can Enhance Communication Skills. *Business Education Forum*, 52 (4), 28-30.

O'Neil, S. L. (1998, December 23). [Telephone interview].

Raisfeld, R.D. (1998). Human Resource Implications of Diversity Programs. *Dangers in Litigation of Corporate Diversity Programs*. [Online]. Available: http://www.orrick.com/news/emplaw/diverse/3.htm.

Riccucci, N. M. (1997, Spring). Cultural Diversity Programs to Prepare for Workforce 2000: What's Gone Wrong? *Public Personnel Management*, 26 (1), 35-41.

Richard, O. C. (1997, June). Cross-National Human Resource Diversity as Value Added: The Contingent Role of International Strategy. *Mid-Atlantic Journal of Business*, 93–101.

Rundles, J. (1997, July). The Multicultural Corporation. *Colorado Business Magazine*, 24 (7), SS12-16.

Silverstein, S. (1997, April 27). Job Prospects Look Hot for 'Geezer Boomers' in *2020*. *Los Angeles Times*, D1.

Solomon, C. M. (1996, April). Big Mac's Mcglobal HR Secrets. *Personnel Journal*, 75 (4), 46-54.

Taylor III, A. (1997, September 8). My Life as a Gay Executive. *Fortune*, 106-110.

The Numbers Don't Lie. (1998, September). *Working Woman,* 61.

Tri-Comm Enterprises. (1997). Diversity in Action. *Diversity/Careers in Engineering and Information Technology.* [Online]. Available: http://www.diversitycareers.com/ diversity/prof/aprmay97/divact.htm.

Tri-Comm Enterprises. (1997). Diversity in Education. *Diversity/Careers in Engineering and Information Technology.* [Online]. Available: http:// www.diversitycareers.com/diversity/coll/sumfall97/divedu.htm.

Wentling, R. (1998). Diversity Initiatives in the Workplace. [Online]. Available: http:// ncrve.berkeley.edu/cw82/diversity.html.

Chapter 12 — Partnership Building and Ideas for Applied Learning Projects

Cynthia Redmond
Bozeman High School
Bozeman, Montana

Byrdeen Warwood
School District No. 7
Bozeman, Montana

Partnerships are creative unions that go well beyond the typical business agreement used to teach basic accounting principles. As discovered by the Teesside Industrial Technology Partnership (1997), partnerships create bridges among schools, communities, parents, and the workplace by recognizing that these entities have similar missions and goals:

- Establishing a solid base for and improvement of teaching.

- Supporting development of concepts such as teamwork, problem solving, and decision making at an earlier age.

- Encouraging higher levels of learning through working with real-life applications.

- Developing fresh and fluid teaching styles that "link" with other systems.

- Creating a climate in which all players can gain confidence, enhance communication skills, and increase self-esteem.

- Involving all players to create ownership of the project.

- Reinforcing the idea that partnership—and learning—activities are both interesting and fun.

- Fulfilling needs, directives, and goals of the school and community at large.

Active participation in partnerships can help students develop skills in communication, problem solving, and interpersonal relations. Partnerships can in turn attract a wide variety of people who give participants even greater opportunity to grow in social, business, and economic competencies—and to understand how heretofore "separate" parts of the community are, in fact, connected.

Whether between business and schools, schools and communities, or community schools within different geographic regions, partnerships offer students first-hand experience in taking learning beyond the classroom and into real-world contexts. Learning based on practical experience produces lasting effects in other decision-making situations. Students exercise higher-order thinking skills and learn the Z-shaped skills—that is, the skills necessary to function across varied situations and contexts—that are so vital to today's and tomorrow's businesses (Meister, in Gary, 1998). Finally, because partnerships foster personal and societal responsibility, students are able to develop and practice personal leadership skills.

Successful educational/business/community partnerships reflect well-strategized planning that articulates distinct outcomes for student success. All components of the partnership must necessarily be identified, present, and active in order for true partnership benefits to occur.

Components of Effective Partnerships

Participants committed to the vision. Educators, parents, students, nonprofit agencies, corporations, government agencies, service organizations, senior citizens, grant-making entities—any and all of these groups can form successful partnerships. All that is needed is a commitment to the envisioned outcome of the partnership and a desire to work collaboratively to make that vision a reality.

Potential participants include not only those with similar interests but also those who will inspire those standing on the periphery. The accurate and timely identification and inclusion of prospective partners cannot be overstated. Whether the partner is a student, the parent of a student, the Rotary Club president, or the CEO of a multimillion dollar business, all share equitable responsibility for the development, promotion, and implementation of the partnership. Partners not only bring a list of needs to the table but also offer resources that will benefit the overall goal and direction of the partnership. The bottom line is that all partners benefit from the arrangement.

Clearly defined goals and activities. "A partnership is a mutually supportive arrangement between a business and a school or school district, often in the form of a written contract in which the partners commit themselves to specific goals and activities intended to benefit students" (McDonald et al., 1990).

All participants in the partnership define needs, develop objectives, identify resources, agree on the administrative structure of the partnership, set the rules and regulations under which it functions, identify resources, create implementation strategies, and assess results. Together they describe the level of interaction between partners, the role each is expected to play, and the wish list of dreams, hopes, and expectations each wants to fulfill and have fulfilled. Each player contributes, and each player benefits.

Appropriate and mutually agreed-upon time lines. The National Association of Partners in Education (NAPE) recommends a 12-step process for creating a partnership uniquely suited to the schools and businesses in a specific community. The process includes awareness, needs assessment, resources, goals, design, management, recruitment, assignment, orientation, training, retention, and evaluation (NAPE, 1999).

The design, development, and implementation of partnership activities demand year-round attention. Proper planning necessarily requires allowing enough time for needs, interests, and activities to be assessed and addressed. Identification of specific strategies for achieving the partnership's goals can be accomplished through work committees and/or advisory groups throughout the year.

Partnerships may be single- or multi-year engagements. A suggested cycle for a one-year partnership, based on the school-year cycle of August through June, appears in Table 1.

Choice of appropriate settings. Learning occurs anywhere there is a "teachable" moment. Depending on the project, necessary equipment and other resources must be available and readily accessible. This means any environment—classroom, workplace, community areas—can and should be considered as a potential site for the fulfillment of partnership projects.

Thorough and detailed planning processes. It might be surprising to realize that most, if not all, components for partnerships are already in place; players need to "walk down the hall," so to speak, and talk, agreeing, for example, on one appropriate project.

Organizing meeting places and times acceptable to the majority of participants is critical. Creating agenda items that are meaningful and that will fulfill partnership goals is another important element of effectively launching a successful partnership. It is also desirable, if possible, to have one person

Table 1. Suggested Time Line for a One-Year Partnership	
Date	**Task to Complete**
Prior to summer	Identify need; determine mission and goals; canvass potential business, community, agency, or education partners.
By late summer	Target and commit resource materials, projects, and staff.
By October	Complete all training, if necessary; acquire project materials; finish necessary reporting.
October-December	Fine-tune project details.
December	Activate partnership.
June	Celebrate accomplishments.

responsible for facilitating partnership endeavors and another person assigned to the task of record keeping, whether for recording meeting minutes, noting group decisions or brainstorming items on flipcharts, or for creating general correspondence, if needed.

When players agree to a goal or project, it is important to assign participants specific responsibilities, such as who will be responsible for materials, resources, etc.; and to develop a time line that will facilitate the details of goal and/or project development. It is suggested that players create an implementation agreement, outlining project particulars. To determine if the project fulfilled intended goals, solicit, record, and report feedback from all participants. To improve the project process, implement follow-up activities that will build on perceived strengths and indicate the lasting implications for future and/or ongoing partnerships.

Organizations such as Future Force 2000, the National Association of Partners in Education, and School-to-Work offer additional planning resources to teachers who wish to engage in partnership activities (see Table 2).

Case Study: Real-World Partnership Articulation in School District 7, Bozeman, Montana

In a work-oriented society, education ought to be goal-oriented and lead to a practical outcome. That is why the partnership connection among schools, businesses, and community is so important. Partnerships let students apply their learning in a real-world context and appreciate the connections among school, the workplace, and society. Following are some examples of how this has been achieved in School District 7.

Connecting high school and elementary school students. Students in Bozeman High School's computer applications course participate in a longstanding project that connects their high school and the local elementary school.

Table 2. Resources for Planning Partnerships

Future Force 2000 (NY Vocational Training Center), Staten Island, NY; 718-273-8200; http://www1.k12.nycenet.edu/stw/stwhtmls/future.htm.

National Association of Partners in Education, Alexandria, VA; 703-836-4880;http://www.PARTNERSINEDUCATION.org

National School-to-Work Learning and Information Center, Washington, DC; 800-251-7236; http://www.stw.ed.gov/. For publications about partnerships/collaborations, go to http://www.stw.ed.gov/Database/productSubject1.cfm.

School-to-Career Resource Center, Denver, CO; (303) 861-8661; http://www.stcresource.org/index.htm. For checklist of results and descriptors, go to http://www.stcresource.org/infrastr.htm.

The project began several years ago and concerned the implementation of technology and how it could be applied. The high school students, who continually work with new hardware and learn new and upgraded software programs, sought a project that would let them apply what they were learning and integrate that learning with student projects in local elementary schools.

The high school, therefore, invited local elementary schools to participate in an integrated learning project. A third grade class accepted the invitation and completed a writing project in which they created autobiographies and submitted them to the high school students for editing and "finish work." The high school students asked the elementary students to submit a picture of themselves that could be scanned and placed in the finished document. The high school students also incorporated a paragraph or two about themselves into the document, along with information about the computer applications class.

This partnership has expanded to include several different writing projects connecting elementary and high school students. For example, a fourth grade class wrote letters to Santa Claus. The letters were answered by high school students on letterhead they designed.

Connecting students, law enforcement agencies, and the community. In 1995, Gallatin County District Court Judge Larry Moran called a meeting of community people who were concerned about the steady increase of cases coming before the youth court. Bozeman Public Schools worked with Judge Moran, the Youth Probation Office, law enforcement staff, and the Gallatin County Attorney's Office to determine the merit of pursuing the development of a Court of Peer Review. After appropriate investigation and discussion, a model for such a court was designed and implemented.

The Court of Peer Review lets juveniles serve in a serious citizenship role, one that promotes responsibility and accountability—they become part of the juvenile justice system. Once a juvenile offender has admitted guilt or has been adjudicated guilty, a jury of juveniles is convened for the purpose of recommending an appropriate disposition to the Youth Court Judge—by jury "verdict." The District Judge considers that recommendation, along with recommendations from the Youth Probation Office and the County Attorney's office, in deciding the ultimate disposition of the case. By receiving the juvenile jury's advisory "verdict" from the Court of Peer Review proceedings, the Youth Court Judge will have added to the sentencing process the ideas, insight, and perceptions of the offender's peers.

The main objective in establishing the Court of Peer Review was to create a real forum that could effectively exert "peer pressure" through a procedure easily administered in a short time. Six jurors are summoned, advised of the facts, permitted to ask questions, then allowed up to 40 minutes to reach a verdict.

Several cases have been brought to hearing, incorporating jury verdicts in "dispositional orders." These orders immediately launched the process of amending and fine-tuning procedures on a case-by-case review and ultimately culminated in Judge Larry Moran's *Court of Peer Review General Order and Practice and Procedure Manual.* As part of this process, a jury pool of more than 200 prospective volunteer jurors from several high school classes (business law students look forward to being selected) has been developed, and more than a dozen members of the Gallatin County Bar Association agreed to preside over cases as Judges Pro Tempore.

The Court of Peer Review is now fully operational. Communication has been established among the Court, the schools, the students, and the community regarding issues of general public concern as they relate to juvenile behavior.

Connecting with School-to-Work (STW) programs. Seven middle school and two high school teachers have been matched to pilot a Business-in-Residence program in Bozeman. Together, a local businessperson and a classroom teacher will develop opportunities to explore, with students, all aspects of a business and a career. A partnership handbook that provides guidelines and expectations for teachers and businesspeople working together as partners has been developed. The handbook will be used at all grade levels, elementary through secondary.

Coordinated efforts between Bozeman's two middle schools and the business community will allow all eighth grade students to participate in a job-shadowing experience. A local philanthropic organization is driving and supporting this endeavor.

Plans are also underway for a Teens & Tourism/Youth Leadership Bozeman summer camp. A team representing various components of the community (students, teachers, Bozeman Chamber of Commerce, Bozeman Job Service, and others) will attend training to help develop the camp. The desired outcome is for students to become better prepared for the service industry.

Connecting across the curriculum. Junior and senior English classes at Bozeman High School are collaborating on two projects with the Computer Application I and II classes.

In the first project, computer class students instruct English class students on how to utilize presentation software. The English class students must then create a presentation, for a community service organization, utilizing the software. Before "going live" at the community service organization, the English class students first practice, using the computer class students as their audience. Students in the computer application classes evaluate the presentation and slide show (see Table 3).

In the second project, the computer classes help the English classes create a simple Web page. Students use basic Hypertext Markup Language (HTML) and Microsoft FrontPage 97 software. Since the Internet is probably one of the fastest-moving media ever to infiltrate popular culture, this project is an appropriate one to enhance students' use of the Web and orient them to the future possibilities of this communications tool. The evaluation tool used for this project is shown in Table 4.

Table 3. Evaluation of PowerPoint Presentation

	Excellent	Good	Fair
INTRODUCTION			
Effective title	☐	☐	☐
Effective graphics/design	☐	☐	☐
BODY			
Successful coverage/development of:			
five slides	☐	☐	☐
one slide per section	☐	☐	☐
appropriate topics selection	☐	☐	☐
appropriate graphics	☐	☐	☐
CONCLUSION			
Effective/positive conclusion	☐	☐	☐
PRESENTATION			
Appropriate for wide audience	☐	☐	☐
Appealing both in text and graphics	☐	☐	☐
Preparation:			
awareness of audience	☐	☐	☐
delivery	☐	☐	☐

COMMENTS

_____

_____

_____

_____

Partnering with adult education instructors. Bozeman High School's computer applications class students learn to use Microsoft Office 97—learning Word, Excel, Access, PowerPoint, and Outlook. Bozeman's adult education customers take classes that teach each component of the Microsoft Office 97 program. Because of high enrollment in the Word and Excel classes offered for adults, a teacher assistant was needed to help adults who might be having problems or who just needed a jump start to stay on task with the instructor. Two students from the Computer Applications I class filled the teacher assistant positions. The students applied their knowledge of the software, and the adults received help in implementing the instructor's lessons.

Connecting across state boundaries. Bozeman High School computer application students use the Internet to correspond with sophomore English

Table 4. Evaluation of Web Page Design

	Excellent	Good	Fair
INTRODUCTION			
Effective title	❑	❑	❑
Effective graphics/design	❑	❑	❑
BODY			
Successful coverage/development of:			
seven topics	❑	❑	❑
explanation of each event and its significance	❑	❑	❑
clear relationship between text and graphics	❑	❑	❑
CONCLUSION			
Effective/positive summation	❑	❑	❑

students from Coldwater High School in Coldwater, Ohio. The purpose of this project is to use technology to encourage students to learn about places, communities, schools, and cultures outside their direct experience.

The project began as a simple Internet correspondence project and expanded into a video project. Students in each classroom decided that simply exchanging digital photos of themselves through the Internet was not enough. The students wanted to show one another what each school looked like and what the towns and communities were all about. Each school's students made a video and edited it using the computer. They dubbed in music for effect. The videos showed the school layout, classrooms, and programs, and introduced each student involved in the production. The video then showed the town's interesting attractions along with activities the students like to do outside of school. The two schools then exchanged videos.

Partnering with the business department. Bozeman High School's business department wanted to develop a logo and slogan that would define the essence and purpose of the department and which could be printed on all departmental documents. Because the department wanted to encourage student involvement in the project, teachers devised a contest inviting students to create and submit a logo and slogan. The submissions were judged on the following criteria:

- Graphics must be simple and easy to reproduce.

- Slogans should be short and to the point.

- The logo and slogan would be suitable for use on all documents in the business department including letterhead, newsletters, progress reports, and curriculum of study.

- The graphic should send a message of what the business department is all about.

The project inspired much competition and collaboration among the students.

Connecting with the world of work. The Bozeman High School business department is currently working on implementing a program that is already operating in 22 states. This program involves changing the ways students learn, setting targeted learning concepts in a work-based environment and integrating them across traditional disciplines. Students who participate in the program experience what it is like to work in a real business office and be treated as employees.

The centerpiece of this simulation is the Company. The integrated learning environment promotes the skills necessary to succeed in a competitive, higher-learning environment such as a college or university and emphasizes the employ-ability skills required for attaining a job or developing a career.

The Company simulates a computerized electronic office and prepares students for the challenges and rewards they will encounter in the real world. Using the latest technology, employees work toward mastering competencies in a chosen area (for example: business management, computer applications, desktop publishing, financial records, information processing, and office support technology). The employees' work is self-directed (within param-eters), and they do not progress to the next level until they have successfully completed a competency.

Universities and employers want people who know their individual capabilities; who are dependable, self-motivated, independent, and organized; and who possess and command good communication skills. Employees must be able to apply these abilities, attributes, and skills in a variety of situations. The Company simulation gives students the opportunity to implement the knowledge and practice the skills—specifically communication, problem solving, and teamwork—that make employees attractive to high-performance companies. Student-employees in the simulation will be exposed to such topics as time management, dressing for success, psychology of achievement, job resumes, interview techniques, and telephone etiquette. They will also interact with guest speakers from the business world.

All facets of the program will be built into the company structure and all subjects will be taught in one classroom setting, thus minimizing scheduling conflicts.

Summary

Expansion of partnership projects should be considered any time partners and projects can be combined to promote applied learning that can be transferred to other aspects of life—now and in the future. Reviewing other technology partnerships of varying types and levels indicates that much can be learned from participating in partnerships (for further information, see Chapter 13, "Corporate Relationships With Business Education Programs," by Terry D. Roach).

It is important to remember that partnerships do not live by goodwill alone. They require hard work, good management, deep commitment, clear communication, and attitudes of inclusiveness and personal/societal responsibility. In examining the prospects and origins of business education partnerships, McDonald et al. (1990) concluded that "Well-constructed partnerships ... are a good response to concerns Americans feel about education." There are three basic concerns. First, almost all future jobs will require a high degree of literacy and critical thinking skills. Second, schools cannot alone solve the problems associated with recent and pervasive social and economic changes in American life. Third, schools require assistance to prepare America's students to participate in businesses that must compete in the international marketplace. Technological development, McDonald et al. (1990) emphasize, is directly dependent on the knowledge, expertise, and leadership of the workforce.

When resources are combined to meet the identified needs and concerns of a community, everyone wins, especially students. This is the measurement of success.

References

Gary, L. (1998, October). Corporate Universities: The New Pioneers of Management Education (an interview with Jeanne Meister, author of *Corporate Universities: Lessons in Building a World-Class Work Force).* Harvard Management Update. Reprint #U9810B. [Online]. Available: http://www.hbsp.harvard.edu/educators/index.html.

McDonald, Merenda, Spinner, Sysak, Tangeman, Walker, Yuan. (1990). *Business & Education: A Practical Guide to Creating and Managing a Business/Education Partnership.* Alexandria, VA: National Association of Partners in Education, p. 7.

Moran, L. W. (1996). *The Court of Peer Review General Order and Practice and Procedure Manual.* Bozeman, MT: Eighteenth Judicial District Court, Department II.

National Association of Partners in Education (NAPE). (1999). Twelve-Step Partnership Process. [Online]. Available: http://www.napehq.org/4.html.

The Teesside Industrial Technology Partnership. (1997). Teesside Industrial Technology Partnership. [Online]. Available: http://www.aesnet.demon.co.uk/tip.htm 1997.

Chapter 13 — Corporate Relationships With Business Education Programs

Terry D. Roach
Arkansas State University—Jonesboro
Jonesboro, Arkansas

Businesses and schools form partnerships for mutual benefit. Though philanthropic motives draw many employers to initiatives such as School-to-Work programs, others participate out of self-interest, for example, to access a pool of qualified workers (Olson, 1998).

The need a partnership is designed to serve determines the form a partnership takes. Alliances may be modest one-to-one local initiatives or comprehensive collaborations that involve multiservice organizations with long-term commitments based on a shared vision, mission, and goals. Contracts or other agreements that outline the partnership's purposes and goals are signed by representatives of all parties. Goals may include the following: curricula revisions, apprenticeship or internship programs, classroom presentations, participation in career days, site tours, faculty externships, and donations of cash and/or equipment. These partnerships will become increasingly important to both groups during the 21st century (Zimmerer and McIntire, 1996).

Projected cuts in federal funding and recent business trends such as mergers may threaten the existence of business-education partnerships or cause them to re-emerge in another form, perhaps bundled with other school-reform initiatives (Kubota, 1993). Facilitating partnerships and encouraging projects that "enhance curriculum and facilitate a framework for teaching the competencies that are the intellectual barter of the new workplace" (Public Education and Business Coalition, 1998) will be among the challenges business educators face in the 21st century.

History of Corporate Partnerships

Businesses and schools have been involved with each other since the late 1800s, although public calls for education reform acted as a catalyst to formalize the relationship. Three factors—the education crisis in the public schools, the low skill levels of entry-level workers, and the demands of an evolving economy—caused partnerships to more than triple between 1984 and 1987 (Grobe et al. in Lankard, 1995).

Traditionally, schools were seen as the primary beneficiaries of business-education partnerships. Businesses most often provided local schools with guest speakers, special demonstrations, or use of their facilities; special awards, scholarships, or incentives for students; and curriculum supplements and equipment such as computers. In return, businesses benefited from enhanced goodwill and community relations. Today, businesses look for bigger returns, often in the form of benefits that improve their operations, productivity, and bottom line.

Examples of Corporate Involvement With Business Education

Just as types of partnership vary, so, too, do the level and kind of interaction between the partners. Whether the alliance is a one-to-one partnership, a jointly planned and governed cooperative agreement, or a comprehensive collaboration, each tends to focus in one or more of four major areas: classroom teaching and learning; vocational education program development; apprenticeships; and work experience programs (Lankard, 1995).

Businesses may work indirectly with students, by providing equipment or scholarship incentives, or directly, in training programs, internships, or preceptorships. They may work with teachers to plan integrated academic and vocational courses or include them in work experience initiatives specifically geared to bring them into the business world. Or businesses may work to improve their own practices and systems by employing the services of educators in human resource departments or corporate university settings.

Specific examples of corporate relationships with business education are described below.

Partnerships that exchange goods or services. Businesses may donate cash or equipment, award scholarships, provide educational materials and specific training, and sponsor other student activities. Local schools, in turn, allow businesses to call on the expertise of their faculty, offer use of the school plant for meetings or other functions, and connect them with students who will be prospective employees. In successful business-education alliances, benefits radiate from one partner to another, resulting in rewards for all constituencies: business, education, higher education, parents, and communities (Lankard, 1995).

Groups like the Business Economics Education Foundation (BEEF) in Minneapolis, Minnesota, for example, piloted projects that combined the efforts of educational institutions, government, social service organizations, and companies such as General Mills, Ecolab, and 3M. BEEF community volunteers aimed to help students improve their understanding and attitude toward business as well as help them better prepare for their futures. An offshoot of the program, Classroom Plus, coordinates speakers and tours and provides articles and videos to supplement business, economics, and career curricula (Business Economics Education Foundation, 1999).

H & R Block, Wal-Mart, Boatman's Bank, and Coca-Cola Distributors are among the many corporations that make scholarships available for students in financial need. These businesses hope to recoup their investments by hiring the recipients upon graduation. The expectation is simple: a better-educated employee makes a better candidate for job promotions and long-term employment.

Other corporations make industry-specific learning opportunities available to students. Lincoln Industries (Booneville, Indiana) and Allegiance Health Care Systems (McGaw Park, Illinois), for example, have identified particular schools in which to invest money, time, employees, and equipment to prepare students for specific job functions in their industries. The intent of these programs is to train students using specific company software, databases, and product information. When the students complete these training programs, the companies hire them.

Another example of what can arise from a successful partnership between the business community and business educators is the Industry Certification Program (ICP). The Atlanta Chapter of the Society for Human Resource Management and the Alabama Business Education Advisory Committee worked with business educators to describe competencies characteristic of quality instructors and effective business education programs (Yelverton, 1996). Business education programs seeking to become ICP-certified must meet specific requirements that involve instruction, equipment and facilities, learning resources, instructional staff, student organizations, administrative services, advisory committees, and related services (Yelverton, 1996, p. 9). Schools that obtain ICP certification receive the "stamp of approval" from the business community and are recognized for developing a curriculum and a workforce to meet employers' needs.

Integration of academic and vocational courses. Businesses continue to insist that students develop excellent skills in communication, problem solving, interpersonal relations, computer applications, and business ethics. By integrating the curricula of traditional academic courses with vocational/technical courses, students have a greater opportunity to develop these important abilities (Schmidt, 1996). Businesses are willing to help develop courses that support an integrated curriculum.

It is important for teachers to meet and discuss course objectives from academic and vocational perspectives. By working together, teachers will help one another formulate a curriculum that includes the best methods, objectives, and components for all courses. Flexibility in defining what constitutes education, who will provide it, and how to assess it will be needed (Stone, 1991, p. 12).

A precursor of such an integrated system was established in Germany. The dual apprenticeship-vocational education program combines formal apprenticeships with vocational education and is jointly operated and financed by private industry and the government. A student spends one day/week in school and four days/week on the job. Schools use uniform curricula developed jointly with industry representatives to ensure consistent training. The government also maintains technical training centers to supplement what employers provide. After three years of training and passing both a written and a hands-on exam, apprentices become journeymen with nationally recognized credentials (Stone, 1991, p. 10).

Job shadowing, internships, work/cooperative agreements, and service learning. Employers work directly with students when they sponsor job shadowing experiences, internships, part-time jobs, apprenticeships, and other cooperative work agreements with local schools.

The Greater Washington Society of Association Executives (GWSAE), for example, partners with schools in Washington, DC, to participate in National Groundhog Job Shadow Day. Every year, on February 2, students arrive at workplaces nationwide to shadow adults and learn about careers, industries, and the world of work. Students observe and share the responsibilities of volunteers whose occupation reflects the student's career interest. Volunteers provide first-hand information and direct experience about the specific requirements, benefits, and challenges of their career choices.

A "deeper" version of the job shadow is the internship. Internships may be paid or nonpaid agreements. Their intent is to provide on-the-job training for potential employees and "lend" the company an extra employee at minimal or no cost. D'Arcy, Masius, Benton & Bowles, a New York-based advertising conglomerate, is one company that offers more than 70 percent of its interns positions after graduation (Tooley, 1997).

High school student interns typically wait until their senior year before being admitted to internship programs. However, at state-funded metropolitan Regional Career and Technical Center in Providence, Rhode Island, public high school students begin in ninth grade to work with teachers and their parents to construct individual learning plans centered around workplace projects based on adult roles, careers, and issues they want to explore. This school-to-work project uses real-world contexts to teach rigorous academics, higher-order thinking skills, and interdisciplinary competencies (Steinberg, 1998).

Students also learn about work through a program called service learning in which they study for specific careers by working a specified number of hours for service agencies. Work sites include nursing homes, schools, public health offices, state and local government offices, and day care centers. Service learning agreements, developed between the local school and the business, usually include such components as the methods of monitoring student learning and evaluation, the expectations of the student and work site supervisor, liability agreements, and learning objectives.

Preceptorship. Though a preceptorship resembles an internship, there are striking differences. A preceptorship requires that a student be assigned to a cooperating supervisor who has earned at least a master's degree in the specific field of study for the preceptorship. Thus, learning outcomes are more stringent and written at a higher level of responsibility than those for regular internships.

Because students in preceptorships may be involved in difficult decision-making situations and receive more authority than is normally allowed in other cooperative agreements, preceptorships are usually offered only to students enrolled in programs at the baccalaureate level or beyond. Students who successfully complete a preceptorship are usually considered first-choice employees for higher-than-entry-level positions (Alford, July 1998).

Teacher-in-the-workplace initiatives. Like work experience programs that match students to mentors in specific businesses, teacher-in-the-workplace programs such as the San Francisco Bay Area's Industry Initiatives for Science and Mathematics have placed teachers in summer employment programs designed to enhance their professional development and directly affect the way they teach. These programs expose teachers to new technologies, give them authentic work with real-world business problems, and help them transfer work experiences into the classroom. Other programs such as University of Washington's Ford Fellows Science/Mathematics Project prepare teacher leaders to act as change agents in their school systems (Kubota, 1993).

Students have benefited from such programs as teachers introduce updated business content into the curriculum, increase the use of computers in the classroom, and seek ways to maintain connections to the business in which they worked. Businesses gain a new appreciation for teachers' skills in organizing, setting objectives, and communicating (Kubota, 1993).

Human resources/corporate universities. Education for employees is a growing concern for corporations and is predicted to be a substantial part of all business budgets for the immediate next decade (Webber, 1996). Many businesses have established education directorates within their human resource departments so that employees can benefit from training they provide. Orbit Value, Little Rock, Arkansas and Hytrol Conveyor Company, Inc., Jonesboro, Arkansas, for example, offer many in-house education programs geared specifically toward job training or personal enrichment.

Traditional training has been criticized as being reactive and decentralized, thus more forward-thinking companies are replacing training departments with corporate universities. In corporate universities, the curriculum involves training in workplace competencies such as technological and global business literacy, creative problem solving, and leadership development, but also includes courses that develop "Z-shaped skills"—cross-functional abilities that are vital in contemporary business (Meister, in Gary, 1998).

Corporate universities rely on mentoring to meet educational objectives, emphasizing a holistic approach to learning with technology as the tool that helps create a continuous learning community. They tend to be strategic in focus and use education and training to solve business issues and to improve job performance. For example, Southern Company in Atlanta, Georgia, used its corporate university to retrain managers in how to market its utility services in the competitive deregulated utility industry of the 21ˢᵗ century. And Sears relied on Sears University to engineer its recent turnaround (Meister, in Gary, 1998).

Characteristics of Model Programs

Not all business education programs, of course, take advantage of corporate involvement, but those that do share a number of characteristics. They are usually schools that have implemented Tech-Prep initiatives and School-to-Work processes, included business leaders in curriculum development, purchased appropriate computer technology, hired an appropriately trained and educated teaching staff, and updated business programs with annual reviews for improvement. Their teachers continually implement the latest technology into their programs and are up-to-date with respect to emerging legislation that affects education and evolving business trends. They continue to survey their stakeholders for employment needs, industry trends, and other demographics that may impact business education curricula.

Such educational environments make it more likely that businesses will continue to partner with schools to better ensure success for all. Merrill Lynch Financial Consultants and K-Mart, for example, provide funding as well as business and employee services to schools (Cofer, 1997). A model of how businesses can better "connect learning with earning" in School-to-Work-type programs was developed by the National Employer Leadership Council (see http://www.nelc.org/model-s.html).

Schools are developing better programs, and businesses are beginning to provide students with appropriate work experiences (Bunn, 1996). However, in the new economy, where school and work will be ever more entwined (Stone, 1991; Lankard, 1995), there will be a need for extending and creating new links among companies, students, and schools. As school reform efforts progress and standards continue to be raised, students will need more incentives to work hard, even beyond current scholarship and mentoring opportunities that now exist and have been proven successful. They will need to see that grades, not just performance in internships or other school/work cooperative agreements, matter (Stone, 1991, p. 9-10).

An example of an entity that evolved in this direction is the Boston Compact, established in 1982 to provide high quality education for all children in the Boston school system. Initially, the compact guaranteed a job for every high school graduate in exchange for the school board's commitment to raise student performance levels, yet there was no clear connection between the grades students earned and the jobs they eventually received. Later, however, a number of companies and schools agreed informally to use grades, teacher evaluations, and attendance to match students with white-collar jobs (Stone, 1991, p. 10).

Trends and Issues Influencing the Future of Business-Education Partnerships

Despite, or perhaps because of, the success of corporate involvement in education, controversy about business' role in America's schools has emerged. Critics say programs like School-to-Work "open the door to corporate control of the schools and narrow education to the preparation of worker drones" (Steinberg, 1998). Ironically, just when school reform efforts are making headway, corporate America's commitment to educational reform may be showing signs of strain (Walsh, 1998). Recent business trends, such as mergers, have resulted in less support for the initiatives of the merged companies.

In addition, federal funding for the School-to-Work Opportunities Act of 1994 will end in 2001, leaving the decision of whether to sustain School-to-Work efforts up to individual states (Zehr, 1998, December 2). Critics of School-to-Work perceive the program as separate from reform efforts to raise academic standards. Unless the program helps students score better on standardized tests, they say, the program will not receive much respect. Yet even experts disagree on the effectiveness of standardized tests (Zehr, 1998, July 8).

A hallmark of school reform is the call for authentic learning, however, and School-to-Work allows students to be "taken seriously in an enterprise worthy of adult concern"; the program doesn't "just get jobs for kids" but engages students in applied learning approaches as the intellectual and the practical are combined (Steinberg, 1998). Such programs are especially popular in urban settings, and their emphasis on certain key practices that contextualize curriculum, assessment, and pedagogy make an easier transition to the adult world of learning and work for all—not just vocational education—students (Steinberg, 1998).

If it is true that the worlds of school and work will be even more closely entwined in the 21st century, then one could reasonably expect more, not less, corporate involvement in education, perhaps in different forms or incorporated into other reform efforts (Kubota, 1993).

Considerations for Creating and Strengthening Effective Partnerships

Teachers who wish to engage in business-education partnerships may want to model their programs after "best practices" suggested by Jobs for the Future:

- Create a real-world context for rigorous academics emphasizing higher-order thinking skills.

- Expand academics to include problem-solving and interdisciplinary competencies.

- Extend learning beyond the classroom through internships, field-based investigations, and community projects. Engage adult mentors and coaches to work closely with students.

- Incorporate exposure for high-quality student products through exhibitions, portfolios, and other assessment vehicles informed by real-world standards (Steinberg, 1998).

The School-to-Career Resource Center in Denver, Colorado, offers guidelines for designing projects appropriate for partnership initiatives. According to its newsbrief, *Blueprints,* projects should be characterized by authenticity (Does the project originate from a problem or question that has meaning to the student, and is there a real audience for the result of the work?); adult relationships (Will students meet and work closely with at least one adult who has expertise in the problem at hand?); academic rigor (Will students develop the work habits necessary to complete complex tasks?); active learning (Is the learning inquiry-based?); and assessment (Have both adults and students collaborated on the criteria for success, and has time for reflection and self-assessment been built into the program?).

Business-education partnerships will continue to evolve. Creating a checklist of benchmarks and descriptors may prove useful to measuring and maintaining accountability. A complete description of an infrastructure to support and sustain a comprehensive school-to-career system is available from the School-to-Career Resource Center (http://www.stcresource.org/infrastr.htm). Overall, such a system allows for the following:

- Vesting ownership in all partners in the school-to-career system;
- Prioritizing school-to-career to accomplish the organization's mission;
- Implementing all components of the program across the system and community;
- Allowing all students to participate in the full range of school-to-career opportunities; and
- Documenting proven results to support the school-to-career initiative.

Summary

Businesses will increasingly rely on successful business education programs to supply the critical mass of trained employees for the future (Spinks, Wells, Duggar, and Mellington, 1996). Through cooperative agreements, corporations and business education programs have been successful in meeting the employment needs of business and in helping students prepare for their chosen careers (Penningwerth, 1997).

Businesses are becoming involved in school systems not only to help strengthen the educational infrastructure, but to develop career-ready students who will become better employees. Business educators must continue to discover ways to increase their students' potential for success. Work-based apprenticeship programs, internships, and other efforts to integrate academic and vocational learning can help prepare students to operate within systems that have interrelated business functions. As a result of such programs, students will enter the workforce with marketable skills in problem solving, critical thinking, teamwork, human relations, and work site protocol.

To prepare for the work environment, students must transcend curricular boundaries; accounting concepts, for example, must be applied to situations presented in management classes, and management skills must be used in marketing classes. Students need to recognize that the different aspects of their business courses in such areas as accounting, communication, marketing, and law contribute to a total educational experience that will enable them to solve problems, make decisions, and manage a business.

Federal funding and individual state vocational initiatives such as Tech-Prep and School-to-Work may act to support business-education partnerships and encourage projects that intertwine the worlds of school and work. Changes in funding sources and corporate priorities, and the emphasis on accountability in school reform, will challenge these objectives and may cause these programs to be reevaluated. By working with community and business leaders, parents and other major stakeholders, business teachers can build on the exemplary programs already developed and ensure positive, supportive agreements that help our nation's students succeed in the work-place of tomorrow.

References

Alford, L. (1998, July 12). Personal Interview. Mr. Alford is the Chief Financial Officer at St. Bernard's Hospital, Jonesboro, AR.

Bunn, P. C. (1996, Spring). School-to-Work: We've Been Doing This for Years. *SBEA Newsletter*, 9–10.

Business Economics Education Foundation (BEEF). (1999). About the Business Economics Education Foundation/Classroom Plus. [Online]. Available: http://www.beef-mn.org/about.htm and http://www.beef-mn.org/class.htm.

Cofer, B. (1997, November 23). Businessmen Make Schools Their Business. *Arkansas Democrat-Gazette*, pp. B1, B3.

Gary, L. (1998, October). Corporate Universities: The New Pioneers of Management Education (an interview with Jeanne Meister, author of *Corporate Universities: Lessons in Building a World-Class Work Force*). Harvard Management Update. Reprint #U9810B. [Online]. Available: http://www.hbsp.harvard.edu/educators/index.html.

Griffin, B. (Spring, 1996). School-to-Work Transition: America's Future? Yes, It Is. *SBEA Newsletter*, 8–9.

Kubota, C. (1993, March). Education-Business Partnerships: Scientific Work Experience Programs. Columbus, OH: ERIC Clearinghouse for Science, Mathematics, and Environmental Education. ERIC/CSMEE Digest ED359045. [Online]. Available: http://www.ed.gov/databases/ERIC_Digests/ed359045.html.

Lankard, B. A. (1995). Business/Education Partnerships. Columbus, OH: ERIC Clearinghouse on Adult, Career, and Vocational Education. Document ED383856 95. [Online]. Available: http://www.ed.gov/databases/ERIC_Digests/ed383856.html.

Olson, L. (1998, April 8). Study: More Student Interns Finding Work. Education Week on the Web. [Online]. Available: http://www.edweek.org/ew/vol-17/.

Penningwerth, P. L. (1997, December 8). Internships. *U.S. News & World Report*, 32.

Public Education and Business Coalition (PEBC). (1998). Linking Business and Education. [Online]. Available: http://www.pebc.org/business.htm.

Schmidt, B. J. (1996, February). The Instructional Environment: Student Experiences in Business, Vocational, and Nonvocational Classes. *Business Education Forum*, 50 (3), 14–17.

School-to-Career Resource Center. (1998, October). Resource Highlight: from A. Steinberg's *Real Learning, Real Work*, New York, NY: Rutledge Press. Blueprints, 2 (1). [Online]. Available: http://www.stcresource.org/blueprin.htm.

Spinks, N., Wells, B., Duggar, J., and Mellington, B. (1996, April). Community Involvement: Business internship Programs. *Business Education Forum*, 50 (4), 27–30.

Steinberg, A. (1998, March 25). Trashing School-to-Work. Education Week on the Web. [Online]. Available: http://www.edweek.org/ew/vol-17/.

Stone, N. (1991, March-April). Does Business Have Any Business in Education? Harvard Business Review. Reprint #91209. [Online]. Available: http://www.hbsp.harvard.edu/educators/index.html.

Tooley, J. A. (1997, November 17). Working for Credit. How to Make the Most of a Semester-Long Internship. *U.S. News & World Report*, 76–78.

Walsh, M. (1998, April 1). Business Leaders Urged to Step Up Support for Schools. Education Week on the Web. [Online]. Available: http://www.edweek.org/ew/vol-17/.

Webber, A. M. (1996). Chris Turner of Xerox Business Systems Learns to Grow. *Fast Company*, 41–51.

Yelverton, S. (1996, Fall). Alabama Business Education Industry Certification Program. *SBEA Newsletter*, 9–10.

Zehr, M. A. (1998, July 8). Test Scores Loom over School-to-Work Programs. Education Week on the Web. [Online]. Available: http://www.edweek.org/ew/vol-17/.

Zehr, M. A. (1998, December 2). School-to-Work Movement Faces Test, Study Says. Education Week on the Web. [Online]. Available: http://www.edweek.org/ew/vol-18/.

Zimmerer, M. E., and McIntire, H. B. (1996, February). Business and Education in Partnership. *Business Education Forum*, 50 (3), 8-10.

Chapter 14 — Educating for Business: Keeping Pace With the Changing Marketplace

J. William Murphy
Winona State University
Winona, Minnesota

College business education programs have been eliminated in some areas of our country. In Minnesota, for example, only one of the seven state universities continues to offer an active undergraduate program leading to certification as a business educator. The demand in the upper Midwest for secondary business education teachers has dramatically increased from 64 openings in 1994-95 to 186 openings in 1998-99, according to statistics provided by the Placement Department at Winona State University (Decker, 1999). What, then, is the future for business education?

By its very nature, business—and business education—involve lifelong learning. New trends and technologies continue to affect how business is conducted, which markets it serves, and how it provides those services. Business educators, therefore, must stay in step with the fast-paced marketplace in order to align as closely as possible the skills taught to students with the demands of an ever-changing business environment.

Students want what they learn in school to be relevant to their future in the workplace, and business educators need to adjust content and teaching strategies accordingly. Further, teachers must balance what students want to learn with what the workplace needs them to know. Teachers who intend to prepare the most qualified workers face a difficult, but not impossible, task: looking beyond the classroom for opportunities to expand their expertise while providing real-life learning for their students.

Trends in the Workplace of Tomorrow: Corresponding Implications for Business Educators

Research conducted by the American Society for Training and Development

(ASTD) on the future of the training profession identified 10 trends that will likely also affect the future of business education. Awareness of these training trends will help business educators prepare for forthcoming and inevitable changes (Bassi, Benson, and Cheney, 1996). Six of theses trends have specific applications for business educators and are examined here.

1. The American workforce will be significantly more educated and diverse. The workplace of tomorrow will include more women and minorities; the marketplace in which future business operates will become increasingly more global. Between 1987 and 1992, the number of women-owned business firms increased 43 percent; they now represent 31 percent of all firms. Black-owned businesses rose by 46 percent; Hispanic by 82.7 percent; and Asian, Native American, Alaskan Native, and Pacific Islander by 87.2 percent (Small Business Administration, 1997). Total world trade increased from $629 billion (in 1995 dollars) in 1960 to $5 trillion in 1995 (Small Business Administration, 1998).

Trainers and business educators therefore need to understand and utilize instructional strategies that prepare students to operate in a global marketplace and teach them to accommodate diverse learning styles and cultures. Instructors will be called upon to teach current and future workers the skills needed to operate as part of a diverse workforce as well as help them recognize the benefits diversity brings to companies willing and ready to embrace it. (For additional information on this issue, please see Chapter 11, "Fostering a Diverse Workforce for Today's Global Marketplace.")

2. Corporate restructuring will continue to reshape the business environment. Neither today's nor tomorrow's employees can count on working for the same company until retirement. Between 1990 and 1996, the U.S. economy reinvented itself. "Rightsizing" replaced "downsizing." Restructuring led to a focus on core competencies, and firms outsourced business that was peripheral to those core competencies (Small Business Administration, 1998). From 1992–1996, almost all new jobs were generated by firms with less than 500 employees; microbusinesses with one to four employees generated 50.2 percent of those new jobs (Cognetics, Inc., in Small Business Administration, 1997).

The electronic age has affected where work is done and how it is accomplished. For example, businesses such as Motorola and IBM not only allow employees to work at home, but encourage it. The number of people working out of their homes is expected to continue to grow well into the next century and will spur a greater need for retraining (Klayton-Mi, 1999). In addition, trends in outsourcing reflect a respect for intellectual capital: large businesses are outsourcing research, product development, human relations, accounting, legal work, marketing, logistics, and market research (Outsourcing Institute, 1999).

When work is "distributed" outside the company, be it to contractors or to telecommuters, workers must develop and perfect skills in self- and time-management, organization, and interpersonal communication. They must maximize the potential of electronic communication tools such as e-mail, voice mail, and fax.

Business educators themselves must model using such tools effectively (including emerging conventions for related business etiquette [Okula, 1998]) so that they can enhance their students' use of these evolving technologies.

Social interaction, once a major feature of the work environment, will be less available. Workers may need to counter possible isolation by finding opportunities to socialize outside the office, perhaps in training sessions and other continuing education settings such as workshops, conferences, and professional associations.

3. Skill requirements will continue to increase in response to rapid technological change. Business, industry, and the service sector have been technologically driven since the advent of the computer. The Internet has revolutionized communication. Web pages attract immediate attention for a product or service while e-mail has provided employees, students, and homebound individuals with the ability to communicate quickly, conveniently, and economically. Teleconferences bring individuals together from remote locations, and training once confined to a classroom environment now takes place across the country via distance learning.

All these technological advances require new thought processes, systems, and procedures to achieve maximum effectiveness. Even so, they have not eliminated the need for basic skills or for human contact. Communication skills continue to be critical for success, and critical thinking and decision-making skills take on added importance. Individuals must be able to create analytical reports and interpret data. They must be able to work independently and as members of a team. As responsibility shifts further down the corporate ladder, line workers must demonstrate management and leadership skills as they contribute to business plans and develop proposals for new ventures or grants. As workers create their own small firms or sole proprietorships, they will need to rely on the critical thinking skills important to making realistic plans for innovative products or services (Graduate School for Industrial Administration, Carnegie Mellon University, 1999).

Worker training and development therefore continue to be areas of rapid growth. "Both in school and after our school years, we need to keep learning if we're going to grow jobs and keep jobs that will support our families in the challenging marketplace of the next century," stated Indiana Governor Frank O'Bannon in an announcement regarding state grants for training and retraining workers at three companies in Indiana (O'Bannon, 1997).

More and more companies are realizing the necessity of helping employees upgrade their skills. In a survey on the state of the training industry, ASTD found that most firms increased the amount of money they spent on individual employee training by $150 in 1996–97. However, leading-edge firms averaged increases of $300 per employee, believing that employee training enables their companies to remain competitive. Companies that invested the most in workplace learning reported higher net sales and gross profits per employee compared to companies that invested less in learning (ASTD, 1999).

4. Advances in technology will revolutionize the way training is delivered. Distance learning, the Internet, computer-assisted training (now enhanced by video technology and courseware authoring tools), and interactive CD-ROMs have created new opportunities and new challenges in how training is delivered.

Distance learning has expanded educational access, but requires high levels of interactivity to keep remote audiences focused and attentive. The Internet makes access to such resources as museums and libraries a simple click away, but raises the issue of "authenticating" information from the wealth of home pages that have been produced and registered on various search engines by educational institutions and individuals.

Business trainers and business education teachers will need to adopt appropriate strategies to maximize the power of these new training tools. For example, course syllabi can now be posted to Web pages. Students can e-mail assignments to instructors, who can then e-mail evaluations back. Classes can correspond with students and teachers in other parts of the country or the globe and internationalize their education.

Courses conducted over the Internet offer several advantages: the ability to make immediate updates to Web pages; the ease and cost-effectiveness of distributing course materials, and the convenience of adapting a course to the learner's schedule. Business education teachers preparing students for the lifelong learning requirements of the 21ˢᵗ century must make mining the variety of training media a natural part of the education process.

5. Training professionals will focus more on interventions in performance improvement. Leading-edge firms invest in technology and in the training that leads to high performance. (They also invest in management practices that lead to high performance: self-directed teams, access to business information, and innovative compensation and training practices.) Job-specific technical skills were the most frequent kind of training delivered, followed by management and supervision, computer literacy and applications, and professional skills training (ASTD, 1999).

Businesses understand that they need more skilled employees. They expect educators to teach the skills and knowledge that will enable students to perform effectively on the job. Recently, state legislatures have mandated standards required for graduation. Such standards have two purposes: (1) they measure abilities in the basic skills area; (2) they set expected outcomes deemed important for becoming contributing members of society. The phrase so often associated with education standards, "what students know and should be able to do," is itself performance-based.

As in business, classroom assessment and continual upgrading of skills will necessarily become ongoing rather than being end-of-project or end-of-term activities. Assessment is evolving from a paper-and-pencil exercise to a measure of the ability to perform certain tasks. For example, written and oral communication skills are evaluated on whether they "work," i.e., whether they accomplish their intention. Computer literacy is not evaluated by the ability to understand how a computer works, but rather by the ability to use it to gather information, manipulate data, and produce documents and reports.

6. Integrated high-performance work systems will proliferate. Companies are recognizing that their critical resources are people, education, and software (Outsourcing Institute, 1999). Successful organizations will tap their employees' commitment to mastering five skills identified by Peter Senge as essential to learning organizations: systems thinking, mental models, personal mastery, building shared vision, and team learning (Fricker and Wehrle, 1996, p. 3).

The challenge for business educators becomes finding more opportunities for students to develop these higher-order thinking skills and work cooperatively in decision-making and problem-solving activities. One approach is to use shared inquiry and case studies that involve students in group discussions of a selected text or specific subject. The instructor asks carefully prepared interpretive questions and guides discussion. Students learn to look at complex ideas from multiple perspectives, listen and respect the ideas of others, think on their feet, look for connections they might not have considered earlier, and articulate their ideas clearly (Fricker and Wehrle, 1996, pp. 5–6).

To foster team building (which will become increasingly important in the business education curriculum either as a unit in an existing course or as a stand-alone course) and lead to a better understanding of how teams function, instructors should use any activities that involve trust, interdependence, and cooperation. Successful teams are comprised of hard-working, effective individuals capable of developing the team spirit, camaraderie, and human relations skills needed to achieve their goals.

Distance education and other Internet outreach activities provide opportunities for collaborative work relationships among students from various classes and schools. For example, Project Globe (http://www.unc.edu/depts/cmse/programs/GLOBE.html) is a hands-on environmental science and education program that teams students, educators, and scientists from around the world in collecting observations and data for studying the global environment. Another project, Electronic Recycling in an Urban Environment (http://www.materials4future.org/computer.html), a pilot program of The Materials for the Future Foundation, involves students and other citizens in identifying electronic recycling and revenue-generating opportunities for local businesses.

The Challenge: Providing a Relevant Business Education Curriculum

The trends identified above and the nature of business as a continually evolving entity challenge business educators to reexamine how they can best modify the curriculum in order to prepare students to cope with a changing business environment. In addition to teaching specific performance-based skills, individuals educating students for business must focus on creating learning situations that accomplish the following:

- Celebrate and embrace the diversity characteristics of the emerging global economy;

- Expose students to strategies that will help them deal with constant changes in corporate environments and work performance standards;

- Demonstrate the value and need for lifelong learning;

- Take advantage of multimedia educational opportunities; and

- Introduce authentic, real-world projects that let students practice communication, teamwork, critical thinking, and decision-making skills.

Such reexamination of the curriculum will require educators to look beyond the classroom and align themselves more closely with the workplace to ensure that what they teach reflects current business trends. And because technology permeates not only business but also society and the home, they will need to stay in step with students' acquired skills (for example, their exposure to computers and the Internet) and necessarily adjust the agreed-upon scope and sequence of basic business skills. For example, because students are exposed to computers at younger and younger ages, the scope and sequence of learning at secondary and postsecondary levels will continue to change as students extend competencies developed at elementary or middle school levels.

Adapting certain business practices, such as goal-oriented work teams comprised of teachers from various grade levels and departments and partnerships with stakeholders such as the local business community, may assist this reevaluation of the business curriculum. In addition, to remain relevant in the 21ˢᵗ century and beyond, business educators must participate in ongoing professional development opportunities, such as becoming active members of business- and education-related professional organizations, reading trade publications, and staying in step with new developments in both business and training.

Developmental Issues in Adjusting Scope and Sequence

Coordination among educators at different grade levels is required to achieve the adjustments to curricula needed to prepare students for the workplace. Specific curricular issues are discussed below.

Elementary school. Although keyboarding is being taught as early as the third or fourth grades, the most frequent level is at grade five and involves preparing students for word processing and information retrieval (Jackson, 1991). Minnesota, in its *Profiles of Learning,* has mandated technology instruction that includes these same skills at the primary level (Minnesota Department of Children, Families, and Learning, 1997).

Correct keyboard techniques and mastery at an early age will lead to increased efficiency and improved skills later in life. The most immediate problem is ensuring that trained keyboarding professionals or elementary teachers receive the instruction in required keyboarding methodology (McLean, 1995). Reinforcement of techniques and development of speed and accuracy will become the focus of later keyboarding courses. To accomplish these goals, computer labs must replace the lone computer in elementary classrooms.

Middle school. Students should extend their basic keyboard learning and expand their computer proficiencies. Incorporating voice input with keyboard input will offer relevant options in some business applications. In addition, computer applications such as databases and spreadsheets should be taught to students finishing their elementary education or beginning their middle school years.

Teaching these applications should be grounded in relevant projects. For example, middle school students can learn to catalog their sometimes extensive collections of such items as sports cards or compact discs, using a database. Every textbook includes graphs and charts to depict relationships; students can increase their understanding of these concepts by creating their own graphs and charts relating to these collections or to other investigative learning projects. They can learn word processing concepts and applications to produce reports. Not only do such applications encourage interdisciplinary learning, they also make evaluation less time-consuming for teachers because the assignments are submitted in more legible form.

Middle school also lends itself to explorations in career awareness. Students can use e-mail and the World Wide Web to address questions such as educational requirements, certifications, and marketplace demand for professions in which they are interested.

Secondary level. Computer applications that allow students to apply earlier learning to more complex situations should be offered at this level. Hands-on activities that pertain to students' personal desires, career interests, or educational futures will help them understand these issues. Personal money management and consumer economics courses also provide students with the knowledge to use money wisely.

Project-based learning provides opportunities for students to see how varied and individual tasks can be important in solving a much larger real-world application. For example, concepts such as budgeting, insurance, and depreciation can be applied to students' real-world experiences, such as purchasing a first car. Multimedia, Internet research, oral and computer presentations, and data analysis—which all reflect real-world business applications—lend themselves to projects based on authentic student concerns.

Students will typically be interested in more in-depth career exploration at this stage, and many students want to start their own businesses after completing their education. However, most have had little or no exposure to entrepreneurship. Courses that explore the world of small business and entrepreneurial ventures offer another opportunity for interdisciplinary learning experiences, perhaps offering products or services in either a school-based business or a short-term entrepreneurial setting. Internet sites, such as *Entrepreneur Magazine* (http://www.entrepreneurmag.com) and the Mining Company's guide site for entrepreneurs (http://entrepreneurs.miningco.com/blwhat.htm?pid=2737&cob=home) offer additional content resources.

Partnerships between business and education should be established and nurtured whenever possible at this level. Every opportunity to work in the business environment will provide invaluable experiences that will transfer into the classroom, not only for students, but also for instructors. Indeed, one of the best ways for trainers and business educators to stay current is to become involved in the everyday workings of local businesses. (Chapter 12, "Partnership Building and Ideas for Applied Learning Projects," and Chapter 13, "Corporate Relationships With Business Education Programs," offer information and resources for incorporating partnerships into the business education curriculum.)

Involvement in partnership activities is an excellent way to demonstrate how business education disciplines—such as marketing, accounting, communications, and management—are integrated, rather than isolated, in the real business world. All jobs incorporate aspects of marketing, accounting, communications, and management principles—these topics should be connected rather than taught separately.

Making business courses attractive—and relevant—to students is a major task at the secondary level. New courses and attention-getting titles may interest students. Teachers must seize opportunities to create and sell new courses to the school board, administration, and students. To create these new courses, business educators must keep in touch with and involve local businesses so that courses reflect relevant and necessary business skills.

Postsecondary. Training for employment and/or continuing education becomes the focus at this level. Competencies consistent with the demands of business and industry are the expected exit standards for students, who must achieve or exceed expectations for entry-level employment. Computer skills, subject-matter skills, and the soft skills of human relations and work ethic are central to the curriculum.

Certificate programs and certifications, such as those offered by software companies to proficient users of their applications, should also be identified and offered to postsecondary students. Programs leading to certification are attractive not only to job-seeking individuals, but also to current employees anticipating either career changes or promotions.

Apprenticeship and mentoring programs can benefit both experienced professionals and trainees. The position of being an expert and sharing knowledge in a particular field can be especially rewarding to the mentor, and the interest invested by a mentor in a student can be instrumental in career development. In addition, these real-life experiences make textbook theories come alive.

Business education partnerships will again provide learning beneficial to businesses, students, trainers, and teachers. Employees may experience improved productivity and morale; students will learn more about current business practices; trainers and teachers may be offered training and consulting opportunities. Every consulting or training opportunity should be viewed not only as a financial opportunity, but also as a chance to grow professionally.

University level. Teaching the touch operation of the keyboard and basic computer skills may be phased out at this level. If students lack these essential competencies, they must remedy their situation through computer-assisted training or remedial work. Once students have achieved the basic skills, course work at the university level should require the application of these skills in case analysis, decision-making, and critical thinking exercises.

Knowledge of what will promote and improve human performance is vital. University students must recognize the importance of motivation, interpersonal relations, ethical behavior, leadership styles, systems, and communication in a culturally diverse global economy—and this understanding becomes a key mission in business education. In addition, being able to assume leadership responsibility, share knowledge with others, and continue to learn on the job so that an individual continues to grow with the company are equally important.

Teachers can model these concepts by becoming actively involved in professional organizations and in the community at large and then sharing these experiences with students. Teachers can also involve students in discipline-specific professional organizations by informing them of meetings, taking them along to conferences, and making sure that such conferences and conventions have sessions specifically tailored to students. Besides the obvious values of leadership and personal growth, these activities are beneficial for networking and for developing a perspective wider than one's desk.

Because the training market is expected to increase, the university level is an excellent place to provide courses in training and presentation skills. These courses will, in turn, expand students' career opportunities. For example, trainers are called upon to present sessions ranging from interpersonal relations to communications to computer applications. Students may be able to incorporate training courses into an existing minor.

Highly developed presentation skills and training techniques are essential for workers who may be called upon to brief managers or departmental directors, develop a marketing proposal, or conduct on-the-job training for staff. A course requiring oral presentations with accompanying visuals will provide aspiring trainers with an invaluable experience. Indeed, proficient use of presentation software should be a requirement. "Train the Trainer" courses should also instill the importance of creating a classroom environment in which learning is comfortable, enjoyable, and enriching. Resources that can be included in such courses are training games, icebreakers, and motivational exercises.

The need for business education will exist as long as there is a demand for skilled workers and managers. Business educators at the university level are in a good position to recruit prospective teachers and to be alert to the qualifications these future teachers will need in order to secure employment and become successful.

Summary

Even though some undergraduate programs for certification in business education have disappeared, the need for competent business educators has not. To remain viable, business educators must adjust content and teaching strategies and more closely align themselves with current business practices so that what is taught in the classroom reflects current and emerging business trends.

ASTD identified six business trends that have implications for business educators: an increasingly diverse workforce, continued corporate restructuring, the need for constant skills improvement, changes in training delivery, emphasis on performance improvement, and the proliferation of high-performance work systems. To prepare students for inevitable and ongoing changes in business and technology, business educators must create learning situations that celebrate and embrace diversity, develop coping strategies for change, underscore the importance of lifelong learning, take advantage of multimedia educational opportunities, and develop students' communication, teamwork, critical thinking, and decision-making skills.

Business educators must work together at all levels to offer up-to-date and relevant courses, reexamining the curriculum, its scope and sequence, and the terminology selected to identify course offerings. They must look beyond the classroom for professional and personal development opportunities to expand their expertise while providing real-life learning for their students. (See Table 1.)

Revision of the business curriculum cannot be accomplished by one individual or even one district. National, regional, and state organizations must join forces and implement the changes that will best serve students and employers.

References

American Society for Training and Development (ASTD). (1999). ASTD Releases 1999 State of the Industry. [Online]. Available: http://www.astd.org/CMS/templates/ template_1.html?articleid=21020.

Bassi, L. J., Benson, G., and Cheney, S. (1996, November). The Top Ten Trends. *Training and Development, 27–42.*

Decker, V. (1999). Personal Interview. Career Planning and Placement. Winona State University, Winona, MN.

Fricker, R. D., and Wehrle, R. A. (1996, June 11). Essential Business Skills: Educating the Future Workforce. Personal paper of the authors. An edited version under the title "Shared Inquiry: Learning How to Really Succeed in Business" appeared in *National Productivity Review*, vol. 16, pp. 71–5.

Graduate School for Industrial Administration, Carnegie Mellon University. (1999). Entrepreneurship Education (Donald H. Jones Center for Entrepreneurship). [Online]. Available: http://www.gsia.cmu.edu/e-ship/education.html.

Table 1. Opportunities for Professional Development

The following organizations and publications offer resources to educators who want to keep pace with today's changing business market.

American Society for Training and Development (ASTD), Alexandria, VA; http://www.astd.org.

America's Learning Exchange. A partnership between the ASTD and the U.S. Department of Labor to support learners, employers, and training suppliers. Web-based; available at http://www.astd.org/CMS/templates/template_1.html?articleid=20820.

The Business Education Network. Based at Utah State University, Cache Valley, Utah; contains links to other business-oriented entities. On the Web at http://biseben.bus.usu.edu/.

***Fast Company* Magazine.** Available on newsstands, by subscription, or online (selected articles) at http://www.fastcompany.com.

International Society for Performance Improvement (ISPI), Washington, DC; http://www.ispi.org.

National Business Education Association (NBEA), Reston, VA; http://www.nbea.org.

Jackson, T.H. (1991, Winter). Building Keyboarding Skills at the Elementary Level. *The Balance Sheet*, 19–21.

Klayton-Mi, M. (1999, January 19). Telecommuting. Presentation at the meeting of the Potomac Chapter of the International Society for Performance Improvement, NOVA Community College, Annandale, VA.

McLean, G.N. (1995). *Teaching Keyboarding*. Little Rock, AR: Delta Pi Epsilon.

Minnesota Department of Children, Families, and Learning. (1997, April). *The Profiles of Learning*. St. Paul, MN: Minnesota Department of Children, Families, and Learning.

O'Bannon, F. (1997, November 26). O'Bannon Pushes Jobs, Lifelong Learning. Press Release. [Online]. Available: http://www.ai.org/gov/pr/nob26.htm.

Okula, S. (1998, October). New Etiquette for Evolving Technologies: Using E-Mail and Voice Mail Effectively. *Business Education Forum*, 53 (1), 6–9, 51.

Outsourcing Institute. (1999). Managing Outsourcing and the Intellect: Discussion With Dr. James Brian Quinn. [Online]. Available: http://www.outsourcing.com/articles/managingoursrc/main.htm.

Small Business Administration (SBA). (1997, September). The Facts About Small Business, 1997. [Online]. Available: http://www.sba.gov/ADVO/stats/fact1.html.

Small Business Administration (SBA). (1998, June). The New American Evolution: The Role and Impact of Small Firms. [Online]. Available: http://www.sba.gov/ADVO/stats/evol_pap.html.

Chapter 15 — Strategies for Success: A Guide for Preparing Future Teachers

Patricia Arneson
Wayne State College
Wayne, Nebraska

Movies like *To Sir With Love, Lean on Me,* and *Dangerous Minds* reinforce publicly what teachers today already know: they are often forced to deal with violence and gangs, nonsupportive parents, sexually active youth, unmotivated learners, outmoded curricula, inadequate teaching facilities and resources, and, unfortunately, sometimes even school administrators, staff, and faculty who are out-of-touch or out-of-date with today's education and today's youth.

Such negative publicity, coupled with noncompetitive beginning teacher salaries which often drive prospective teacher education students into other better-paying majors, often makes it difficult to recruit and retain qualified teachers. Predictions of an impending teacher shortage capture national headlines as schools scramble to hire qualified personnel.

According to recent National Education Association projections (NEA, 1998), America's schools will need at least 2,000,000 teachers over the next 10 years to meet the demand caused by school enrollment increases and teacher attrition due to retirement. One-half to two-thirds of these teachers will be first-time teachers. Government reports predict that the shortage, including the demand for business and vocational teachers, is likely to get worse before it gets better.

More than ever before, Congress, as well as teacher-training institutions all over the country, have a vested interest in recruiting, preparing, and retaining qualified teachers for our nation's schools. In October 1998, Congress, enjoying an unexpected budget surplus, approved a massive appropriations bill that included $1.1 billion for the recruitment of 100,000 new teachers.

Raising Standards for Teacher Training

Goal 4: By the year 2000, the nation's teaching force will have access to programs for the continued improvement of their professional skills and the opportunity to acquire the knowledge and skills needed to instruct and prepare all American students for the next century (NEGP, 1997).

Goal Four of the *National Education Goals Report* is a reminder that student achievement depends foremost on the quality of the nation's teaching force. Colleges of education find themselves countering both perceptions and realities about the quality of the teacher training they deliver. In its 1996 report, the Carnegie Foundation's National Commission on Teaching and America's Future effectively "flunked" the nation's teacher colleges for separating theory from practice, presenting superficial curricula, and allowing uninspired or outmoded instruction.

"Most prospective teachers learn to work in isolation rather than in teams, and to master chalkboard and textbooks instead of computers and CD-ROMs," according to the Carnegie report.

In his October 1998 speech, President Bill Clinton called for states to raise teacher standards. Controversial furor over teacher training, minimum standards for teacher education graduates and teachers, and alternative certification soon followed. Although many states have made progress on improving teaching training in recent years, others have a long way to go.

Roundup: The "State" of Education Nationwide

Massachusetts. A few weeks after Clinton's speech, Massachusetts' governor, legislators, and educators were demanding a revolutionary overhaul of their teacher-training system. Their outcry, which reverberated throughout the nation, was prompted by the results of the first-ever Massachusetts Teacher Test. Fifty-nine percent of prospective teachers failed the first exam. Three months later, a second exam was administered; 47 percent failed.

Critics of the test claimed that prospective teachers were told the test would not affect their ability to get jobs—only to be notified two weeks before the exam that it would. "Our teachers are being tarred and feathered with being incompetent and illiterate," said former Massachusetts Education Commissioner Frank W. Haydu III, who resigned during the fiasco. "It's so inaccurate and unfair" (Hardy, 1998).

California. While Massachusetts battled over the politics of teacher training, California legislators were collaborating on legislation to improve the size and quality of its state's teaching force. One bill provides $10,000 bonuses to as many as 500 teachers who achieve National Board Certification (Hardy, 1998).

Pennsylvania. With 91 programs, Pennsylvania has more teacher-training institutions than any other state except New York. Pennsylvania's State Board of Education is considering raising the minimum grade point average for prospective teacher education majors from the current 2.5 to 3.0.

"We think it's important that people who go into teaching are able to demonstrate excellence in the classroom," says Pennsylvania Education Secretary Eugene Hickok (Mezzacappa, 1998).

Pennsylvania is also proposing an alternative that would allow people who pass certification exams to begin teaching immediately, under an intensive one-year apprenticeship supervised by an experienced teacher or principal. Pennsylvania also plans to raise the cut-off scores on many of its subject matter certification tests and would like to make data on certification test scores and job placement rates public.

New York. New York State education officials approved a policy (July, 1998) that will abolish lifetime teaching licenses and require teachers to take 175 hours of course work every five years (Mezzacappa, 1998). It will also decertify teacher education programs if fewer than 80 percent of a program's students pass licensing exams.

Texas. In three years, Texas will also decertify colleges of education that have high failure rates on the licensing exam. The state set the following standard for success: 70 percent of students from each ethnic group—white, black, and Hispanic—must pass (Mezzacappa, 1998).

New Jersey. New Jersey's decade-old alternative certification program requires teachers to take a certain number of education courses after they begin to teach and assigns them a mentor for their first year of teaching.

Model Standards for Beginning Teachers

Regardless of the controversy surrounding the content, direction, and focus that teacher education programs should take, there is growing support for standards describing what preprofessional teachers should know and be able to do. Irrespective of content area specialization or grade level, this expertise consists of the knowledge, skills, and dispositions an individual entering the teaching profession should demonstrate. When this expertise is embodied in a set of standards that all prospective teacher education graduates are expected to meet, employers are assured that graduates have been held accountable to institutional, local, state, and national benchmarks established by colleges and universities, state departments of education, professional associations, and accreditation agencies.

The National Business Education Association and the role of standards. According to *This We Believe About the Role of Standards for Business Education*, Policy Statement Number 62 (NBEA, 1998), standards provide a framework for judging the quality of business teacher education programs. Such standards identify what teachers should know and be able to do in terms of content area mastery, learning theories, and knowledge of instructional delivery and classroom management techniques.

According to this policy statement, standards encourage business teacher education programs to prepare teachers who meet the following criteria:

- Command a core body of knowledge for and about business;
- Integrate vocational and academic learning, including school-based and work-based activities;
- Understand how individuals develop and learn;
- Create instructional opportunities that meet the needs of diverse learners;
- Assist students in processing information and making decisions at progressively higher cognitive levels;
- Provide articulated instruction and programs that allow students to progress smoothly from one educational level to the next; and
- Value diversity and cultural differences.

INTASC Standards. The *INTASC Standards,* set forth by the Interstate New Teacher Assessment and Support Consortium, established model performance-based standards for teacher licensing. This model is the basis for teacher preparation and assessment of effective practice in many states and institutions nationwide.

The *INTASC Standards* model consists of 10 principles that guide the philosophies, curricula, goals, and outcomes of teacher preparation programs (see Table 1).

Guide for Successful Student Teaching

Successful student teaching begins three to four years before the onset of directed teaching. The years that precede the student teaching semester provide the preliminary foundation for success. During this time, the preprofessional is mastering subject matter content, acquiring knowledge of educational teaching and learning theories, and implementing such knowledge through a variety of field experiences.

Once engaged in the "professional" semester, the student teacher is often surprised to learn that the "formula for success" includes the active involvement of four key people: the *student teacher*, his or her *cooperating teacher* and *secondary administrator*, and the *university supervisor*. The following sections list responsibilities for each person involved in the student teaching experience and are based on the model standards mentioned above.

Formula for success — student teacher responsibilities. The primary responsibility of the student teacher is to learn how to become an effective teaching professional in a prolonged, natural classroom setting, under the direction of a qualified, experienced mentor and role model. Student teachers are expected to do the following:

- Regard themselves as members of the cooperating teacher's team and perform those tasks necessary to ensure the proper functioning of the business classroom.

Table 1. Recommended INTASC Standards for Beginning Teachers

Standard One: Subject Matter. The teacher understands the central concepts, tools of inquiry, and discipline he or she teaches and can create learning experiences that make these aspects of subject matter meaningful for students.

Standard Two: Student Learning. The teacher understands how children learn and develop and can provide learning opportunities that support their intellectual, social, and personal development.

Standard Three: Diverse Learners. The teacher understands how students differ in their approach to learning and creates instructional opportunities that are adapted to diverse learners.

Standard Four: Instructional Strategies. The teacher understands and uses a variety of instructional strategies to encourage students' development of critical thinking, problem solving, and performance skills.

Standard Five: Learning Environment. The teacher uses an understanding of individual and group motivation and behavior to create a learning environment that encourages positive social interaction, active engagement in learning, and self-motivation.

Standard Six: Communication. The teacher uses knowledge of effective verbal, nonverbal, and media communication techniques to foster active inquiry, collaboration, and interaction in the classroom.

Standard Seven: Planning Instruction. The teacher plans and manages instruction based upon knowledge of subject matter, students, the community, and curriculum goals.

Standard Eight: Assessment. The teacher understands and uses both formal and informal assessment strategies to evaluate and ensure the continuous intellectual, social, and physical development of learners.

Standard Nine: Reflection and Professional Development. The teacher is a reflective practitioner who continually evaluates the effects of his/her choices and actions on others (students, parents, and other professionals in the learning community) and who actively seeks opportunities to grow professionally.

Standard Ten: Collaboration, Ethics, and Relationships. The teacher communicates and interacts with parents/guardians, families, school colleagues, and the community to support students' learning and well-being.

- Review district and classroom discipline and management policies. Anticipate behavioral problems and be able to take appropriate action.

- Dress, act, talk, and conduct themselves as members of the teaching profession. Consider themselves members of the community and act accordingly.

- Attend school faculty meetings, parent-teacher conferences, and other professional meetings and school events. Become familiar with school and classroom facilities, building routines and policies, and teacher responsibilities for student safety.

- Develop student rapport. Make every attempt to learn names and faces as quickly as possible. Develop seating charts for each class. Be aware of students' special learning needs and how to meet these needs through modified instruction.

- Utilize a variety of instructional methods and materials to accommodate various learning styles. Use appropriate audio-visual, multimedia, and instructional technology. Learn how to operate all equipment, as well as how to repair and maintain equipment, computers, and printers.

- Prepare weekly and daily lesson plans. Make copies available to the cooperating and university supervisors. Participate in open, honest communication with both the cooperating teacher and university supervisor.

- Plan and arrange classroom displays and bulletin boards.

- Participate in parent-teacher conferences, help develop progress reports and grade sheets, and attend extracurricular school events.

- Develop a student teacher portfolio (recommended). Student teachers can develop student teaching notebooks for each class taught, including a professional portfolio that contains lesson plans, school and classroom policies and rules, copies of cooperating and college/university supervisors' evaluations, and a teaching journal. This daily or weekly journal should include reflections about classroom planning and performance. Student teachers should also videotape at least two or three classroom presentations throughout the student teaching semester.

Formula for success — cooperating teacher responsibilities. The secondary school cooperating teacher performs three primary roles when working with student teachers: (1) serves as a mentoring role model, (2) shares wisdom of experience and practice, and (3) encourages the preprofessional student teacher to inquire and reflect on educational processes. To prepare for the student teaching semester, the cooperating teacher is encouraged to take on the following tasks:

- Meet with the future student teacher for an introductory conference and give the student teacher curriculum guides, school calendar, handbooks and policies, necessary teaching manuals and materials, and other professional materials. During this preliminary conference, the cooperating teacher should also review his or her teaching expectations and those of the school district.

- Define the student teacher's role in terms of duties and responsibilities.
- Establish the student teaching schedule or timetable, which ensures that the student teacher's induction into actual teaching is at an appropriate rate.
- Review school district dress and conduct codes.
- Explain record keeping, grading, attendance, and classroom management procedures.
- Familiarize the student teacher with the school building, provide a facility map, and visit other classrooms and/or buildings.
- Review school safety procedures, including appropriate drills (fire, tornado, earthquake).
- Introduce the student teacher to school administrator(s), other faculty, and, if possible, the students and classes the student teacher will ultimately teach.

After the student teaching experience actually begins, the cooperating teacher is encouraged to do the following:

- Provide a desk or work area for the student teacher. It is important that the student teacher have his or her own individual work space and not share the teaching desk of the cooperating teacher. A secure location for the student teacher's belongings, coat, and teaching materials should also be provided.
- Distribute required teaching materials, manuals, grade book, and other related teacher resources.
- Review daily and weekly lesson plans prepared by the student teacher and guide him or her in the preparation of lesson plans, units, and testing materials.
- Evaluate the student teacher regularly. Weekly evaluations are recommended. Be specific in evaluative comments, compliments, and suggestions for improvement. Be sure to examine both strengths and weaknesses. If a student teacher's work is unsatisfactory, notify the secondary school administration, the college/university supervisor, and other cooperating teachers—whoever is appropriate—that intervention is necessary.
- Conduct regularly scheduled conferences with the student teacher (no less than once a week for 15–30 minutes) to review teaching progress, make suggestions and constructive criticism, and review lesson plans. Make sure the student teacher has planned adequately before he or she is permitted to teach.
- Maintain appropriate records for use in conferences with the student teacher and supervisory university personnel. Participate in open, honest

communication with both the student teacher and the university supervisor. Regularly discuss the student teacher's progress with the college/university supervisor. Telephone and e-mail conversations between visitations are also encouraged.

Formula for success — college/university supervisor responsibilities. The college/university supervisor serves an important role as the liaison between the student teacher and the high school cooperating teacher and its school administration. These supervisors have responsibilities that begin even before student teachers are placed in a directed teaching assignment. In many colleges and universities, the supervisor is responsible for arranging the actual placement of student teachers with schools, while at other institutions, the supervisor advises student teachers on appropriate placement. The supervisor may also be asked to assist the student teacher in advance planning and preparation for the student teaching assignment, including which lessons, units, or courses are to be taught or observed.

After the initial placement is completed and the student teacher is on site, the college/university supervisor should:

- Review the evaluation forms to be used during observations of the student teacher. If possible, inform the student teacher of how many observations will be made, how long each visit will last, and what criteria will be used in making the observation.

- Review the student teaching timetable created by the student teacher and the cooperating teacher.

- Make an adequate number of visits to observe the student teacher. University supervisors typically make a total of four to five on-site visits. Some supervisors make fewer actual visits/observations, but spend an entire day with the student teacher, whereas others make several visits, observing one or two class periods at a time. Still others rely on technology (videotapes; e-mail conversations among the student teacher, cooperating teacher, and college/university supervisor) to enhance the visitation process.

- During the student teacher visitation/observation, take notes about the lesson plan, delivery of instruction, student teacher's demeanor, and classroom management. While conducting the on-site visit, review the student teacher's professional notebook, including the student's journal of daily self-evaluations or reflections, lesson plans, teaching materials used or prepared, and weekly evaluations completed by the cooperating teacher(s).

- Allow enough time during the visitation/observation to meet with the student teacher and the cooperating teacher(s), as well as the school administrator(s). Make recommendations, using concrete examples. Be sure to praise, as well as constructively criticize, what is observed. Give a copy of the evaluation and any accompanying notes or comments to both the student teacher and the cooperating teacher. Copies should also be retained for the supervisor's own records.

- Intervene if the student teacher's performance is unsatisfactory.

Formula for success — administrator responsibilities. Although often overlooked, secondary school administrators play an important role in the professional development of successful student teachers. Administrators may choose different roles when working with student teachers. Some assume a more active role in guiding the student teacher through observations and conferencing, while others choose to serve more as a problem solver.

The administrator is encouraged to carry out the following activities:

- Welcome student teachers to the school, staff, and community. Describe general and specific expectations for student teacher/faculty conduct and responsibilities. Advise student teachers of faculty policies (meeting attendance, in-service attendance, dress code, discipline policy).

- Maintain a school environment in which faculty, staff, and students are accepting of student teachers and supportive of the college's teaching program.

- Help student teachers become familiar with the school's philosophy. Give student teachers a description of the building and district policies, procedures, and regulations (calendar, handbooks, report cards, daily schedule, schedule of events, maps, fire/tornado drill, play/recreation areas, use of cafeteria/gym/library).

- Encourage student teachers to participate in parent-teacher conferences, extracurricular activities, and other school events. Encourage student teachers to attend a school board meeting. If possible, arrange for all student teachers to be recognized by the board during one of the meetings.

- Confer regularly with cooperating teachers on the performance of their student teachers.

- Confer with the college supervisor if any serious problem concerning student teachers arises.

- Occasionally observe student teachers and provide feedback about classroom performance.

- Provide at least one formal school or district evaluation. If possible, provide student teachers with a sample job interview.

Implications for Business Teacher Education Programs

Like their teacher education colleagues, those who prepare business education graduates for successful student teaching experiences are accountable for training teachers who can demonstrate exemplary teaching practices.

More so than any other content area, teacher education programs in business must also address the impact of technology. Although the prevalence of computers in our lives is already evident in today's elementary and secondary schools, the majority of America's schools remain seriously underequipped to take advantage of what technology has to offer. According to an analysis of school technology programs by the CEO Forum on Education and Technology, 59 percent of America's schools are classified as "low technology" schools, with limited access to computers or to the Internet (CEO Forum, 1997). Furthermore, only about three percent of U.S. schools have achieved the CEO Forum's top designation as "target technology" schools.

Though there have been strides made in supplying schools with computers, too little attention is being paid to training teachers to integrate computer technology into their curriculum (Oldenburg, 1999). Making the most of technology as a teaching and learning tool requires intensive staff development and teacher training. In the majority of school districts, there is neither instruction, time, nor incentive for teachers to receive technology training. In fact, only one in five teachers feels "very well prepared" to use computers in the classroom (Oldenburg, 1999).

Because technology defines how business is and will continue to be conducted, business education graduates must emerge from their collegiate programs equipped not only to *utilize* technology for instructional delivery but also to *teach* technology to their students. Business education, more so than any other discipline, exemplifies how technology, while revolutionizing each aspect of our daily lives, has also revolutionized how we teach students and train future employees.

The term "classroom" no longer means a room, designated for learning, with desks and a chalkboard. Through the Internet and widespread use of e-mail, as well as the instantaneous transmission of data and information, the world is literally at the fingertips of today's students and teachers, trainees, and trainers. The explosion of technology in the workplace has made employers ratchet up the skill level requirements for their employees. Preparing vocational business students to effectively use technology is a challenge—and a mandate—facing today's business educators. Resources for incorporating technology into the curriculum can be found in Chapter 5, "The Promise of Technology," by Rodney G. Jurist.

Summary

Educators are entrusted with parents' most prized possessions—their children. Such public trust and responsibility require that teachers—and the educational institutions that prepare future teachers—do their utmost to be well prepared, knowledgeable, highly skilled, caring, sincere, and dedicated.

America's schools will need at least 2,000,000 teachers over the next 10 years. This impending teacher shortage has caused renewed concerns about the quality of teacher education programs and the teachers they produce. Goal 4 of the *National Education Goals Report* reinforces the importance of teacher competence with respect to student achievement.

Groups such as the National Business Education Association and the Interstate New Teacher Assessment and Support Consortium have identified performance-based standards that state what teachers should know and be able to do. These standards include developing professional attitudes and behaviors; knowledge of educational pedagogy and content area specialization; specialized training for working with a diverse student population with a variety of special needs; effective classroom management skills; and the use of sophisticated technology for instructional purposes.

The responsibility for preparing qualified, successful business teachers cannot rest entirely upon state or national standards nor solely with college/university teacher education institutions, programs, and faculty. A high level of dedicated, committed involvement is also required of those schools, administrators, and teachers that accept student teachers. Ultimately, the greatest responsibility rests with student teachers themselves in taking a proactive role in the educational process and professional development that will complete their transformation from that of *student* to *teacher of students*. The guidelines suggested in this chapter can be used as starting points for creating successful student experiences that lead to competent, effective future teachers.

References

CEO Forum on Education and Technology. (1997, October 9). *School Technology and Readiness Report: From Pillars to Progress.* [Online]. Available: http://www.ceoforum.org.

Hardy, L. (1998, December). Education Vital Signs 1998—Main Events. A supplement to the December 1998 *American School Board Journal.* Alexandria, VA: National School Boards Association.

INTASC Core Standards. (1998). [Online]. Available: http://develop.ccsso.cybercentral.com/intasct.htm.

INTASC Standards. (1998). [Online]. Available: http://www.soe.stthomas.edu/websoew/WHATSHAP/INTASC.html.

Mezzacappa, D. (1998, August 2). Training Teachers: Should Colleges Set Higher Standards? *The Philadelphia Inquirer*, B2 and B5. [Online]. Available: http://www.phillynews.com.

Murray, B. and Murray, K. (1997). *Pitfalls and Potholes: A Checklist for Avoiding Common Mistakes of Beginning Teachers.* NEA Checklist Series, Stock #2151-7-00-C4. West Haven, CT: NEA Professional Library.

National Alliance of Business. (1997, December). Workforce Economics Trends: Enhancing Education and Training Through Technology. [Online]. Available: http://www.nab.com.

National Business Education Association. (1998). *This We Believe about the Role of Standards for Business Education.* Policy Statement 62. Reston, VA: National Business Education Association.

National Education Association. (1998, May). *A Qualified Teacher in Every Classroom.* [Online]. Available: http://www.nea.org/qps/qtc.htm.

National Education Goals Panel (NEGP). (1997). *National Education Goals Report.* Washington, DC: National Education Goals Panel.

Nebraska Department of Education. (1998, May 4). Rule 20: Regulations for the Approval of Teacher Education Programs—Title 92, Nebraska Administrative Code, Chapter 20. [Online]. Available: http://nde4.nde.state.ne.us/LEGAL/Rules.html. State of Nebraska Department of Education, 301 Centennial Mall South, Lincoln, NE 68509.

Oldenburg, D. (1999, February 22). The Teacher Technology Gap. *Washington Post,* C4.

Riley, Secretary of Education Richard W. (1998, September 15). Annual Back to School Speech. [Online audio from U.S. Department of Education's Speech Webcast Site]. Available: http://www.connective.com/events/deptedu/#2.

Society for Human Resource Management. (1998, May-June). *Workplace Visions— Education* (Executive Summary). [Online]. Available: http://www.shrm/org/issues.

Wayne State College. (1998). *Student Teaching Handbook.* Wayne, NE: Wayne State College.

White House, Office of the Press Secretary. (1998, October 7). Press Release: President Clinton's Call to Action for American Education in the 21ˢᵗ Century: Improving Teacher Quality, Recruitment, and Preparation. [Online]. Available: http://www.pub.whitehouse.gov/urires/12R?urn:pdi://oma.eop.gov.us/1998/10/8/2.text.1.

White House, Office of the Press Secretary. (1998, October 15). Press Release: President Clinton, Vice President Gore, and Congressional Democrats Win on the Budget, but There Is Still More Work to Do. [Online]. Available: http://www.pub.whitehouse.gov/urires/12R?urn:pdi://oma.eop.gov.us/1998/10/16/ 4.text.1.